D1114898

BITTERROOT

BITTERROOT

ECHOES OF BEAUTY AND LOSS

STEVEN FAULKNER

BEAUFORT
BOOKS

BITTERROOT

Excerpts from:
Smet, Pierre-Jean De, Hiram Martin Chittenden, and Alfred Talbot Richardson. Life, Letters and Travels of Father Pierre-Jean De Smet: Missionary Labors and Adventures among ... the North American Indians ... New York: Francis P. Harper, 1904.

Library of Congress Cataloging-in-Publication Data On File

For inquiries about volume orders, please contact:
Beaufort Books
27 West 20th Street, Suite 1102
New York, NY 10011
sales@beaufortbooks.com

Published in the United States by Beaufort Books
www.beaufortbooks.com

Distributed by Midpoint Trade Books
www.midpointtrade.com

Printed in the United States of America

Interior design by Mark Karis
Cover Design by Seth Faulkner
Maps Designed by Seth Faulkner

In the dark times

Will there also be singing?

Yes, there will be singing.

About the dark times.

—BERTOLT BRECHT

Another species [of root] was much mutilated but appeared to be fibrous; the
parts were brittle, hard of the size of a small quill, cilindric and as white as
snow throughout...this the Indians with me informed me were always boiled
for use. I made the exprement, found that they became perfectly soft by boiling,
but had a very bitter taste, which was naucious to my palate, and I transfered
them to the Indians who had eat them heartily.

—THE BITTERROOT, AS DESCRIBED BY MERIWETHER LEWIS

CONTENTS

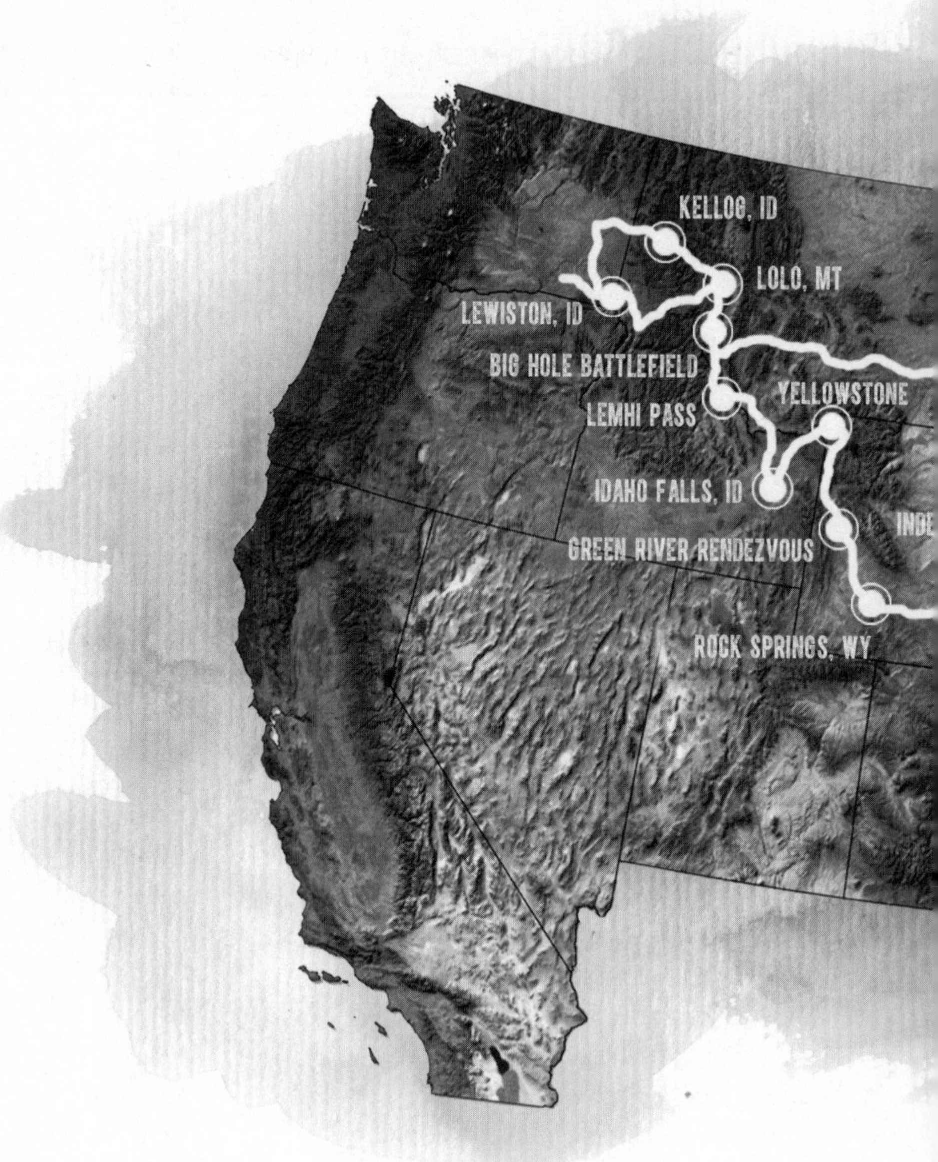
KELLOG, ID
LOLO, MT
LEWISTON, ID
BIG HOLE BATTLEFIELD
LEMHI PASS
YELLOWSTONE
IDAHO FALLS, ID
GREEN RIVER RENDEZVOUS
ROCK SPRINGS, WY

UFFALO, WY

BLACK HILLS

ROCK

CHADRON, NE

RAMIE

ASH HOLLOW

TOPEKA, KS

FAULKNER TRIP

STEVEN, (JUSTIN), ALEX

THE OREGON TRAIL

In the long darkness before dawn, we follow the Oregon Trail west along the Kansas River: black, moonless fields of growing corn, erratic white moths picked up in the headlights, the eyes of a deer catching fire as it bounds into trees standing against a starlit sky. At about four in the morning we cross the river into Manhattan, Kansas (they call it The Little Apple), and turn north into the night, the highway heaving up over hills of long-grass prairie, cutting though pale limestone bluffs, then sagging into dark little valleys of corn and milo and soybeans, more or less following the Big Blue River where the old wagon ruts ran. These are the Flint Hills, where I grew up with tornados and blizzards.

I'm telling Alex that when I was his age I hitchhiked this highway one sunny afternoon with a friend named Paul. Farmers in their mud-splotched pickups and flatbed trucks wouldn't stop for us, so I climbed onto Paul's shoulders. With him walking backwards beneath me, we both stuck out our thumbs—a double incentive.

A sheriff's car pulled over.

I slid off Paul's shoulders, thinking we were in trouble for sure. The sheriff, with a white cowboy hat and grey sideburns, leaned across the seat and motioned us to get in. We climbed in.

"Where you boys headed?"

"Back to college in Chicago."

"That's a far piece. Cain't take you that far, but I kin git you boys up to the county line."

As he drove us over the hills, he told us stories about the farmers and ranchers whose homes we were passing, whose ancestors had followed the westward hopes. He turned a thumb toward a passing farm: "That there's old man Carter's place, over thataway in the stone two-story. His cows got into green alfalfa last year. Swole 'em up like roadkill in August. Moanin' and fartin' and shittin' and bawlin' till they cain't stand up straight. Well, the old man had to chase 'em through the fields with a stick till they done cleaned theirselves out. Old Carter his own self was pretty wrung out."

Suddenly, he practically threw us out of the car, swerving hard left to run down a coyote that was loping across the road. The coyote escaped—as, in a few miles, did we.

My son Alex grins, puts his pillow against the window, and closes his eyes. In a few miles he's asleep in the early morning dark.

We had driven for a day and a night and a day.

Leaving our current home in the southern forests of Virginia, we had stopped briefly in Charlottesville, hometown of Thomas Jefferson who sent his secretary Meriwether Lewis with William Clark on their epic exploration of the unknown. We searched a sporting goods store for a few last requirements—hiking boots and two first aid kits—then headed west, twisting over the Blue Ridge Mountains, winding down into the Shenandoah Valley, then up, up and over the entire breadth of the Appalachian Mountains into the foothills and horse farms of Kentucky. The sun went down and we hurried west with the night across the flat, black farmlands of Indiana and Illinois, chasing a quarter moon down the sky and driving it into an Illinois cornfield about one in the morning. An hour later we rolled onto a concrete Mississippi River bridge into St. Louis.

There, just beyond the big river, the tall silver arch bends like a steel rainbow into the night sky. They call it the Gateway to the West, a stainless steel construction that vaults 630 vertical feet. Two sets of cable cars mechanically crank sightseers up the legs to the summit where they can peer out small portholes at a thicket of skyscrapers and down upon a tangled maze of highways, abandoned warehouses, train tracks, barges, and bridges: a fitting monument to America's industrial expansion westward.

In 1764, a French fur trader named Pierre Laclede and his stepson Auguste Chouteau, traveling up the Mississippi from New Orleans with 30 men, hauled their boats ashore here and told their men to start building. Forty years later Laclede's fur-trading post had developed into a scruffy, crowded riverside town, home to French, Spanish, and American traders who ranged the fringes of the known West. The Spanish held the far coast of California and captains of trading ships had found the mouth of the wide Columbia River flowing into the Pacific Ocean, but the maps of the continental interior were featureless blanks.

There is an odd thing about those early nineteenth-century maps. French explorer Marquette's 1673 map of the Mississippi River included the names of every Indian tribe he could find and sank them along the tributaries of the Mississippi as far as the Kansa Indians hundreds of miles to the west. Historian Richard White says that maps of the sixteenth and seventeenth centuries "portrayed a densely occupied continent teeming with people... But by the nineteenth century, all this had changed." These later maps of the West were blank. Why? The answer seems obvious: land portrayed as an empty wilderness is ready for the taking.

Lewis and Clark spent the winter of 1803-1804 across the river from St. Louis procuring supplies and hiring boatmen in the town. They set off into the wilderness in mid May, rowing, poling, and when the wind was right, sailing west and north up the Missouri River in a keelboat and two pirogues. Alex and I plan to catch up to Lewis and Clark far to the west near the Bitterroot Mountains and accompany them along the most difficult part of their great adventure.

St. Louis was also the American home of the Belgian Jesuit priest Pierre Jean De Smet, whose 1840 and 1841 journeys up the Missouri River and out along what would soon be called the Oregon Trail helped popularize that arduous journey west. De Smet was almost 40 when he left St. Louis for the Rocky Mountains. He was a short, powerful man with shoulder-length hair, a square face, and a mouth he said was made for laughing. He was intensely interested in everything he saw: plants, fossils, animals, geography, and especially in the many tribes of Indians he encountered on his journeys west. He came to respect them and they him, so much so that De Smet became one of the few intermediaries trusted by both Indians and whites.

Alex and I are catching De Smet along the Missouri River. From there we will follow him across the High Plains to the fur trappers' rendezvous on the Green River, then on to the Lewis and Clark Trail which will take us across the Rockies into the homeland of the Nez Perce Indians, whose fate is strangely tied, for better and worse, to these emissaries from the east. Through the journals of Lewis and Clark, the letters of de Smet, and the accounts of a young Nez Perce warrior named White Thunder, we will try to capture a three-legged understanding of the northern half of what was then called the Far West, an understanding supported by many chance encounters with modern residents. I want to see this vast landscape with eyes both old and new.

I have always loved travel and history. Reading history is, of course, a means of travel—time travel. Alex reads little and loves socializing with friends, which means that he would rather spend time with his friends than with a parent, but we have a good relationship and he's willing to humor me by joining me on this journey. He has little experience with self-discipline and hard work, and I think that this month-long trip to the West will be good for him, a trip that will include humping 60-pound packs up very steep mountains and canoeing the rough waters of three mountain rivers. Though history doesn't particularly interest him, adventure does.

Within minutes the silver arch fell behind us, and we sped out of St. Louis and skimmed 'cross the wide Missouri. We were rushing west on busy I-70, a multi-lane highway of concrete and petrified oil slag, while the mysterious Missouri River that the early emigrants traveled wandered away to our south and west, lapping quietly by limestone bluffs, soaking through marshlands, skirting summer forests.

Six hours later we arrived exhausted in Topeka, Kansas, where Alex was born eighteen years ago. We slept. We took a few days to see his brothers, his sisters, his mother (my wife Joy—who still lives and works in Kansas: a complication of my low wages in Virginia and our not being able to sell the house in Kansas).

***

The night wears on as I drive and Alex sleeps. Distant lightning is jumping, echoes of light shaking a black horizon. Out there, on the outer rim of the dark prairie, thunder beings suddenly stand up: two-legged, three-legged, jitter-step sideways, and leap back to the clouds— uncertain guides to the north and west. Black Elk, the Sioux medicine man, told of thunder beings who came to him in a dream, flying head-first out of the clouds, their lances tipped with lightning. They carried him up into the rainbow-arched clouds and told him to save his people. But his elaborate visions, ceremonially reenacted by his village, did not save his people during the bitter years of the western wars.

Driving north, the prairie hills to the east are black silhouettes against a slowly awakening dawn, and the highest clouds of the thunderstorm ahead are catching sunlight as we drive into Nebraska. One cloud resembles a grey-white grizzly pointing its snout to the sky and sniffing the coming day. Silent lightning flares through the cloud banks as the bear leans gradually into the dawn, its huge head disintegrating into a wicked smile. We will meet that bear again in about four weeks' time and he will have his way with us.

These hills were hard on those early emigrants walking muddy miles beside their covered wagons. Historian S. C. Gwynne tells us that "the contrast between the dense eastern woodlands and the 'big sky' country of the west would have been stark" for the emigrant. "It would have seemed to him a vast emptiness. At that point, everything the pioneer woodsman knew about how to survive—including building houses, making fire, and drawing water—broke down."

Father De Smet took this route in 1840—before anyone had discovered a way for wagons over the Rockies. De Smet was happy to be heading into this wilderness, hoping at last to meet the tribes that had, over the last nine years, sent four groups of emissaries to St. Louis asking that black-robe priests teach them the white man's powerful book of mysteries.

The first leg of De Smet's long journey was up the fast-flowing Missouri River on a steamboat. De Smet, who could not swim, describes the difficulties and dangers:

> With the exception of the snags which raked and scraped us now and then and the sandbars which opposed our passage, and which had to be crossed at all hazards, our journey was pleasant enough. The boat has to be lifted over these bars, which is not any too easy. Two heavy timbers are set in the water in front and the boat made fast to them. Then the engine is started full speed, and by means of posts it lifts the stern and shoves the boat forward a yard or two or three. Then the same thing is done over again, and so on until the bar is crossed. This often takes a whole day.
>
> The Devil's Rake, which has to be passed through, is a place much dreaded by the rivermen. It has the appearance of a whole forest, swallowed up by the immense river. Gigantic trees stretch their naked and menacing limbs on all sides; you see them thrashing in the water, throwing up foam with a furious hissing sound as they struggle

against the rapid torrent. Add to these inconveniences the fear of the boiler exploding, which often causes loss of life among the unhappy travelers. At the same time the weather was excessively hot: the warm, muddy water of the Missouri was our only drink, and myriads of mosquitoes, fleas, and other insects were our traveling companions... I fear the sea, I will admit, but all the storms and other unpleasant things I have experienced in four different voyages did not inspire so much terror in me as the navigation of the somber, treacherous and muddy Missouri.

When De Smet remarks that this journey was "pleasant enough," I expect he's joking. Hordes of biting, flying insects, dirty drinking water, sandbars, and other serious hazards do not a pleasant journey make.

After several days on the Missouri, De Smet and his two Iroquois guides joined members of the American Fur Company led by the mountain man Andrew Drips who was heading a supply caravan through wild country toward the fur-trappers' rendezvous at the Green River, just beyond the continental divide. De Smet had contracted malaria and was too sick to ride, so he found a place to lie down in a wagon. "Very often," he writes in a letter, "we would have to cross deep and perpendicular ravines, throwing me into the most singular positions; now my feet would be in the air, now I would find myself hidden like a thief between boxes and bundles, cold as an icicle or covered with sweat and burning like a stove." The trappers told De Smet he was too sick to go on, but he had promised the Flathead (or Salish, as they now prefer) Indians of the distant Rockies that he would meet them that year at the trappers' rendezvous on the Green River, and he was determined to keep that promise.

***

For Alex and me, travel is easy: air-conditioned miles and miles, slowing only for sharp turns in the highway or the stop signs of Beatrice, Nebraska. The hills roll away to every horizon gathering colors from the dawn: the early summer grasses coming up green between last fall's shades of pale yellow, ochre, and burnt sienna. This is the long-grass prairie of tall bluestem, grama, and Indian grasses that fed the massive herds of buffalo, elk, and antelope. Wooded creek banks ease down from the hills and open onto meadows and fields now knee-high in yellowing wheat and green corn.

In 1846, twenty-three-year-old Francis Parkman traveled this route for pleasure and adventure and recorded the hardships: "The thunder here is not like the tame thunder of the Atlantic coast. Bursting with a terrific crash directly over our heads, it roared over the boundless waste of prairie, seeming to roll around the whole circle of the firmament with a peculiar and awful reverberation...and the wind blew with such fury that the streams of rain flew almost horizontally along the prairie, roaring like a cataract." Even after taking shelter in their canvas tents, the men were miserable, the rain beating all night "through the canvas in a fine drizzle. We sat upon our saddles with faces of the utmost surliness, while the water dropped from the visors of our caps, and trickled down our cheeks." On nights like that they ended up sleeping in pools of water. If the clouds passed, then by day the sun beat down "with a sultry, penetrating heat."

Near Lincoln, Nebraska, we run into our own fury of thunder and rain, a nearby grain silo nearly washed from sight in windy sheets. Black cows turned tail to the slashing downpour, but it did not discomfit us. We turn straight west and roll into a clear, windy morning and on into a blustery afternoon along the broad and shallow Platte River, its several currents passing through reedy swamps and braiding together tall groves of cottonwood trees, the flat river valley expanding to distant hills. Alex wakes when we stop for gas, but the steady singing of the tires soon shuts his eyes.

In time the long-grass prairie hills lose their trees and diminish to yellow-white hills of what the pioneers called buffalo grass. Off to our right, the meandering currents of the Platte are still bordered by cottonwoods, junipers, and scattered Russian olives, but the hills and gullies beyond are now almost treeless. A strong wind whips the roadside grasses, shaking whole hillsides of yellow sweet clover. Down in a river meadow, six wild turkeys are pacing through the blowing grass, leaning into their search for grasshoppers and crickets. Beyond them, a dust cloud chases a red dump truck along a sandy river-bottom road and blackbirds are crossing with the wind beneath a wide sky of palest blue.

We pass the sawed-off trunk of a giant cottonwood tree, maybe six feet in diameter. The limbs of the fallen trunk lie shattered, scattered, and weathered to smooth silver, a fitting symbol of the old West as we see it today. Beyond the fallen tree, a distant feedlot, where thousands of cattle line the feeding troughs hoof-deep in mud.

For the early emigrants from the eastern forests, this treeless journey along the shallow streams of the Platte River became several bewildering weeks of moving into an increasingly hostile prairie: their precious herds of cattle chased off at night by large packs of wolves, Pawnee Indians stealing their horses and shooting men who strayed too far, Dakota Sioux helping themselves to their supplies, the mud and heat intolerable. There were arguments between wagon leaders with some wagons turning back for civilization, others breaking into smaller groups under new leaders, and the inevitable deaths from dysentery and fevers. Anger and fear and mistrust cut into dreams of the beautiful Willamette Valley in far away Oregon.

I turn up the air conditioning and step on the gas, rolling along the straight, flat concrete of Interstate 80 hour by hour, the low hills of the far horizon rising slowly and falling away.

De Smet writes of seeing herds of several hundred antelope at a time along the Platte River plain: "Other animals are rare, but there are evident indications that game has not always been lacking. For several days' journeys, we found the whole plain covered with buffalo bones and skulls arranged in circles or half-moons and painted with various devices. It is in the midst of these skulls that the Pawnees are wont to practice their divinations when they go forth to war or to the chase. In this desert, the traveler, wearied of living so long on salt meat, is rejoiced at sight of these weather-bleached bones, which announce to him the vicinity of the buffalo."

Though he would suffer the weakness and fevers of malaria for another three months, he forced himself one early morning to walk out alone to see the herds of bison:

> I approached them by way of the ravines, without showing myself or allowing them to get the wind of me. This is the most keen-scented of animals; he will detect the presence of a man at a distance of four miles, and take flight at once, since that odor is insupportable to him. I gained, without being perceived, a high bluff, resembling in shape the Waterloo monument; from it I enjoyed a view of perhaps a dozen miles. The vast plain was so covered with animals, that the markets or fairs of Europe could give you only the feeblest idea of it. It was indeed like a fair of the whole world assembled in one of its loveliest plains. I looked with wonder...and for two hours I watched these moving masses in the same state of astonishment.

Roaming herds of buffalo as far as the eye could see. Thirty years later, a herd fifty miles long and twenty-five miles wide, estimated to number four million, was seen near the Arkansas River in what is now southern Kansas. And there were many, many herds that wandered from Canada to southern Texas. Estimates put their numbers at sixty million.

***

Having reached the place where the North and South Forks of the Platte join, we soon cross the South Fork and turn northwest, not far from the place the old wagons forded the river. For us it's a few seconds' skimming over a concrete bridge. For the emigrants in their loaded wagons it was a dangerous struggle. Parkman watches from shore: "First the heavy ox-wagons plunged down the bank, and dragged slowly over the sand-beds; sometimes the hoofs of the oxen were scarcely wet by the thin sheet of water; and the next moment the river would be boiling against their sides, and eddying around the wheels. Inch by inch they receded from the shore...until at length they seemed to be floating far out in the middle of the river."

De Smet describes a more dangerous crossing of the Platte on a later journey. The party's hunter put his horse into the strong current while pulling the lead rope of a colt that carried his one-year-old daughter and slapping with his quirt the horse on which his wife was mounted. After seeing the one-year-old safe across the swift current, De Smet, who could not swim, was embarrassed to hold back, so he plunged in with his horse. Those on horseback walked and swam their horses across, but "the largest wagon," De Smet reports, "was carried off by the force of the current, in spite of all the efforts, shouts and cries of the men, who did all they could to keep themselves from being drowned. Another wagon was literally turned over. One of the mules showed only his four feet on the surface of the water, and the other [mules] went adrift entangled in the [straps and halters]. On one side appeared the American captain with extended arms, crying for help. On the other, a young German traveler was seen diving with his beast, and soon after both appearing above the water at a distance from each other. Here a horse reached the shore without a rider; further on, two riders appeared on the same horse; finally, the good Brother Joseph dancing up and down with his horse, and Father Mengarini clinging to the neck of his, and looking as if he formed an indivisible part of the animal. After all our difficulties, we found that only one of the mules was drowned."

ASH HOLLOW

We're on our way to visit Ash Hollow, a spring along the Oregon Trail that tells stories both bitter and beautiful. Beyond broken, chalky hills to our right, we catch a glimpse of the river dammed into a long lake of intense blue. Somewhere along here, Parkman, riding with his French guide Henry Chatillon, hunted buffalo for the first time. Chatillon dismounted and crept close, then shot two bulls. Parkman mounted up and soon found himself riding alone, chasing a dozen bulls on horseback through "the intricacies of the hills and hollows." He gained the top of a ridge but found the buffalo had vanished. "Reloading my [heavy, single-shot] pistols in the best way I could, I galloped on until I saw them again scuttling along at the base of the hill, their panic somewhat abated. Down went [his horse] old Pontiac among them, scattering them to the right and left; and then we had another long chase, scouring over the hills, rushing down the declivities with tremendous weight and impetuosity, and then laboring with a weary gallop upward. One bull at length fell a little behind the rest, and by dint of much effort, I urged my horse within six or eight yards of his side. His back was darkened with sweat: he was panting heavily, while his tongue lolled out a foot from his jaws. Gradually I came up abreast of him, urging Pontiac with leg and rein nearer to his side, when suddenly he did what buffalo in such circumstances will always do: he slackened his gallop, and turning toward us, with an aspect of mingled rage and distress, lowered his huge, shaggy head for a charge. Pontiac, with a snort, leaped aside in terror, nearly throwing me to the ground. I raised my pistol to strike [Pontiac] on the head, but thinking better of it, fired the bullet after the bull, who had resumed his flight."

Having missed his shot, Parkman found he was utterly lost in the maze of hills: "I looked about for some indications to show me where I was. I might as well have looked for landmarks in the ocean. How many miles I had run, or in what direction, I had no idea; and around me the prairie was rolling in steep swells and pitches, without a single distinctive feature to guide me."

He wandered for hours. "The face of the country was dotted far and wide with countless hundreds of buffalo. They trooped along in files and columns, bulls, cows, and calves. They scrambled away over the hills to right and left; and far off, the pale blue swells in the extreme distance were dotted with innumerable specks. Sometimes I surprised shaggy old bulls grazing alone, or sleeping behind the ridges I ascended. They would leap up at my approach, stare stupidly at me through their tangled manes, and then gallop heavily away. The antelope would approach to look at me, gaze intently with their great round eyes, then suddenly leap aside and stretch lightly away over the prairie. Squalid, ruffian-like wolves sneaked through the hollows and sandy ravines. Prairie dogs sat, each at the mouth of his burrow, holding his paws before him in a supplicating attitude, and yelping away most vehemently...checkered snakes were sunning themselves, demure little gray owls with a large white ring around each eye were perched side by side with the prairie dogs. The prairie teemed with life."

Not any more. Even the cattle that have replaced the buffalo are missing. Coyotes, which the trappers called prairie wolves, will still waken the night with their yips and yells, but the wolves so idealized by city-living Americans have disappeared and are only now making a reappearance in the Rocky Mountains where their decimation of elk herds and threat to cows and sheep have created competing howls from packs of sportsmen and ranchers on the one hand and packs of environmentalists and tourists on the other. Almost every reference Parkman makes to wolves involves words like *squalid, sneaking,* or *ruffian.* They were not then the ideal emissaries of all things wild and wonderful that they have become for American urbanites.

In the empty hills ahead, I see a woman dressed in construction gear standing on the highway, holding a stop sign. I slow to a stop on the hot tarmac. She is a thin, middle-aged woman with a deep tan. Alex looks up from his pillow. The woman leans down to get a look at us. She has eyes the same blue as the sky, and short windblown hair the color of the summer grasses.

I say hello.

"Where you headed?" she asks.

"Ash Hollow."

She nods her head. "I been there. Fact is, just visited the place a couple weekends ago. Just down from your turnoff you'll see a cemetery with a grave. First white woman on a wagon train to get sick and die. And there's a real sod house down there off on the left."

She tells us about the visitor's center and museum, the old prairie school house that burned down and has now been rebuilt, how the emigrants had to winch their wagons down steep slopes and up again and raft them over the deeper rivers by taking off the wheels and covering the wagon boxes with buffalo hides, how cholera epidemics ravaged the later wagon trains. "And don't wear flip flops when you're climbin' around out there, might be rattlers. But it's a fine place to learn about stuff, there at the museum. I know I need to learn something new every day. Your brain never has enough information."

After twenty minutes, a pilot car drives up and pulls around for us to follow it past the roadwork. "You ought to see my boy on up ahead there. He's about five-feet-ten, big boy, 260 pounds, got glasses. It's kind of a family business." She reaches out to shake hands with me and then reaches her lean brown arm across to shake Alex's hand.

A mile down and up the road big yellow machines are grinding up asphalt with a terrific roar while a conveyor belt pours it into waiting trucks. Behind them, tanker trucks are spewing hot black oil onto the scarred undersurface while sweaty, half-naked men with dirty bandanas tied around loose, blowing hair walk with their blackened shovels either side of another monster machine that smashes down the new layer of tarred gravel. We catch the reek of oil and tar while heat waves shimmer off the hot new tarmac. The pilot car pulls off and lets us by.

In one of the asphalt trucks I see a heavy young man with glasses. Part of the family business.

***

The visitors' center is closed, open only on weekends. I tell Alex I want to look around.. For some reason, he's still sleepy and not in the mood for my explorations of history, so he pulls a red blanket and a couple of pillows from the car, shakes the blanket out under a shade tree, drops the pillows, and lies down in a warm summer breeze. You cannot get him to go to bed at home, but put him on a long trip and he will not stay awake.

We are on a high bluff of whitish-grey, speckled limestone, much of it silted over with a thin soil and fringed in blowing prairie grasses. Beyond, on all sides, low hills scattered here and there with dark green junipers roll to a blue, hazy horizon. Far off in a valley to the northeast I see the Platte River reflecting the wide sky, but not a buffalo nor an antelope, nor a single prairie dog. I make my way down from the bluff toward the spring, which is no longer "a number of springs of cold, crystal water gushing forth" from beneath the bluff as an early traveler wrote. After weeks of drinking water from the silted Platte where buffalo and elk and cattle and hundreds of previous travelers often muddied and contaminated the waters, the emigrants loved this flowing spring. Now it has been reduced to a long, stagnant pool of brown water; a few picnic tables stand in a cutout clearing baking in the sun.

The early mountain men knew of the gushing springs too. Here, or near here, a party of Indians and frontiersmen arrived in 1837 (just three years before De Smet's journey), coming from the Green River Rendezvous of fur trappers and Indians. They were an interesting collection.

A Presbyterian missionary named William Gray was leading a party out of the Rocky Mountains and back to St. Louis, on his way to recruit more missionaries for the mountain tribes. Two years before, a handful of Presbyterian and Methodist preachers, including two of their wives, had pushed on beyond the rendezvous site to be the first Protestant missionaries to settle among the western mountain tribes. Gray had been a part of that expedition. Now he was solemnly entrusted with the care and education of two Indian boys whose father was a Salish war chief called The Grand Face. The chief had warned Gray that he did not want Gray to "make fools of the boys by making them drunken and bad men" like many of the mountain men. Accompanying Gray was a Nez Perce headman called The Hat, because he had taken to wearing a tall silk hat a mountain man had given him. With Gray, The Hat, and the two Salish boys were three French Canadians and two more Salish Indians, friends of the last member of the group, Big Ignace La Mousse, an Iroquois who years before had left Canada and had married a Salish wife. Previously, Big Ignace had taken his two oldest sons 3000 miles to St. Louis in order to have them baptized by Catholic priests and to ask the black-robes there to start a mission among the Salish. The Jesuits in St. Louis had been sympathetic to his request but said they were unable just then to spare anyone for a mission so distant, as they had begun putting up log buildings for a new university in St. Louis and were trying to start a mission among the Potawatomies on the Upper

Missouri River near Council Bluffs.

Big Ignace and his sons had returned to the Bitterroot Valley, a 6000-mile journey round-trip by steamboat, horse, and foot, much of it claimed by several enemy tribes who would kill them on sight.

After waiting another two years, he and the Salish war chief Insula decided Big Ignace should return to St. Louis to ask again for missionary priests. Apparently Big Ignace, who had been raised a Catholic in Canada, had cautioned his fellow Salish that Protestant missionaries like Gray who had appeared at the Green River Rendezvous in 1835 were "not the long black-robed priests who have no wives, who say mass, who carry the crucifix with them...about whom we have spoken to you."

Perhaps another reason the Salish and their allies were so eager to bring Catholic priests is that a Salish medicine man by the name of Shining Shirt had made a prophecy long ago that fair-skinned men wearing long black robes would come teach the Indians a new medicine dance and a new moral law. The black-robes would bring peace, but their arrival would also mean the beginning of the end of all the people who then inhabited the land.

Gray had been entrusted by the Nez Perce to trade a herd of horses for cattle when he got to St. Louis—a risky proposition, since it entailed a journey through almost 2000 miles of hostile territory—one way. Henry Spalding, one of the missionaries and an associate of Gray, was determined to bring cattle to his new mission among the Nez Perce so that the Indians would not be tempted to leave the mission for their annual trek eastward across the Rockies to hunt buffalo.

The mountain men at the recent rendezvous thought Gray "was courting disaster by starting east" with such a small party, says historian Alvin Josephy, "but there was no stopping him." Gray had no interest in the drunken uproarious singing, the gambling, cursing, horse racing, and general mayhem of the gathered trappers and Indians at the Green River rendezvous. "His impatience and officiousness," says Josephy, "had already got him in trouble with the Flatheads; and the trappers, who thought he was about as obnoxious a human as had ever come to the West, sided with the Indians against him whenever argument arose. Gray pestered Drips, Jim Bridger, and others to hurry the rendezvous" so he could continue his journey.

The mountain men refused, so he started east with his few companions and the herd of horses. The mountain men warned him again not to go, but Gray, by faith or foolishness, left anyway. Gray was warned once again at Fort Laramie on the North Platte, where one of the French Canadians decided to leave him. But Gray and the others pushed on down the North Platte with their herd of horses.

On August 7, near the springs of Ash Hollow, the nine travelers were suddenly attacked by a large war party of Sioux. A running skirmish broke out with Gray getting two bullets through his hat, one creasing his scalp. The men scrambled up one of the nearby bluffs (perhaps the very one where Alex is now sleeping), but they were terribly outnumbered. A Frenchman who was with the Sioux called up to them that the Sioux wanted to kill only their traditional enemies and that the whites should walk away. Big Ignace, dressed like a white man, was mistaken for a white man and perhaps had the opportunity to save himself, but he refused to abandon his Salish and Nez Perce friends. "What happened next," says Josephy, "brought lasting disgrace to Gray's name among the trappers who later heard of the fight. Prevailing on the two whites and a [half-blood] youth to accompany him, Gray abandoned the Indians and walked out in open surrender."

I climb up from the pool of brown water through grass and brush to the base of the bluffs: swaying columns of white rock, eroded buttresses of limestone capped by grey, weathered slabs that in some places have been colonized by swallows, which have built clay nests that look like quart-size clay bags with a hole at the end of a small neck, all made of little balls of clay. Beneath an overhang, globular clusters of very white round stones have been dropping off the wall, leaving a white pebble path along the base of the bluffs. Golden dragonflies like delicate, living jewelry, flit this way and that, decorating the dark green juniper trees or alighting on the prairie grasses where even brighter yellow flowers grow between rocks flaked with orange lichens. I find a way to climb back up the bluff and return to Alex, still safely asleep in the shade.

I think of those two Salish boys, sons of The Grand Face, on their way into a new world past their reckoning, to learn the ways of the strange white man, to see his vast, fabled cities, to ride the great canoes that can carry a hundred men and horses and are said to paddle themselves up rivers against the currents while coughing out the smoke of twenty bonfires and bellowing so loud they can be heard for miles. Two boys on their way to see an unimaginable world, on their way to be taught the meaning of the magic scratchings in the missionary's big black book. I see them standing there on that windblown bluff watching the four white men make their way down the hill toward three-hundred mounted warriors, a great crowd of restless war ponies slapped with paint, their manes and tails tied and braided with bones and feathers and teeth, the men fierce, half-naked, impatient, jerking the reins of twisted horsehair one way then another, their faces streaked with white clay or smeared about the eyes with boneblack or spotted red like fever blisters; they are howling and chanting and shaking their rawhide shields, stabbing the air with lances strung with human hair as the Frenchmen and Gray approach.

And I think of the Nez Perce headman in his stovepipe hat standing on this remote hill so far from the mountains of home, standing beside the two young brothers and singing his Nez Perce death song, while Big Ignace and the two Salish men cross themselves and recite the prayers Big Ignace has taught them while Big Ignace checks the priming of his Hudson-Bay rifle and the Salish pull four or five iron-pointed arrows from their otterskin quivers, knowing there will be no time for more when that calamitous horde charges.

They come. A rumbling thunder of hooves and a screaming of eagle-bone war whistles, and perhaps none of the Sioux shooting a single arrow nor firing a shot, because each one yearns for the reputation of having charged in with nothing but a lance or a coup stick, or a swinging club of rawhide and rock.

19

The two boys stand beside each other, breathing hard, and, perhaps too soon let fly their brief, useless arrows at the gaudy, harlequin horde yelping and barking and thundering toward them...

But the story doesn't end there. Two years later, a son of Big Ignace, called Little Ignace, joined a party of fur trappers heading for St. Louis. Little Ignace, along with another Iroquois named Pierre Gaucher, safely arrived in St. Louis and finally obtained the bishop's promise to send a black-robe. That black-robe was Pierre Jean De Smet, who, by all accounts, became one of the best friends the mountain tribes ever had in the years of loss and destruction.

The wind is blowing in my face on this high and beautiful ridge. I can see for miles across the lower, cedar-feathered hills all around me. We need to head west, so I wake up young Alex. He gets up and stuffs his pillow and red blanket in the car.

I take a last look around the lovely landscape of Ash Hollow. Even on this windblown crest of the bluff, the delicate, golden dragonflies flick here, there, glinting in the sunlight, and far over the valley a hawk appears out of clear air, like a sudden memory of murder.

FORT LARAMIE

Then it's on into the high, treeless pastures of Wyoming. We spot our first mountain slowly raising its solemn grey head above the horizon, a far-flung relative of the higher Rockies beyond. Alex is awake now, gazing out the window, watching the sagebrush for the occasional antelope. We have a longstanding family game: a candy bar for the first-sighted deer or antelope.

We find the turnoff to the Fort Laramie National Historic Site. It is a remarkable collection of barracks, officers' quarters, and a museum, but the buildings date from a period later than 1840 when De Smet with the Andrew Drips party passed, later than 1846 when Francis Parkman spent some singular days watching the comings and goings of Indians and white emigrants. It was then an outpost of the American

Fur Company, largely populated by French trappers and their Indian wives (American soldiers were still hundreds of miles to the east). The fort Parkman saw was built of adobe bricks stacked fifteen feet high and surmounted by a wooden palisade. The modern historic site has no stockade, but a visitor can walk the grounds and see the very landscape Parkman described. He had his biases, and was not one to romanticize the early West, as evidenced by his description of pioneers who camped near Fort Laramie:

> A crowd of broad-brimmed hats, thin visages, and staring eyes, appeared suddenly at the gate. Tall, awkward men, in brown home-spun; women, with cadaverous faces and long, lank figures, came thronging in together, and, as if inspired by the very demon of curiosity, ransacked every nook and corner of the fort.

Our own demon of curiosity satisfied, we drive west to the little town of Guernsey and find our way to a range of hills where the steel-shod wagon wheels cut deep ruts in solid rock. The evening is misty and cool and the light is fading as we climb among juniper trees to the sandstone hill where you can walk the ruts that cut the rock, some so ground down by wheels and rain that the rock rises on either side above our heads.

Darkness overtakes us, and we hurry west from Guernsey, then take Interstate 25 north, looking for steak. An hour later we find it in Douglas, Wyoming, at the Clementine Cattle Company, a gabled building with unpainted lap siding. We slip through the door two minutes before closing and order our potatoes and meat. Only one table is occupied this late: four men in cowboy boots and greying hair talking the evening away. The lights are dim, the wood-slatted cathedral ceiling rises into darkness, and the steaks are delicious.

But the motels of Douglas are full. We drive the streets, circling twice through the town till at last we find a hodgepodge place with a bronze statue of an elk and two rusted oil-well pumpjacks out front beneath a huge cottonwood tree. It's called the High Plains Motel, and seems to have been assembled from a line of shops attached to a two-story building behind. There are two rooms available: one, a confined, windowless room thick with the smell of cigars and cigarettes, and a large attic in the rear building. We choose the attic. It contains six double beds beneath a low ceiling. The clerk tells us migrant workers often split the night's rent, a dozen workers dividing the cost. The bathroom is old, dilapidated, but the shower works, and we're soon cleaned up and asleep.

DESERT

I t's mid-morning when we eat our eggs and biscuits and drink coffee in a restaurant across a side street from the motel. The place is darkly paneled and divided into several dimly lit rooms, one with a fireplace—clearly someone's home, once. In back we have found a table beside construction workers who are wolfing down their biscuits and sausage gravy and pancakes. The waitress refills their coffee cups and some of them kick back and light up cigarettes. We slept too late, so we hurry through our omelets and hashbrowns, pay at the cash register and walk out into a bright Wyoming morning.

We're off to Casper, skirting the darkly forested Laramie Mountains to our left, where Parkman spent three nomadic weeks with a band of the Dakota Sioux, hunting antelope and buffalo and listening to

Indians tell tales of war, torture, and the hunt. He returned to the East, where he became one of our most notable historians of the American and Canadian frontiers.

We are heading deeper into the wide landscapes of the old West. Nearing Casper, we see smoke drifting from a forest fire in the mountains above the city, the white smoke blowing north over pale, treeless hills. We drive into the city and stop for a box of .357 magnum bullets for my bear pistol, then head south. The highway follows the North Platte River into dry-grass and sagebrush desert that stretches far away through occasional white salt flats to barren, rock mountains on either hand.

By midafternoon we reach Independence Rock, a long, grey mound of granite 130-feet high, lying on flat, sagebrush prairie like a giant, stranded, petrified whale. We walk around to the north side and climb the steep incline to the top to take in the 360-degree view of alkaline rangeland. North lies another white salt flat; east are jumble-rock mountains, the western horizon is rimmed by distant, serrated mountains, a cool blue in the hot sun.

Andrew Drips' mule train and wagons, with De Smet and his two Indian guides, stopped here. A plaque commemorates De Smet's arrival. By the summer of 1840 when they camped nearby, travelers had already carved their names into the rock. Now there are many, many more. I find that a Miss L. B. Faulkner visited on July 4, 1920, exactly 90 years after fur trapper William Sublette named the rock. Sublette arrived here July 4, 1830 with wagons headed toward a fur traders' rendezvous. In 1843, the explorer John C. Fremont chiseled a big cross into the granite and covered the cross with a preparation of black, India rubber to prevent erosion, but emigrants, thinking it a symbol of Catholicism, blew it away with dynamite four years later.

De Smet called the rock "the great register of the desert" and he scraped his own name into it as witness of "the first priest to reach this remote spot." I look for his name, but like so many others engraved here, time and wind have worn them away. I do find a rabbit sleeping high on the rock in the shadow of a long ledge. Even though I step within twenty feet and its eyes open, it doesn't move. Perhaps it's bored by the presence of another tourist. He reminds me of Alex, sleeping away the day, so I leave him to his slumbers.

One day's wagon journey to the southwest of Independence Rock, up the Sweetwater River, travelers had to bypass what they called the Devil's Gate, a nearly vertical cleft in a 1500-foot granite ridge too rocky and narrow for the wagons to pass. De Smet smiles at the name: "These gentlemen have frequently on their lips the words devil and hell...Be not then alarmed [he tells his European readers] that I examined the Devil's Pass, went through the Devil's Gate, rowed on Satan's Stream, and jumped from the Devil's Horns." He writes that several of these locations, particularly the Devil's Rake, very much deserved their names.

It's late in the day, so we leave the Oregon Trail and head south, looking for a motel: 170 miles across the flat, scraggly Red Desert, a death sentence for the emigrants, who avoided it by crossing and re-crossing the Sweetwater River nine times as it flowed out of the Wind River Range. The wagons often left the winding river for miles at a time, cutting up toward South Pass to cross the continental divide. It was touch-and-go for everyone involved: the venemous sun overhead all the livelong day, burning against a white, dry sky, the arid winds drying out the wood of their covered wagons, loosening the wheel spokes in their sockets, the axle trees creaking, sometimes cracking, breaking; the parched mules and oxen pulling heavy weight up the rocky slope, moaning, huffing, straining, sometimes collapsing to leave their hard, blackened skins and bleached bones among the countless discarded dressers, implements, and the occasional rock-covered grave that marked this rutted, wind-gutted trail. De Smet describes the passage: "Presently the river was crossed, and the line of our wagons spread out as best they could, twisting and straying in almost every direction, amid a labyrinth of mountains and valleys, obliged to open a road, now in the bottom of a ravine, now on the slope of a cliff, often through brush; in one place the mules would have to be unhitched, in another teams must be doubled, and again all hands would be called upon to support the wagons on the

inclined edge of an abyss or hold them back in some too rapid descent...
and how many overturnings did we not behold?"

ALEX

Hours later, we turn west onto Interstate 80, now following the Transcontinental Railroad, the industrial successor of the wagons, just as the wagons replaced the fur trappers' pack trains, which succeeded the wild, nomadic tribes that followed the bison.

The sun declines toward distant mountains, and I flip down the visor. It has recently rained and sagebrush stands in bright pools of water. A herd of multi-colored wild horses gallops away, the sun behind them catching the crystal spray kicked up by their hooves. Alex points out little families of antelope beyond the fences (he long ago won his candy bar), and sometimes we see oilwell pumpjacks standing among the rocks like chained prehistoric birds, wasted to bone, pecking mechanically at the shadowed sands.

After a long day of watching desert, Alex settles back to sleep again. He is the last of our children. Thin and tall, a face growing leaner as he enters manhood, thick brown hair, pebble-grey eyes, the first traces of a beard. He is a lover of pickup basketball games and beat-box rhythms self-created, of free-styling hip-hop songs, and jokes.

He was born in a hundred-year-old, three-story farmhouse now in the city limits of Topeka, Kansas. I remember walking to an upstairs window and watching his doctor, her long red hair tied back, pulling a wheeled oxygen tank up our sidewalk to come deliver our new baby. A difficult birth, my wife refusing all medications. She had been busy all day, enduring the contractions, laundering sheets, making beds, boiling corn on the cob for the other children. After her doctor arrived, she agreed at last to lie down in the upstairs bedroom and take on the labor pains. The doctor had told her that the child would be very small because Joy had been unable to eat much in the past months, piecing on salads, picking at food the rest of us devoured. However, the new baby turned out to be larger than expected and resisted coming into this world. She endured the hard contractions and the boy finally made his wet, squalling entrance—ten pounds, nine ounces, a little big boy.

I looked at his scrunched up red face, his squashed and pointed head, his matted hair, and remarked that he was in fact a very ugly child. Our red-headed doctor who had constructed her life out of loving babies was highly offended that the boy's father would say such a horrible thing. So I shut my mouth. Joy knows me and my quirks; she wasn't offended. We named him Alexander, after Alexander Solzhenitsyn, Russian writer and dissident.

***

It's four or five years later, late in the evening. Winter in Kansas. Alex climbs up the cold, creaky stairs of the old farm house in bare feet and finds me in my office typing a college paper or paying the bills. He grabs my hand and says, "Bedtime, Daddy. Es go to bed." I lay aside my work and follow his brown thatch of hair into the bathroom to brush our teeth, then we walk down the hall and into the bedroom to that same bed on which he was born so I can read him poetry or a bedtime story. He is by this time a beautiful child and he loves the evening routine. On winter nights he giggles when he pokes his icy little feet between my warm thighs, making me jump half out of the bed.

Then I read him a familiar Mother Goose rhyme: "Goosey goosey gander,/ Where shall I wander,/ Upstairs and downstairs,/ And in my lady's chamber./ There I met an old man./ Would not say his prayers;/ Take him by the left leg and throw him down the stairs!" He has no idea what it means (nor do I), but he soon falls into the rhythms of the words, reciting: "Where thall I wander, Uptares and downtares,/ And in my wady's kameber." He loves the sound of the words, and I love the sound of his voice.

**

He's already seven. He lies beside me asleep. Summer has come again. Through the open window of the old farmhouse, I hear the Russian olive tree receiving and translating a night wind for my listening. We've been reading a story about a boy of the Teton Sioux who is guided and mentored by an older boy named Hump. They ride the Dakota prairies hunting birds and prairie dogs. The younger boy, Curly, will one day become the Sioux war chief Crazy Horse. A few minutes before, Alex lay staring at the ceiling as his imagination picked up the tales of those wild riders of the western plains, but now he's chasing them into his dreams where I cannot follow. His mom has cut his dark brown hair into a strange bowl cut that lies scattered across the faded green pillowcase. In the warm night he lies shirtless and I see a small cut on his neck, another small scab on his backbone, and an inch-long white welt on one foot where he once kicked a piece of glass. None of these marks of misadventure minded long—all resulting from and overcome by the joys of play.

Joy comes up the stairs. Rather than carry him to his own bed and wake him, she slips in beside me. I scoot him over and we three sleep.

***

He is eight or nine and time is running faster. To slow it down, he and I have camped with our friend Frank and his boys near the shore of a Kansas reservoir. At dawn Alex and I are walking across a meadow through prairie grasses weighted with a heavy dew. Dew-whitened webs of the wolf spider lie here and there across the meadow, stitched like random patches to the thick fabric of knee-high bluestem and grama grasses. I lead the way, weaving between the white spider patches, my jeans wet to my knees, my shoes soaked, our trail leaving a winding seam of darker grasses where we've brushed off the dew. We come down through dark junipers and lighter hackberries to the lake where we've hidden our canoe. Across the grey water, the growing light whitens the fog that lies quiet and cool, rising faintly blue-green where it dims a forested hill beyond. Dead trees stand in the water, gesturing stiffly, misshapen victims of another project of the Army Corps of Engineers.

I tell him to step through the middle of the canoe, and hand him a paddle. He settles on the webbed seat in the prow. I step in and shove off into the pale fog. A wet spring morning. Our paddles dip the water and pull, sliding us out into grey water. The wings of unseen ducks in the fog are suddenly drumming the air, then we see two dark forms hurtling away into milky daylight. We move slowly among the dead trees, dipping our paddles quietly, winding through the old, lost forest. There are spider webs here, too, long, glinting strands of drawn glass and beaded silk. The day coming, the mist thinning, we see five or six white pelicans floating out of the naked grey trunks of old elms and oaks. Turning toward them, we see the nervous flicker of their white tail feathers as they turn away, swimming steadily, each one moving its sagging-beaked head to keep an alien eye upon us. As we approach, they arch their enormous white-and-black wings. At once they are all moving quickly forward, hammering the fog with their wings, their running feet slapping the water...soon gone.

Alex looks back at me and smiles. "That was cool!"

"Yes, it was."

An hour later we beach the canoe and walk up to the campfire where Frank is boiling coffee and frying up a big batch of scrambled eggs and sharp, summer sausage.

***

Winter again. A snowpack on the streets. Alex is twelve, and time is skipping by. He sits with four other boys his age in a snowy yard a few doors down from our house. They've had their snowball fight and are now waiting out the evening, talking, telling stories, laughing, enjoying each other's company. To his left is Daniel, Alex's lifelong friend, whose house lies just behind the seated boys. Chinese Alex lives next door; he's a heavy-set boy in an orange-and-blue winter coat. He scrunches together another snowball. Jake from down the block is there, and Malcolm, a black friend from a few streets away.

Two blocks to their left a big SUV pulls onto the snowy street. Its windows are tinted stone black, a heavy bass beat pounds from the approaching car. It looks dangerous. Topeka is a city of many street gangs: Bloods and Crips moved in years ago to sell drugs. Hispanic gangs and Kansas meth dealers have now added their crimes. Our next door neighbor's oldest boy is in prison for murder. A boy across the street loved to be called a "gangsta" and took the title to jail with him. A few years ago Topeka had the highest per capita murder rate in the nation for a city of its size. The boys know about gang violence.

Chinese Alex stands up with the big snowball in his hand. He has never taken part in snowball attacks before, never been part of the spoken plans that precede the ambush; his mother, or perhaps his preference for video games, keeps him inside most of the time. But here he is standing up for the first time in his bulky winter coat, warning no one of his intentions, clutching a huge snowball.

Daniel looks up. "Alex," he says.

The boy steps forward, his arm moving back.

Then my Alex notices: "Alex! What are you doing?"

The car moves slowly by over the icy street. Chinese Alex lets fly.

The snowball smashes into the passenger window. The boys are suddenly all on their feet. The SUV slides to a stop and the driver's door opens. They see a big black man come sliding around the corner of the car. The four boys turn and sprint toward the alley, in a mad scramble into Daniel's backyard, ducking into the shadows behind Daniel's house, listening closely over their pounding hearts for pursuit.

They hear nothing. Chinese Alex, in his big orange-and-blue winter coat is, for some reason, whirling around, dodging back and forth between the boys, jumping up and down.

My Alex whispers, "Alex, what are you doing? Chill out."

Chinese Alex's winter coat whirls toward my Alex and seems suddenly to grow larger; the face is not Chinese Alex's; it's the face of a very large and very angry black man who happens to be wearing the same kind of coat as Chinese Alex.

"What the fuck was you trying to do!" the man yells.

Alex freezes.

"Who done it?" The man jumps from Alex to Daniel. "Who done it?" He stares into Malcolm's face.

One of the boys manages to mutter, "He's not here. He got away."

"Got away! I should kill all you sons of bitches! I got my wife and kids in that car! You scared the hell out of her! I should beat the shit out of you!"

None of them move.

"What the hell was you doin'!"

He's in a fuming rage—as well he should be. He is stomping back and forth, his hands clenched into fists. "Don't you ever let me catch you again. You hear?"

The boys stand there wide eyed, mute, but manage to nod.

The man turns on his heel and stomps away through the snow.

Daniel, feeling terrifically relieved, suddenly thinks to offer thanks. He calls after the man: "Thanks for teaching us a lesson."

The man whirls about and charges in a spray of snow. "If I wanted to teach you a god-damned lesson, I'd pound your sorry ass into the snow!"

Daniel holds his breath.

The man turns and stalks away.

***

But such occasions will not stop boys bent on play. Through the long hot summers it is league baseball, basketball in the park, or lofting water balloons at passing cars and then running like crazy for blocks, dodging through back yards, leaping fences, slipping into garages. Or it's hiding at night in the dark bushes, then sneaking onto someone's porch, knocking hard, then diving, giggling, back into the bushes to await the mystified neighbor come to the door. Annoying behavior, but given the gang killings and drug addictions across the city, I was glad, when I finally heard these stories, that it wasn't worse.

***

After I found a teaching position in Virginia, Alex and I moved, expecting Joy to follow within six months. But the house didn't sell and the national economy collapsed. Alex and I were marooned. Still, it turned out to be a good four years for Alex and me, living like bachelors, learning to cook chili, spaghetti, and hamburger gravy, occasionally hunting squirrels or fishing for bass, enjoying Alex's football, basketball, and baseball games.

But I have not raised him as I should. He has learned little of self-discipline and hard work—most of what Alex was required to do came from sports, work enhanced by play. Of course he had his homework, but a student can maneuver through many modern high schools with little work outside of class. Now he will need a strong dose of self discipline to make his way through college while keeping a part time job.

ROCK SPRINGS

By the time we reach Rock Springs, I'm worn out. The dying sun has soaked the western clouds in deepening shades of red as the highway drops us down, down, down past all sunlight into some kind of wide canyon of shadowed streets and streetlights, roadside motels, and restaurants. Dark stone cliffs to the west blot the fading sky.

Rock Springs, Wyoming looks like a town thrown up in a rock quarry, a quarry cut into a corner of 9000 square miles of unrelieved desert. Not the desert of the majestic saguaro, organ pipe cactus, and painted canyons, but a wide, dry plain of baked alkali and laterite crust, with an occasional mesa or butte of red sandstone layered over chalky limestone. An arid landscape of sagebrush, saltbush, clump grass, and yellowing cheatgrass ravaged by strong winds that grind down stone and sand smooth the grey limbs of drought-killed cottonwoods. The first church built in Rock Springs blew down three times during construction. A bad omen, if you ask me.

The brackish stream, Bitter Creek, that winds through the town is alkaline, the water undrinkable; when the town was first settled, water had to be transported by rail from the Green River, twelve miles to the west.

Why would anyone choose to live here?

Coal. Coal is often the answer chosen for energy-hungry America.

In September 1852, almost 50 years after Lewis and Clark's exploration had opened the west to immigration, Captain Stansbury of the U.S. Topographical Engineers and his guide, mountain man Jim Bridger, discovered a giant vein of coal. A lack of coal and wood to fuel the trains had been the fundamental reason no one had attempted to run a railroad west through the almost treeless Great American Desert. Here was coal in abundance, the richest deposits in the world, and veins of it could be found both east and west of Rock Springs—more than enough for the trains and plenty to send east and west to supply a growing nation. The Union Pacific owned the rights to the coal, and began to build up mining operations soon after completing the transcontinental link with the Central Pacific Railroad May 10, 1869.

The place quickly started adding settlers, but it was not much of a town then—just a collection of weathered shacks, roofed dugouts, and tents. "Streets," said an early visitor, "seemed to wind at their own inclination and they were alternately dusty, muddy, and frozen." An old saying had it that the winter snows never melted, they just wore out blowing back and forth.

I pay for a motel room, then Alex and I walk on over to the Iron Skillet for food. We step in and find a booth near the wall of windows. A pretty waitress with a pert nose walks up and asks for our order.

After a quick look at the menu, I say, "I'll take the steak with wine and mushroom sauce."

"No wine," she says.

"Wine and mushroom sauce," I repeat. "The steak."

"It's just brown gravy," she says. "There's no wine in it. No mushrooms either."

Alex and I glance up from our menus. Her brown hair is tied back in a ponytail and she wears a plaid shirt. She looks me in the eye, waiting for a response.

"All right," I say. "The brown gravy then."

She looks at Alex.

"Chicken-fried steak," he says. His perennial favorite.

"No, you don't," she says.

"I don't?"

"No."

"But I like chicken-fried steak."

"Not this one."

"Why?"

"It's awful. I'll give you a minute to pick something else." She turns and walks away.

Alex is hungry. He calls after her, "How about some mac and cheese?"

She hesitates, and over her shoulder says, "No," and keeps walking.

Alex and I look at each other. I shake my head and smile. I like this waitress.

Alex doesn't.

When she returns a few minutes later, Alex is holding his fingers like a pistol and shooting at me.

The waitress walks up to Alex and asks, "How old are you?"

"Eighteen," he says.

"You're only a year younger than me? Why are you acting like a child?"

Alex smiles. "I'd like a big order of mac and cheese."

"No, you don't."

"But—"

"Do you see a sign out there that says McDonalds or Burger King?"

Alex looks out the plate glass at the darkened parking lot.

"So?"

"That means you can't have it your way. You've got to have it our way."

Alex orders a hamburger and fries.

When she returns with his burger and my brown-gravy steak, I tell the waitress I have read a story by Richard Ford where a criminal's car breaks down near Rock Springs and he finds help from a woman whose husband works at a gold mine.

This doesn't seem to register with her.

"Is there a gold mine outside of town?" I ask.

"Yes. And this is the location of the Chinese Massacre."

"Chinese Massacre?"

"They lined up all the Chinese workers who were laying rails for the Transcontinental Railroad, lined them up on the cliffs back over there and shot them dead. Didn't want to pay them for their work. They'd promised them bags of gold back in California when they started the work, but when they got here, about 50 miles from joining up with the railroad being built from out east, they decided to cut expenses."

Alex is intrigued in spite of himself. "Really? Why didn't that show up in my history books?"

"Where'd you go to school?"

"Kansas."

"Well, that explains it," she says.

"Explains what?"

She smiles.

I look at our waitress's name tag: Daney.

"Danny," I say.

"It's Danéy," she says.

"It could be Danny from the way it's spelled."

"It could." She turns and walks away.

A young man stands up from the adjacent booth, leans over, and whispers, "She's named after a dude, man."

"A dude?"

"Yeah. Our father lost his best friend, Danny, before she was born, so she got named Danéy."

I found out later Danéy was mistaken about the massacre in her home town. It was true that about 50 Chinese workers were shot in and around Rock Springs, but the massacre happened sixteen years *after* the completion of the railroad. The Central Pacific Railroad Company had hired thousands of Chinese laborers who worked hard shoveling the grades, clearing snow, hanging in baskets from granite cliffs while swinging their picks, blasting their way through mountains with gunpowder and lethal bottles of nitroglycerin. Roughly ten percent of their workforce died in blasting accidents, winter avalanches, and other accidents while hammering their way through the Sierra Nevada Mountains and across the Nevada and Utah deserts.

It's also not true that they went unpaid. The man who hired them, big Charlie Crocker of the Central Pacific, knew that the Chinese had saved the western end of the Transcontinental Railroad. Crocker had searched for needed workers all across California and found only 600 white men willing to lay rail into the wilderness mountains and deserts. After he hired them, many slipped away to follow rumors of gold in Idaho or Montana. Crocker had even begun negotiations with the military to send out Confederate prisoners-of-war to build the railroad, but the Civil War ended too soon.

In desperation he hired 5000 Chinese who proved to be tough, capable workers. Crocker, riding his sorrel mare up and down the line, raged "like a mad bull in the railway camps," but he "loved nothing more than to ride into camp on payday in his bearskin overcoat, his beard tinged with snow, his horse steaming, saddlebags bulging, and call out the names of [Chinese] and [Irishmen] and drop the gold and silver coins into outstretched hands," says historian Craig Storti. Chinese and Irish workers were paid $28 a month, a good wage for the Chinese who, in southern China, made from three dollars to five dollars a *year*. By living eight or nine to a room, they could save almost twenty dollars a month (four or five years' wages in China) to take back across the Pacific, but $28 a month was insufficient to support a white man who was often trying to support wife and children while living in rented rooms.

By 1874, the Union Pacific, and hence Rock Springs, were being run by the robber baron Jay Gould, whose biographer Richard O'Connor writes: "None of his contemporaries quite approached his genius for trickery, his boldness in corruption, his talent for strategic betrayal." Jay Gould was a millionaire by the age of twenty-two and he had no intention of letting growing union movements compete with his authority and his investments.

Late in 1874 a new organization, the Knights of Labor, began agitating for higher wages for all workers. With the encouragement of the Knights of Labor, white miners in Rock Springs threatened a strike during the waning months of 1874, but Union Pacific officers countered by hiring hundreds of Chinese workers who would not strike and forced the few white miners who remained to sign so-called "ironclad" contracts that they would never join a union. For nine years thereafter, says Storti, "the coalfields of the West were quiet. In the conflict between organized labor and the Union Pacific for control of the mining camps, Jay Gould and company had won a decisive victory.

"Then, in the fall of 1884, seemingly out of nowhere, the Knights called two successful strikes on behalf of UP shopmen." Within the month, the Knights of Labor had organized railroad workers up and down the lines of the Union Pacific. The coal mines of Rock Springs were key to the strike, because they were the one dependable money maker the Union Pacific could rely upon in hard times when transcontinental transportation was being challenged by fast clipper ships sailing around Cape Horn. The Knights of Labor asked for the cooperation of the Chinese, but the Chinese knew their status with their employers depended on their refusal to strike.

There were other aggravations. The Union Pacific would probably have hired no one but Chinese, but such a policy would have alienated the white population of the territory. They did hire one white for every three or four Chinese, but the UP clearly favored the Chinese laborers. Craig Storti gives the details:

> The Chinese were routinely given the most productive rooms [underground mining pits] and were always allowed first choice of rooms when a new entry was opened. Whites, on the other hand, were assigned to the least desirable rooms—the most dangerous, for example—or the least ventilated or (the most common complaint) rooms where they were obliged to cut through great quantities of rock to get the coal...And even then, when they had such a room in working order, they were often forced to turn it over to a sojourner [Chinese worker who planned on returning to China].

Because each miner was paid by the bushel of coal extracted, hacking through limestone and sandstone, digging ventilation shafts, and other such tasks paid exactly nothing.

Arguments arose. The company regularly sided with their dependable and cheaper Chinese labor force. Chinese, says Storti, "stole the white collier's pit cars, ripped up his tracks, baited him with insults (a reprisal could cost a man his job), and even on occasion stole his coal." The animosity between the Chinese and whites grew. Most white miners were also immigrants, many from Finland, Ireland, and England, with the key difference being that almost all these European immigrants intended to stay in America and not return to Europe, while almost all the Chinese were saving up money to return to China where they would immediately be wealthy men.

Cultural differences made matters worse. The whites saw their Chinese counterparts as "moon-eyed, rat eating pagans" who refused to learn English. The Chinese lived apart in a settlement built for them by the Union Pacific and had little reason to associate with white miners who lived along Bitter Creek in self-made dugouts or in rented buildings in town. The Chinese imported their own food: Chinese bacon, dried oysters, cuttlefish, and abalone, seaweed, mushrooms, salted cabbage, dried bamboo shoots, peanut oil, almond cakes. They drank rice wine and tea, and many smoked opium. The whites ate beef and biscuit, elk and antelope, drank coffee and whisky, and smoked cigars.

Meanwhile, the Union Pacific cut wages and forced workers to buy such necessities as flour, coffee, and tools at elevated rates from the company store while the Chinese were allowed to buy tools for cost and imported their own food by rail.

On the morning of September 1, 1885, a dispute arose over who should work a particularly promising coal room in Coal Pit No. 6. An English immigrant named Whitehouse was appointed to work this room with his partner William Jenkins. Some Chinese miners were working nearby.

Whitehouse and Jenkins laid explosives and then Whitehouse left for the day. When he returned the next morning, September 2, he found that the Chinese had set off the gunpowder charges in the room he had worked the day before and were hauling out the coal. He later reported that he "sat down for about a half an hour, talking with the Chinamen in regard to their shaking the coal down and taking the place." But the Chinese refused to leave. They kept saying, "No savee."

The argument intensified. Whitehouse reported that one of the Chinese miners called him a son of a bitch and swung at him with his pick. Whitehouse said he ducked and threw a fist that knocked the man flat. Chinese miners came running with their picks and drills and shovels while a dozen white miners with their tools joined Whitehouse and Jenkins. Everyone was shouting. Two or three whites jumped the man who had swung the pick and one of them slammed a coal pick into his head three times. Men grabbed their shovels and began hacking at each other. Several company foremen rolled down the tracks in pit cars and put a stop to the fight. The Chinese loaded their dead and wounded on the pit cars and the foremen escorted them out of the mine. Soon the pit superintendent Evans arrived and found the whites were still down in the mine. He took a rail car down and when he found them, he asked what the trouble was about. Some of them were cut and bleeding, all of them were angry. Someone shouted that they weren't going to allow

Chinamen to drive them out of the mines. Evans tried to reason with them, but a man yelled, "Come on, boys! We may as well finish it now, as long as we have commenced. It has to be done anyhow."

Evans wouldn't let the men leave in the pit car, so they all grabbed their tools and climbed out on foot. They had killed a Chinese man, maybe two. They must have known that if the fight stopped there, there would be legal repercussions, so they determined to finish what had started. They hurried to their rented rooms to fetch rifles and pistols, hatchets, clubs and knives, agreeing to meet back on the railroad tracks a half mile from Number 6.

Word spread. People in the town heard that armed miners were coming down the tracks toward town. A few businessmen walked out to meet them and talked them into leaving their weapons in a nearby store, which seems to indicate the miners were initially intending to negotiate. But they continued their march, crossing the railroad bridge over Bitter Creek and turning on Front Street toward the union hall of the Knights of Labor. "White men, fall in!" they shouted, and the crowd was growing.

The bell on the Knights of Labor Hall began tolling, and men from other mines joined the growing crowd. The men from Mine No. 6 reported their version of what had happened and most agreed to a general meeting for six that evening, a meeting that would never take place. The men dispersed and some miners drifted into bars and saloons carrying their anger and arguments with them. Saloon managers could see trouble brewing and wanted no part of it. They began shoving the miners out and locking the doors.

Just after noon, 100 to 150 whites gathered at the railroad tracks. Women and children joined them to listen to the rising furor. Dogs were barking, men shouting, the pent up anger from years of low wages and racial alienation boiled to the surface.

A little after 2:00 p.m., says Storti, a rumor swept through the crowd that railroad officials had wired for federal troops to put down any disturbances. The mob started off for Chinatown. They first retrieved their weapons and headed east along Front Street, passing a store that sold firearms and ammunition where they stopped and bought out the entire stock of ammunition.

The mob then moved toward Chinatown, firing warning shots over the heads of several Chinese who were hiding in a section house near the tracks.

The crowd gathered near the first of two bridges over Bitter Creek where they sent in a three-man delegation demanding that every Chinese pack his goods and leave within the next hour—an outrageous request that the Chinese couldn't quite believe. The leaders of the mob then divided the crowd into three sections; about half crossed a small plank bridge over Bitter Creek while a smaller group continued over the railroad bridge into Chinatown, and the third group circled around to the north side of the Chinese shacks, nearly surrounding the Chinese, many of whom had not gone to work because of a Chinese holiday.

The Chinese now knew the matter was grave. They ran up a red warning flag over their community and sent men to the various mines to bring back miners who had gone to work.

The restless crowd of armed whites spotted Chinese miners running back to their houses and someone called out that they would barricade themselves in their homes and fight. The mob pressed forward. Onlookers along Front Street climbed onto boxcars and cheered them on.

The third group attacked first, charging up the hill behind Chinatown and shooting at men who were hiding in the coal shed and pump house. One man, Lor Sun Kit, sprinted from the pump house and was shot through the back. Leo Kow Boot headed for Mine Number 4 and caught a bullet through his neck. And then everyone was running. A white man named Zwicky later reported that the Chinamen fled "like a herd of antelope, making no resistance. Volley after volley was fired after the fugitives. In a few minutes the hill east of town was literally blue with [blue-shirted] hunted Chinamen. What appeared at first to be the mad frolic of ignorant men was turning into an inhuman butchery of innocent beings."

Two women who were helping guard the railroad bridge spotted Yii See Yen running straight down the hill toward them with Leo Dye Bah close behind. One of the women raised her rifle and shot Yii See Yen in the head. Another woman fired at Leo Dye Bah, hitting him in the chest; he plunged dead into Bitter Creek.

Ah Koon, assistant to the Chinese head man, was running from his house with $1,600 in a bag when he turned to see three or four men aiming their rifles. Shots rang out and he stumbled, dropping the bag, scrambled to his feet and ran again, leaving what was then a fortune behind. Making his way to a railroad section house, he banged on the door and cried out, "Mr., you better open door and let me in."

The white man inside called out, "Who's that?"

"China boy!"

The white man opened the door and Ah Koon stepped in, saying, "I am nearly dead, I got nothing to eat. You give me some bread?"

The man walked to his larder to get some bread and asked what was wrong in Rock Springs.

"Lots trouble, drive China boys out."

Seven to nine hundred Chinese were now on the run, most of them men, but a few women and children too. In the hours that followed, Chinese who hid in their homes were burned out. Those who hid in cellars beneath the burning shacks and clawed their way into the earth also burned to death. Rioters dragged metal trunks from the burning beams and stole what they could. As the sun dropped behind the high stone bluffs, men and women looted homes and systematically torched every single building. A local doctor, Edward Murray, rode his horse up and down the narrow streets waving his hat and shouting, "No quarter! Shoot them down!"

As the sun set, young boys ran through the darkening streets dodging the glaring fires, chasing chickens, ducks, geese, and squealing pigs. One boy made off through the rolling soot and smoke with one pig wrapped around his neck and another held under his arm. Someone heard another boy cry out, "Do you think I'm going to fight all day for nothing?" as he pushed a wheelbarrow with a pig around a corner and down the hill.

After the firing started, most Chinese ran up the hills and into the sage scrub and dry rock of the desert, some of them wounded. It was mid-afternoon when the shooting began and the sun was harsh. But of course there was no refuge in the desert: no shelter, no food, no water. Many had brought no coats; some, having run directly from the mines, were shirtless. That night temperatures would drop below freezing.

One man, with his wife and baby, made his way southeast away from town and over what was called Burning Mountain into the scabrous land of greasewood, rock, and chalky dirt. Behind them they could still hear the distant popping of rifles and pistols. Occasionally they heard the heavy thump of a keg of gunpowder exploding, the blasts accompanied by the distant cheers and jeers of the onlookers and rioters. In the hours of walking through the afternoon heat, the baby must have died of dehydration. Then, with sunset, came the cold. They dared not return to the town, now a seething glow on the horizon. With her baby dead, the mother gave up—she lay down, thirsty and exhausted, and died. When the desert wolves found them, the father had no heart to leave his young family. He put his pistol to his head and pulled the trigger.

Another Chinaman, Yu Kwang, with five others, lost his way in the hills. They wandered into the moon-blanched night, making their way more or less westward toward a coal settlement at the Green River, the only source of water—twelve miles away. But they didn't chart a straight line. For two freezing nights and two burning days they wandered through dry aggregate, scrub and sage, eventually losing each other in the alternately moonlit or sun-blasted wastes. Yu Kwang finally came upon the railroad tracks, where he was picked up by a passing train. The other four were never seen again.

Another five eventually ate their own excrement to stay alive, but four were too weak to fight off the wolves. Only the fifth, Pang Chung, chased by the pack, staggered back into Rock Springs and survived.

Many did find the railroad tracks and walked the twelve miles west to the Green River or were picked up on the way by the train. At the Green River settlement, they found water, but were soon menaced by white miners living there who had gotten word of the riot. The Chinese retreated to an island in the river.

The day of the riot, company officials telegraphed the territorial government in Cheyenne pleading for help. Governor Warren got the message and immediately asked the Union Pacific to send out two trains, one on the tracks east of Rock Springs, and one west to the Green River, to pick up refugees. Rescue parties organized by the railroad were then sent into the desert with blankets and food. By late afternoon of the next day, some 500 Chinese had been picked up and transported 90 miles west to the mining town of Evanston.

Governor Warren, a big man with a handlebar moustache, acted quickly to save them. "I do have an interest," he said, "in protecting, as far as my power lies, the lives, liberty, and property of every human being in this territory...and so long as I am governor, I shall act in the spirit of that idea." A man with the courage of his convictions, he took a train from Cheyenne to Rock Springs himself and confronted the angry rioters. The mob, in no mood for discussions, demanded that mine officials leave; most of them did. But Governor Warren stood fast. He met with remaining mine officials and tried to calm things down.

Several days later, when asked what he thought of the whole affair, he said, "It is the most brutal and damnable outrage that ever occurred in any country. Those fellows actually attacked the Chinese in their own abodes while they were packing to get away, shot them unresistingly and pushed them back into the shanties and roasted them like so many rats!"

Warren's courage and quick action no doubt saved the lives of hundreds, but railroad officials, after promising the terrified Chinese that they would take them to San Francisco, turned the train and carried them back to Rock Springs. The Union Pacific's one concern was not the welfare of their Chinese workers, but coal production. They needed their Chinese to start digging coal again.

When the doors of the windowless boxcars slid open, the Chinese refugees peered out in shock at the smoking ashes of their homes. Stray pigs were rooting around among dismembered corpses, and the stench of burnt flesh was still in the air. Why were they here? They had been promised a safe trip to San Francisco. They were horrified that they had been returned to the scene of their nightmare. They begged for passage to the west coast.

Mining officials refused. To protect their labor force, the Union Pacific had brought along federal soldiers on the train and was asking the government in Cheyenne for more.

The white rioters were incensed at the return of the Chinese and tried to block the mines. The soldiers drove them away, but even so, most Chinese refused to work. They camped out by the boxcars at night and cooked their meals on open campfires while the UP proceeded to build them a new Chinatown with lumber they had loaded on the same train. When additional troops finally arrived, the soldiers built their own semi-permanent camp between Chinatown and Rock Springs as a buffer. Ah Say, the main liaison between the Chinese miners and the UP, asked for the two months back pay owed to the miners, but the UP representative refused, apparently concerned that the Chinese would leave if they received their pay. As historian Storti puts it, "In essence, the Chinese now became hostages of the UP." The Chinese were at last on strike, but the railroad countered by ordering that their UP-sanctioned supply store stop selling to Chinese strikers and threatened to kick them out of the boxcars where they had been living while their homes were being rebuilt.

The Chinese then gave up and went back to work under the escort of soldiers. Little more than a week after the riot, the editor of the Cheyenne newspaper, *The Sun*, wrote, "This great and glorious government is using bayonets and gatling guns to establish a slave market labor system in Wyoming"—this, twenty years after the ending of the Civil War.

The riot and strike were essentially over and it seemed the UP had once again won. Coal production, with some 600 Chinese, and 50 white miners (who had to agree to sign contracts never to join a union) was back to normal.

In the end, however, the railroad's brutal attempt to hold onto a cheap labor force did not work. Reading newspaper accounts of what had happened, whites rioted up and down the west coast. Chinese were driven out of Seattle, Portland, and many towns and cities across eight Western states and territories. Thousands of Chinese workers, fearing for their lives, returned to China, and the U. S. Congress responded in two ways: at the insistence of the Chinese ambassador, they reimbursed the Rock Springs Chinese for their burned homes, but they also passed The Chinese Exclusion Act, which halted Chinese immigration for 50 years.

"The final death toll," says Storti, "was put at fifty-one, the highest ever for a race riot in American history." He also states that Rock Springs has changed little in more than a century. "It is still something of a frontier town and still a mining center. The UP goes through…The centennial of the massacre was observed several years ago, but most residents are not aware of the history their town made that September in 1885."

Not one of the rioters and killers was convicted of his crimes. But neither did the miners of either race win the battle, and they certainly did not win the war—big business did. Most miners were soon replaced by newly invented machines, one mechanized coal digger taking the place of 33 miners. Wendell Berry, writing of another coal field in the Appalachians, says, "The coal industry…held the title deeds to the future and devoured the land, people, and culture with a satanic appetite."

In Cormac McCarthy's *Blood Meridian*, a fourteen-year-old boy runs away from his Tennessee homestead into sparsely settled frontier Texas. There he spends the night with a half-mad hermit who tells him, "You can find meanness in the least of creatures, but when God made man the devil was at his elbow. A creature that can do anything. Make a machine. And a machine to make a machine. And evil that can run itself a thousand years, no need to tend it. You believe that?"

The boy says, "I dont know."

"Believe that," says the old man.

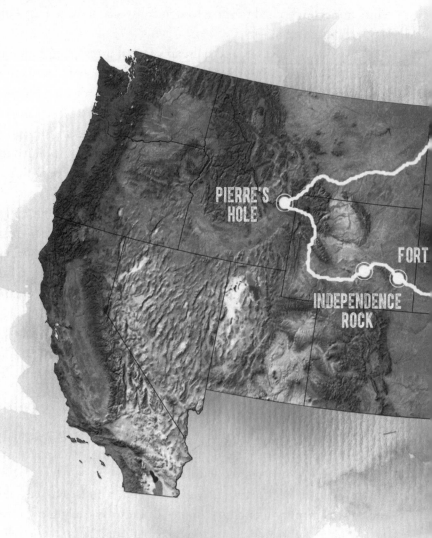

PIERRE'S
HOLE

FORT

INDEPENDENCE
ROCK

ST. LOUIS

DE SMET 1840

RENDEZVOUS

A lex and I drive north out of Rock Springs. A hundred miles of alkaline flats and sagebrush brings us into the foothills of the jagged, snow-flanked Wind River Range that rims the horizon. We stop for gas in the little town of Pinedale, then drive on to the even smaller town of Daniel, where a sign directs us to a gravel road that climbs up and around a high, dry hill of sagebrush and grass where we find a small, open, A-frame structure standing on thin columns of riverstone. A plaque commemorates the first Catholic mass in the northern Rocky Mountains, celebrated by De Smet, and attended by 2000 trappers, traders, and Indians of several tribes.

We gaze down across a wide expanse of sagebrush surrounded by snowy mountains and looped through by the meandering Green River, a tributary of the Colorado. Along the river below us, its banks crowded with willow brush, cottonwood groves, and the rich green grasses that fed the thousands of horses of a Rocky Mountain rendezvous, De Smet would have seen hundreds and hundreds of tepees and tents grouped by tribes and clans and fur trader alliances. He had at last met the Salish and Pend Oreilles, both of whom had been sending emissaries to St. Louis for nine years. "Never in my life," he wrote, "have I enjoyed so many consolations as during my stay among these good Flatheads and Pend Oreilles...Our meeting was not that of strangers, but of friends; it was like children running to meet their father after a long absence." Which seems to our ears a rather condescending description, but his emotion is real: "I wept with joy at embracing them, and they also, with tears in their eyes, welcomed me." Big Ignace's two journeys, and his son's final journey to St. Louis, seemed at last to have achieved their purpose.

Neither side understood the other well. De Smet says the Salish "showed much eagerness to exchange the bow and quiver for the spade and plow." In truth, however, they adapted very slowly to American agriculture and ranching over the decades that followed and what eagerness they showed at the time tended more toward adding the rifle and the pistol to their arsenal of bows and quivers and lances. But there can be no doubt the Salish and their allies were strongly attracted to Catholic practice and spirituality that had been introduced to them by French, British, and Iroquois trappers and traders. De Smet in turn was strongly attracted to the tribes he encountered, not only to the Salish and Pend Oreilles, but to the many tribes he would meet over the following years: the Shoshones, the Coeur d'Alenes, the Kootenais, Crows, Sioux, Cheyenne, dozens more—even the Blackfeet, whom all the tribes he met seemed to fear and hate.

De Smet had a clear eye; he spoke what he saw, neither picking up the Romantic fascination with the "noble savage," nor accepting the devastating prejudices and hatreds of American settlers. Throughout his long life he came to respect the Indians, and despaired at their treatment by the white immigrants, traders, and government officials.

When he reached the Green River Rendezvous of 1840, he was struck by what he saw as the remarkable character of the Salish and Pend Oreilles:

> I was not able to discover among these people the slightest blame-worthy act, unless it was their gambling, in which they often venture everything they possess...They are scrupulously honest in their buying and selling; they have never been accused of having committed a theft...and they abhor a liar. Quarrels and fits of rage are severely punished. No one suffers without his brothers interesting themselves in his trouble and coming to his succor; accordingly, they have no orphans among them. They are polite, always of a jovial humor, very hospitable, and helpful to one another in their duties. Their lodges are always open to any one; they do not so much as know the use of keys and locks. One single man, by the influence which he has justly acquired by his bravery in fight and his wisdom in the council, leads the whole tribe; he has no need of guards, nor bolts, nor iron bars, nor state prisons. I have often asked myself: "Is it these people whom the civilized nations dare to call by the name of savages?"

This assessment is the more remarkable because it is given after witnessing the wild revelry of the fur trappers' rendezvous. Protestant missionaries who had seen these affairs were horrified. The Methodist minister Jason Lee, the first missionary to arrive at a Rocky Mountain rendezvous in 1834, sat in his tent, says historian Josephy, "trying to shut out the noise of the mountain men's carousing and cursing, and wrote in his diary, 'My God, my God, is there nothing that will have any effect on them?'" He was dismayed, too, by the Indians. "One," says Josephy, "an impulsive, fun-loving, young Nez Perce named The Bull's Head, whom the trappers nicknamed Kentuck (because he continually tried to sing the popular ballad, 'The Hunters of Kentucky,' which the Americans had taught him), came charging through the white men's camp one day, chasing a frightened buffalo and yelling, 'Hokahey!' as the mountain men cheered and fired their guns in the air. Another

Nez Perce, Tackensuatis, offended Lee by sousing himself in drink and swearing in English with the trappers."

De Smet, though a deeply religious man, seems to have taken all this in stride. He watched the 1840 rendezvous with a curious eye: "Three hundred [Shoshone] warriors came up in good order and at full gallop into the midst of our camp. They were hideously painted, armed with their clubs, and covered all over with feathers, pearls, wolves' tails, teeth and claws of animals, outlandish adornments, with which each one had decked himself...Those who had wounds received in war, and those who had killed the enemies of their tribe, displayed their scars ostentatiously and waved the scalps they had taken on the ends of poles." It was a wild sight for a man who had spent his youth in Europe, but he expressed no horror, and took no offense.

The Indians liked him. His earnest expression of his faith combined with his ready laughter and willingness to take a joke evidently appealed to them. Even the mountain men seemed to like this priest. The famous fur trapper and scout Kit Carson met De Smet at a rendezvous. In his autobiography, he says:

"Among the missionaries was old Father de Smitt [40 must have seemed old to mountain men whose life expectancy was low]...I can say of him that if ever there was a man who wished to do good, it was he. He never feared danger when duty required his presence among the savages, and if good works on this earth are rewarded hereafter, I am confident that his share of glory and happiness in the next world will be great."

De Smet's hope, and that of the priests who followed him to the early missions, was to see the competing tribes united by faith. A Jesuit, he had read of the remarkably successful missions among the Guarani Indians of South America in the 16th century, where 80,000 Indians settled in 30 towns. The Guarani, according to historians Jacqueline Peterson and Laura Peers, became "town magistrates, sculptors, organ builders, calligraphers, and builders of Baroque cathedrals...For the first band of young recruits like Pierre-Jean De Smet...who left Europe to minister to the Indians of America, it was the memory of the fabled

Paraguayan [missions] that fired the imagination and the soul."

De Smet estimated that 200,000 Indians lived across the northern plains and mountainous west of the United States. He hoped, like Lewis and Clark before him, to unite these tribes in peace, but unlike Lewis and Clark, he hoped the instrument of union would come from the teachings and practice of Christianity rather than from trade and the growing power of the American government. De Smet feared the vices of the approaching invasion: "Soon," writes De Smet, "the cupidity and avarice of civilized man will make the same inroads here as in the east, and the abominable influence of the vices of the frontier will interpose the same barrier to the introduction of the gospel."

DE SMET AND THE SALISH

After meeting the Salish at the Green River Rendezvous, De Smet followed them up the Green River into the mountains toward a major Salish camp. The path was difficult and eventually climbed the rugged Teton Mountains. Every day the priest taught his apparently eager hearers the doctrines of his faith. Ten Canadians who had attended the rendezvous accompanied them as they journeyed up the river and over the granite mountains. One of these Canadians was a Belgian named Jean Baptiste de Velder, a former grenadier in Napoleon's army who had left Flanders thirty years ago and had been a fur trapper in the Rockies for fourteen years. He had almost forgotten his native language, remembering only some prayers and a hymn in honor of the Virgin Mary "which he had learned as a child on his mother's knees." Velder offered to guide De Smet and assist him. His knowledge of the mountains and Indians probably saved De Smet's life, and his understanding of Indian languages helped De Smet communicate.

Crossing these rugged mountains, De Smet, like Lewis and Clark before him, observed plants and birds and animals with a scientific eye: "In this plain, as in all mountain valleys that I have traversed, flax grows in the greatest abundance; it is just the same as the flax that is cultivated in Belgium, except that it is an annual; the same stalk, calyx, seed and blue flower, closing by day and opening in the evening...The slope of the surrounding mountains abounds in the rarest plants, and offers the amateur botanist a superb collection."

His eye for topography was equally keen: "Mountains of almost per-pendicular cliffs rise to the region of perpetual snow and often overhang a rugged and narrow path, where every step threatens a fall...The defile was so narrow, and the mountains on either hand so high, that the sun could scarcely penetrate it for an hour or two of the day.

"After crossing the lofty mountains, we arrived upon the banks of [the Snake River]...The mass of snow melted during the July heat had swollen this torrent to a prodigious height. Its roaring waters rushed furiously down and whitened with their foam the great blocks of granite...The sight intimidated neither our Indians nor our Canadians; accustomed to perils of this sort, they rushed into the torrent on horseback and swam it." But De Smet could not swim and "dared not venture likewise." So the Canadians wrapped all his goods in his skin tent, tied it up, and had De Smet lie down on top. Three Salish jumped in and swam it across the icy torrent, laughing and telling De Smet he made a fine boat.

They followed forest trails through what is now Targhee National Forest, passing up the length of the valley called Pierre's Hole, and came upon the camp of the Salish and their allies the Pend Oreilles near today's Henry's Lake, which lies in a wide valley of sagebrush and buffalo grass near the western entrance to Yellowstone National Park. De Smet estimated 1600 Indians in a camp of between 150 and 200 tepees. "The elders wept with joy, while the young men expressed their satisfaction by leaps and shouts of happiness," writes De Smet. Their chief was The Grand Face, whose sons had been killed by the Sioux at Ash Hollow just three years before. De Smet, dressed in his long black robe, was led to the chief's tepee. The Grand Face "had a truly patriarchal aspect," according to De Smet, "and received me in the midst of his whole council with the liveliest cordiality. Then he addressed me the following remarks, which I report to you word for word, to give you an idea of his eloquence and his character: 'Black-robe, you are welcome in my nation. Today Kyleeeyou (the Great Spirit) has fulfilled our wishes. Our hearts are big, for our great desire is gratified. You are in the midst of a poor and rude people...I have always exhorted my children to love Kyleeeyou. We know that everything belongs to him, and that our whole dependence is upon his liberal hand. From time to time good white men have given us good advice, and we have followed it; and in the eagerness of our hearts, to be taught everything that concerns our salvation, we have several times sent our people to the great Black-robe at St. Louis that he might send us a Father to speak with us. Black-robe, we will follow the words of your mouth.'"

De Smet responded with a summary of his faith, working through his translators, after which the Indians sang together "in a harmony which surprised me very much, and which I thought admirable, several songs of their own composition, on the praise of God."

De Smet then began leading them in morning and evening prayers and preached four times a day. "This zeal for prayer and instruction instead of declining, increased up to the time of my departure," he writes. After about two weeks, De Smet accompanied the tribe as they moved up over the mountains from Henry's Lake, recrossed the continental divide, and found their way to the Jefferson River, named thirty-five years before by the Lewis and Clark Corps of Discovery. Every Sunday and Catholic feast day De Smet said the mass with Indians making the responses in Salish, Nez Perce, and Iroquois, while the Canadians responded in French, English, and Latin, a cacophonous liturgy that gave De Smet hope for the future of his mission.

At length the tribe came to the Three Forks of the Missouri. "In this great and beautiful plain were buffalo in numberless herds," writes De Smet. "From Green River to this place, our Indians had made their food of roots and the flesh of such animals as the red and black-tailed deer, elk, gazelle [antelopes], bighorn or mountain sheep, grizzly and black bear, badger, rabbit and panther, killing also occasionally such feathered game as grouse, prairie-hens, swans, geese, cranes and ducks. Fish abounded besides in the rivers, particularly salmon trout." But once among the buffalo, the Indians relished the meat of the buffalo cows and would eat little else. De Smet followed 400 men to the first hunt. They killed 500 bison and the willow scaffolds around the camp were soon curtained with drying meat while women used sharp buffalo ribs to scrape the skins that were staked out on the ground. The whole camp, says De Smet, resembled "a vast butcher shop."

After spending five weeks with the Salish, Pend Oreille, and their Nez Perce allies, De Smet took his departure, promising to return the next year with priests and supplies to establish a permanent mission among them. He led them once again in prayers and gave them all a sorrowful farewell. The Grand Face then rose and spoke: "Black-robe, may the Great Spirit accompany you in your long and dangerous journey. We will offer vows evening and morning that you may arrive safe among your brothers in St. Louis. We will continue to offer vows until you return to your children of the mountains. When the snows disappear from the valleys, after the winter, when the grass begins to be green again, our hearts, so sad at present, will begin to rejoice. As the grass grows higher, our joy will become greater; but when the flowers appear, we will set out to come and meet you. Farewell."

The tribe sent a bodyguard of twenty to accompany De Smet and his companion Velder on the long journey through the hostile country of the Blackfeet and their allies, the Bloods, Piegans, and Grosventres. "Scouts," writes De Smet, "were sent out in every direction to reconnoiter the country; all traces, whether of men or animals, were attentively examined. It is here that one cannot but admire the sagacity of the savage; he will tell you what day an Indian has passed by the spot where he sees his tracks, he will calculate the number of men and of horses, he will make out whether it was a war or hunting party; he will even recognize, from the impression of the footgear, to what nation they belonged." Every night the travelers laid logs around the camp to fortify it against sudden attack.

One day the hunters killed a grizzly that had a paw measuring thirteen inches, each claw to the end of its root, seven inches. "The strength of this animal is surprising; an Indian has assured me that with a single blow of his paw he has seen one of these bears tear away four ribs from a buffalo, which fell dead at his feet." One of the Indians galloped by a willow thicket and was charged by a grizzly that tore his horse's flesh to the bone and knocked horse and rider down. The Indian leaped up, gun in hand, but the bear disappeared into the thicket.

The party crossed the Bozeman Pass over to the Yellowstone River and followed it down to Clark's Fork, where they climbed a narrow trail over a "chain of rough hills" for six days, suffering from thirst. All the streams and springs were dry. On the fifth of September they came across the tracks of a large company of horsemen. "Were they allies or enemies?" asks De Smet. "In these solitudes, though the howling of wolves, the hissing of venomous serpents and the roaring of the [mountain lion] and grizzly bear are capable of freezing one with terror, this fear is nothing in comparison with that which fresh tracks of men and horses can arouse in the soul of the traveler, or the columns of smoke that he sees rising round him. In an instant the escort came together to deliberate; every one examined his firearm, whetted his knife and the points of his arrows and made all preparations for resistance to the death; for to surrender in such an encounter would be to expose one's self to perish in the most frightful torments." They determined to follow the trail. After some time they came upon a pile of rocks spattered with fresh blood. The Salish leader told De Smet that he thought they were about two hours behind a band of Crows who had stopped here to memorialize the loss of warriors who had died here. "It is their custom," said the chief, "to tear their faces, cut their arms and legs and shed their blood upon these stones, rending the air at the same time with their cries."

At that time the Crows were allied to the Salish, so they continued to follow the trail and soon saw many horsemen about three miles away. The Crows welcomed the little band and provided a great feast for De Smet and his companions. As their languages differed, all the talk was carried on by signs. De Smet was invited to 20 lodges to feast, and was expected to eat in each tepee. He managed not to insult his hosts by paying his companions with "a little piece of tobacco" to eat the food placed before him.

They stayed with the Crows for two days, then passed on to another, larger camp of almost 1000 Crows. De Smet took the opportunity to teach them a little Christianity, after which one of the Crow chiefs stood to say, "I think there are only two in all the Crow nation who will not go to that hell you speak of; those are Otter and Weasel; they are the only ones I know who have never killed, nor stolen, nor been guilty of the excesses which your law forbids. Still I may be mistaken about them, and in that case we will all go to hell together." De Smet doesn't say whether this was said in humor; perhaps in sign language it's difficult to tell.

After leaving the Crows, they found their way to a fort of the American Fur Company where, at De Smet's insistence, the Salish and Pend Oreille bodyguard left him. "I told them that the country I was about to enter was yet more dangerous than that which we had just traveled together, since it was ranged incessantly by war parties of the Blackfeet, Assiniboins, Grosventres, Aricaras and Sioux, nations which had always been hostile to them; that I durst not expose their lives further; that I entrusted my own preservation to Providence...I embraced them all and wished them a fortunate journey."

De Smet and Velder set off together. De Smet's intermittent malarial fevers finally left him, which was fortunate, because the next leg of their journey was hard and exceedingly dangerous for two men alone. They followed the Yellowstone River for days, "crossing rough hills four or five hundred feet high," wrote De Smet. "At every step we were aware of the forts [built of rocks, logs and brush] that war parties put up for their times of raid, murder and pillage; they might contain lurking enemies at the moment we passed them. "Such a solitude," he added, "with all its horrors and dangers, has notwithstanding one very real advantage; it is a place where one is constantly looking Death in the face, and where he presents himself incessantly to the imaginations in the most hideous forms. There one feels in a very special manner that he is wholly in God's hands. It is easy to offer him the sacrifice of a life which belongs less to you than to the first savage who may see fit to take it."

They camped after sunset and rose before dawn. They lit no fires, and rolled themselves in their blankets without eating. De Smet could not sleep through the first long night, but "my grenadier, braver than I, was soon snoring like a steam engine in full swing; running through all the notes of the chromatic scale, he closed each movement of his prelude with a deep sigh, by way of modulation." De Smet did have a sense of humor, often self-deprecating. He once followed a noted German botanist on a walk over high hills along the Missouri River in search of "minerals, petrifications and rare and new plants." They walked up a 300-foot hill, the pathway being "quite practicable, but our descent in another place was different. I followed him, thinking I could go where he had gone, but almost the first step I took, the slippery earth gave way under my feet, and I made a third of the descent at railroad speed. It seemed dangerous and impossible to return by the way I had come, and I found the rest of the hillside was still steeper. Hung up there 200 feet above the river, I did not find myself very well fixed for meditation or reflection. But I took careful measures and partly by jumping from rock to rock and crawling from shrub to shrub, and partly on my hind-quarters without regard to my breeches, which felt this treatment deeply, I reached terra firma in safety. There the lover of Flora was already waiting for me, and being highly pleased with his discoveries he told me 'that he did not think there was any pleasure on earth to be compared to an excursion of this kind.' He was unconscious of the capers that I had been cutting. I answered him in German that 'I had found the promenade fearfully pleasant.'"

When De Smet and Velder awoke one morning, they saw the smoke of a large Indian camp just 400 yards away, beyond the rocks where they had slept. They quickly and silently loaded their horses and moved off up a ravine, trying to keep out of sight, then galloped away without being noticed.

Once, they found a freshly killed buffalo. Only its tongue and marrow bones had been taken and they were afraid enemy warriors were nearby. Velder cut off a supply of meat and they traveled on, turning in the opposite direction of the pony tracks that led away from the carcass. They climbed among some high rocks that night and cooked the buffalo meat. "There I had a good sleep. This time the music of my companion's snoring did not trouble me."

They rode for days. They came upon the fresh tracks of horsemen and passed through the still-burning campfires of a recently abandoned camp where 40 tepees had stood. Coming at last to the Missouri River, they saw that a village of 100 Assiniboine tepees had crossed the river just an hour before. "This," said De Smet, "is only a feeble outline of my dangerous transit from the Fort of the Crows to Fort Union near the mouth of the Yellowstone."

Fort Union was still over 1700 miles from St. Louis, but eventually De Smet and Velder, by horse, by foot, and by dugout canoe completed their journey, stopping at De Smet's former mission among the Potawatomie near Council Bluffs on the very day the river froze over. They had been traveling by dugout canoe, skirting ice floes and being slammed into icy snags and dams of broken ice that almost swamped their dugout.

From Council Bluffs, they headed home to St. Louis by horse and by riverboat. There they began laying plans to return to the mountains the following spring.

FORT CLATSOP

LEWIS

CLARK

LEW

ST. LOUIS

CLARK

LEWIS AND CLARK

Alex and I pass through Jackson Hole where De Smet climbed west over the Grand Tetons to Henry's Lake, but I want Alex to experience Yellowstone National Park and get some small sense of animal populations in the old West, so we drive north into the park. We stop to watch a big grizzly foraging in a creek bottom in knee-high grass and wildflowers, visit the 300-foot-high Yellowstone Falls, pass herds of bison and elk, see a beaver swimming the river, a coyote picking its way through sagebrush, and, just at dusk, watch a black bear ripping apart fallen pine trunks hunting for grubs. A too-short stay, which driving seems to require, but at least we've caught a smattering, running glimpse of the Old West.

We need a canoe, and turn south toward Idaho Falls. Late that night, we find a motel, and the next morning, we buy a canoe. We rope it to the roof of our car, then head north to find the Lewis and Clark trail. We cross the continental divide over Monida Pass—low, rolling, hills of sagebrush and bunchgrass on Interstate 15.

In time, the Pioneer Mountains to the north and the Bitterroot Range to the west fade into grey cloud. Alex puts his seat back and closes his eyes. He tells me he's getting a sore throat. This is very bad news. When we mountain bike and hike the Lolo Trail where Lewis and Clark crossed the Bitterroots, he'll need to be healthy, or we won't go. I tell him we'll look for a cafe. Maybe some hot tea will help.

Driving over another pass in a light rain, the wind jolts the canoe a bit sideways. I find a place to pull over on the empty blacktop to retie the ropes that hold it to the car. West and north the grey clouds have fallen into the mountains, and sheets of rain approach across the valley as horses graze in grasses green for late June. I crawl under the front bumper and rework the rope, cutting holes in the plastic underbelly of the car with my knife, then tying the ropes off to either side. By the time I finish, my jeans and shirt are wet and sandy, and mosquitoes have found my arms and neck.

I climb into the car, slapping them away, grab a towel from the back seat, and wipe my hands and face. "We need a name for the new canoe," I say.

Alex's eyes open briefly and close again.

We drive on. Soon the rain shuts us in. The winding, rising, blacktop keeps fading ahead into a drumming downpour as black fence posts slip by on either side. The radio picks up nothing in these high, sagebrush valleys. Occasionally we see cattle on the irrigated pastures where sprinklers are still kicking out spray against the rain.

Coming over a ridge or passing through gaps in the limestone bluffs, the wind slaps the canoe one way or another, but the ropes seem to be holding.

I glance at Alex. "We're such expert hikers and canoers," I say, "I think we should name the canoe after Lewis and Clark."

His eyes open again and he looks at me sideways.

"Let's name it after Clark and Lewis...Call it Clueless," I say.

I see him smile, though his eyes have closed again. He swallows hard and tries to sleep.

He's a boy given to jokes and surprising displays. Once, when asked to read aloud in Ms. Austin's senior English class, he was dutifully reading through a paragraph when he came upon the word *lion*. He immediately broke out singing the lyrics of "A Lion Sleeps Tonight": "We-ee-ee-ee-ee-ee-ee-ee, we-um-um-a-way! We-ee-ee-ee-ee-ee-ee-ee-ee, we-um-um-a-way! In the jungle, the mighty jungle..." The class looked up in shock. Ms Austin stared. She turned on her heel and exited the room as Alex sang on.

She returned with the assistant principal, Mr. Critzer. By that time the students, including Alex, were quietly reading their assignment—or pretending to. Ms Austin looked at Alex and said, "Oh no, Mr. Faulkner, don't stop now!"

With his eyes fixed on his book, he broke forth again: "We-ee-ee-ee-ee-ee-ee, we-um-um-a-way..." The teacher and assistant principal stood still. His classmates giggled and stared, and Alex sang on. When the verse ended, Alex looked up and smiled. Mr. Critzer shook his head and smiled back. He glanced at Ms. Austin, shrugged, and walked away without a word. By then, Ms. Austin was smiling too, and the class somehow returned to business.

He and his friend Connor were given the job of making the end-of-day announcements to their high school. The students, imprisoned in their classrooms, watched the slow-ticking clocks of late afternoon, waiting for the bell to ring their release. But first they must suffer through the end-of-days' announcements: "Junior varsity volleyball practice has been switched to the old gym at 3:30, varsity girls will practice at..." But Alex and Connor couldn't resist a change from the usual list. Across the intercom one day came a new voice: "Hello, Randolph Henry High School, it's your captain speaking. This is Alexander Faulkner introducing you to the new voice of Randolph Henry High

School, Connor Freeland." At first that was all; Connor would then go on to read the list. But innovations followed. Once they broke into the verbal clicks, spits, and buzzing beats of a beat-box performance: while Alex sang lyrics, Connor beeped and spit the rhythms. Sleepy students and tired teachers sat up. Faces turned toward the speaker on the wall. Of course the boring announcements always followed, but often there was a new twist: a song, a joke, a ridiculous announcement. Students laughed, teachers rolled their eyes. One stuck-in-concrete teacher began protesting and they lost their job.

I myself was a shy and quiet boy in high school. Alex—not so much.

***

We turn west on a narrow two-lane blacktop that skirts Clark Canyon Reservoir, a blue lake lying between sagebrush hills. The rain has passed, but given the high snowpack this winter and the rains of spring, the lake has flooded. Fence posts stand well out in the water. It was here, in 1805, that Lewis and Clark met the Indians whom they hoped would sell them the horses they absolutely had to have in order to pack their supplies over the continental divide, place they named Camp Fortunate.

In their thousand-mile river journey from their winter quarters in what is now North Dakota, the Corps of Discovery, as they called themselves, had not seen a single Indian, not one, though they had come upon old lodges, trails, and a deadfall where Indians had driven buffalo over a cliff. Now, they could not proceed without the help of Indians who owned horses.

Their epic exploration had begun two years before, in the summer of 1803, when they finished construction of a large keelboat in Pittsburgh, Pennsylvania. Several members of The Corps then made their way down the Ohio River to a camp across the river from St. Louis where they wintered. They spent much of 1804 paddling, poling, and sailing far up the Missouri River to winter among the Mandan Indians in temperatures that often plunged well below zero.

Then, in 1805, Lewis and Clark, with 31 men—including York,

Captain Clark's black slave, a French fur trader named Charbonneau (with his fifteen-year-old Shoshone wife Sacagawea and their one-month-old baby), and Clark's black Newfoundland dog, launched six dugout canoes and two pirogues on the seemingly endless, endless Missouri River (they had sent the keelboat back to St. Louis with reports and specimens of their trip so far). After winding west for hundreds of miles and making a month-long portage by the Great Falls of the Missouri (north-central Montana), they followed the river southward to the headwaters of the Missouri at Three Forks. They then paddled and pulled their boats up current for three weeks. Day after day the winds drove fine sand into their eyes and clothes and into every mouthful of elk or beaver tail they chewed. Boils erupted in their skin and the venereal diseases they had picked up in the Mandan and Sioux camps were so common the effects were rarely mentioned. Horseflies and deer flies and green blowflies attacked at daylight, gnats at twilight, hordes of mosquitoes rose from the willows by night. Spikes of the prickly pear stabbed through moccasins, and even needle grass was a plague: its barbed seeds "penetrate our mockersons and leather leggings and give us great pain untill they are removed," writes Clark (he and Lewis were creative spellers). "My poor dog suffers with them excessively, he is constantly biting and scratching himself as if in a rack of pain."

Clark goes on: "The method we are compelled to take to get on is fatigueing & laborious in the extreen, haul the Canoes over the rapids, which Suckceed each other every two or three hundred yards and between the water rapids oblige to towe & walke on Stones the whole day except when we have poleing, men wet all day Sore feet &c. &c... preceeded but slowly and with great pain as the men had become very languid from working in the water and many of their feet swolen and so painfull that they could scarcely walk."

Grizzlies were a present danger. Once, spotting a huge grizzly, six men in the last two dugouts climbed out and sneaked to within 40 yards of the great bear. Four of them fired simultaneously; two of the balls pierced its lungs, but the bear turned on them, roared, and charged. The last two men fired. One shot broke the bear's shoulder and it stumbled but kept coming. They all turned and sprinted for the river, four dodging into thick willows, two jumping into the dugout and shoving off. The men in the willows quickly reloaded and fired again, but the bear charged the sound and smoke and two dropped their rifles and ammunition pouches and leapt off a twenty-foot embankment into the river. The raging, bloodied bear went right in after them, crashing into the water and coming up swimming. He was about to reach one of the swimmers when a man on the bank fired a shot through the bear's head. They found that eight shots had struck, but the first seven had not stopped him.

Once, near the Great Falls of the Missouri, Lewis shot a buffalo through the lungs. The buffalo pitched over, blood streaming from its mouth and nostrils. He walked up to the buffalo without reloading, but suddenly caught sight of a grizzly creeping up behind him. It opened its mouth and charged. He had no time to reload. He turned and sprinted about 80 yards but the bear was almost on him. Lewis splashed into the river. When he was waist deep, he turned to defend himself with his espontoon, a pole with a lance head, but the bear "sudonly wheeled about as if frightened, declined the combat on such unequal ground, and retreated." Later Lewis wrote, "these bear being so hard to die reather intimidates us all; I must confess that I do not like the gentlemen and had reather fight two Indians than one bear."

They named the river they were ascending the Jefferson, after their president who had arranged their expedition. The water was bitterly cold, and became shallower as they approached the mountains. The current was running strong, full of rapids, its many channels tangled by thick willow brush bordered by bogs, pools, marshes, and ponds made by countless beavers that kept waking them at night with the sudden warning slaps of their tails.

Again and again, the men had to rope themselves to the six heavy, cottonwood-log dugouts, loaded with hundreds of pounds of supplies, and drag them and the heavy pirogues through the icy currents and over rocks. The snowmelt waters numbed them to the waste as they yanked and pulled and staggered up the rushing currents, over scrambled flotsam and fallen timber, around bend after bend after bend. One of the men, Whitehouse, was thrown out of a canoe as it swung free in a rapid current, and the heavy canoe ran right over him, knocking him to the bottom. "Had the water been 2 inches shallower," writes Clark, "it must inevitably have crushed him to death." As it was, Whitehouse survived, but with a painful leg injury. The canoe upset and "our parched meal, corn, Indian preasents, and a great part of our most valuable stores," including a keg of gunpowder, were soaked.

One of the hunters, Drewyer, missed his step on a mountain trail while scouting above the river and fell hard; he dragged himself back to camp, barely able to walk. Clark himself had developed a painful, inflamed tumor in his ankle muscle and had come down with a fever. The men were often sick with dysentery and fevers.

At length, the Corps of Discovery passed Beaverhead Rock, a notable mountain that Sacagawea told them was near her people's summer hunting grounds. She pointed out a distant ridge on the horizon and told the men that on the far side of that ridge the rivers flowed westward. With the encouragement that they had the continental divide in sight, Lewis planned to go ahead with three men to find Sacagawea's native tribe, the Shoshones, from whom she had been taken by raiding Hidatsa warriors when she was about twelve. (On that raid, the Hidatsas had killed four men, four women, and several boys, and taken three young girls captive. One girl had managed to bound away across the river and escape. Charbonneau, who was accompanying the expedition and serving as a translator, won the other two, Sacagawea and her friend, as wives in a bet he made with the Hidatsa warriors.)

Sacagawea was a remarkable young woman. During the expedition's winter stay among the Mandan Indians, Clark had assisted at the birth of her first child, a boy Charbonneau named Jean Baptiste and whom Clark nicknamed Little Pompy. Only fifteen years old, Sacagawea walked or boated, carrying her infant for miles every day with a group of men whose language and culture she could not fully understand. Sacagawea's marriage to a Frenchman almost three times her age seems not to have been much of a match. Twice along their journey, Clark severely reprimanded Charbonneau for striking his young wife.

Charbonneau, despite agreeing to join a dangerous expedition, was afraid of water. Lewis called him "perhaps the most timid waterman in the world." A few weeks previously, on the Upper Missouri, a sudden squall caught the white pirogue when under sail and swerved it sideways, tipping it dangerously. The wind-driven waves were high, and Charbonneau was at the rudder. Instead of turning back into the wind, he let the boat slip broadside. A gust slapped into sail and boat and the pirogue began filling with water. Cruzatte, an experienced waterman, shouted to Charbonneau to grab the rudder and turn the boat back into the wind, but Charbonneau could do nothing but cry out in terror as the cold water swirled around his knees and the waves slapped over the gunwales. Meanwhile, Sacagawea managed to keep her baby from drowning and began salvaging sacks and bags of supplies that were floating by. All the while, her husband kept screaming for mercy. Cruzatte shouted he'd shoot Charbonneau if he did not grab the rudder and guide the boat to shore. That brought Charbonneau to his senses; he reached for the rudder and steered the swamped pirogue to shore. Lewis wrote in his journal that night, "had the pirogue been lost," which carried the journals, maps, instruments, medicines, and supplies to trade with the Indians, "I should have valued [my life] but little." He was very grateful for Sacagawea's courage and presence of mind in saving supplies while in such danger, for she herself could not swim.

On August 9, Lewis and three men he had chosen set off walking to find the Shoshones. They spread out to right and left looking for any sign of Indians. After covering some 30 miles that day, they camped and made a fire of willow brush to roast a deer they had killed. Beyond them were high, snow-laced mountains.

The next morning the four men set out very early. After walking five miles, Lewis spotted an Indian on horseback about two miles away.

Lewis was excited. He had no doubt "of obtaining a friendly introduction to his nation provided I could get near enough to him to convince him of our being whitemen." Lewis immediately pulled a blanket from his pack and began waving it up and down, a signal of friendship he had learned from the Plains Indians. The Indian held his horse still, but seemed to look suspiciously at the two men whom Lewis had sent out on either flank to scout for a trail. Lewis left his gun and blanket with McNeil and approached the horseman. Lewis was tense. He could see the Indian watching the two men on either side closing in. Lewis wanted desperately to signal his men to stop walking, but he was afraid this would confirm the Indian's suspicion of a planned attack.

Lewis got within 200 paces of the Indian and held up some beads and a small mirror and pulled up his sleeve to show the Indian that he was indeed a white man. But when he stepped within a 100 paces, the man suddenly turned his horse about, "gave him the whip leaped the creek and disappeared in the willow brush in an instant and with him vanished all my hopes of obtaining horses for the present. I now felt quite as much mortification and disappointment as I had pleasure and expectation at the first sight of this indian."

After this setback, the four men stopped for breakfast, hoping not to further scare the Indian by following him. While they were eating, a heavy shower spitting hail swept over, soaking them and ruining the trail of the single horseman they so hoped to contact. It was a bad day. After hours of searching to find the Indian's trail, they gave up and camped again.

The next day they came upon a worn trail that led toward a pass over the mountains to the west. They ate the last of their venison, then made their way up through the foothills following the trail.

LEMHI PASS

For Alex and me, the paved road from Camp Fortunate has narrowed into a one-lane gravel road that turns and twists into the foothills where Lewis and his men walked. Brown basalt outcroppings appear on the high sagebrush hills. One of the dark brown outcroppings is cut by occasional red-streaked rocks that look as if an ancient giant of Indian legend sliced his hand while arranging the blocks and columns.

A big antelope watches us intently from below a ridge of tall grass. Crowds of yellow buttercups and scattered blue lupine have found the sunny southern slopes. The ranchers who raise cattle here have put up pine-pole fences with two posts nailed together in an X every eight feet or so, and the Xs barred with poles run horizontally, a fence they learned to make from their grandfathers and great grandfathers who couldn't dig postholes in the rocky soil.

The road turns a hill and a neat log home with a red tin roof appears. A weathered buckboard with wooden wheels and rusted rims stands near the front door.

We drive on. The high, gravelly hills stand against a deep blue sky. Tall pine trees begin filling in the valley along the little stream that swirls down this valley through thick stands of brushy willows. The mighty Missouri River, the longest river in North America, is here a slipping, curling stream two yards wide.

Alex is finally awake. We stop and get out to breathe the dry mountain air. Swallows are dipping and swerving before a bluff of black rock, crying softly. I tell Alex we're going to cross the continental divide at Lemhi Pass just up ahead. His throat is still sore, and now he's hungry. I tell him there's a town called Salmon across the divide. "We'll find a cafe."

We drive on.

When we reach the continental divide, a grassy saddle between two low-lying forested mountains, we park the car and take a look. There's the usual historical sign that registers Lewis and Clark's arrival and another sign that mentions the origin of the name Lemhi—from Mormons who later settled the valley beyond. The early trappers and emigrants called this pass North Pass, a relatively low passage across the Bitterroots but a much steeper and more difficult road for wagons than South Pass, which became the passage of choice on the Oregon Trail.

The view attracts me: looking back I see a lovely little valley gathering groves of pine and fir, then weaving away between grass-and-sagebrush hills whose ridges are roughened with rock, whose slopes and vales wander away to the faint blue of the Ruby Mountains. I'm attracted to the view. Alex is attracted to horseflies.

There's a forest service outhouse next to the gravel road, and he has discovered big black horseflies using the place as a refuge. Their bite is vicious, so he takes up a stick and goes to war. (I'm thinking he must not be all that sick.) He slaps the stick against a metal sign fixed to the outhouse and the big black flies come pouring out, buzzing like enraged bees, swinging around his head. He pursues them around the building, ducking and swinging his stick, slapping at dive-bombing biters, whacking them right out of the air, whooping at successful hits. When they take a rest on the building, he bumps the siding beside them, thinking it no sport to bat a sitting horsefly.

When I was a boy of ten, my family moved to Kansas from what was then called the Anglo-Egyptian Sudan. I found a new friend named Mark. He was my age but a sturdier, stronger boy than my skinny self. He lived out in the country in a house I visited as often as I could, because Mark was teaching me how to shoot squirrels and skin them with a razor blade, how to fire a 4-10 shotgun at scattering quail, how to gut and skin a catfish without being cut by its sharp pectoral fins.

When Mark visited my house, we would walk across the gravel road to an old two-story limestone farmhouse long abandoned. We called it The Haunted House. High bushes and tall grass had grown up around the place; a cottonwood tree stood at the southeast corner. All the doors and tall windows had long since lost their wood and glass. We would each break off a good handful of young maple or elm limbs with the leaves still attached, then climb the rickety wooden steps to the bare second floor. Most of the plaster between rooms had fallen, leaving only the rough studs slatted horizontally with lath. We had knocked a few holes in the exposed lath so we could make quick escapes into an adjacent room, for we had discovered a hive of honeybees in the upstairs eaves not far from the spreading limbs of the cottonwood tree and just above a broken-out window so tall a ten-year-old boy could stand in it upright. One of us would take a long stick, step into the window, reach out, and vigorously poke the hive. The bees would respond—a boiling madness of bees would pour out of the hive. Usually the great majority swept out into the pasture and bushes seeking their attackers and only two or three would zing through the window into the dusty room where we waited. But sometimes eight or ten would swing into the room like fighter planes, and we'd be forced back into corners slashing wildly at the kamikaze bees with our leafy branches raising clouds of dust.

We kept score. Our stated goal was to swat ten bees for every one that stung us. Sometimes, when pressed hard, we'd leap backwards, howling, and duck through a hole in the wall or dodge out the bedroom door into the hallway. It was a wild battle. I remember ripping off my T-shirt while a bee buzzed beneath it—trapped between cotton and flesh.

Often the bees scored. The wounded boy would hustle downstairs, out the back door, find some dirt or mud, moisten it with spit, and make a marble-sized ball of mud. He'd scrape the stinger from arm or chest or forehead with a pocket knife, or extract it with dirty fingernails, then squish the mud ball onto the throbbing sting. According to Mark, who had invented this game, the mud pack was an Indian remedy for dulling pain (which it didn't, but having something to press onto the sting seemed to help when the pain was intense).

Alex escaped without a single sting from his marauding horseflies. Lewis and Clark and their company were often stung. The big flies are attracted to sweaty and wet bodies, and during those summer months, the men were almost always one or the other.

We drive over the pass and stop to view what must have discouraged Lewis on that August day in 1805: "I discovered immence ranges of high mountains still to the West of us with their tops partially covered with snow. I now decended the mountain about ¾ of a mile which I found much steeper than on the opposite side, to a handsome bold running Creek of cold Clear water." The view today is much the same. Range upon range of mountains fade away into a blue horizon. Lewis had, for all these months, hoped to find an easy passage over the Rockies, a reliable transportation route that would connect the nation. As he and his three men followed the rushing, twisting stream down the steep gorge. They hoped it would lead to a river suitable enough to launch new canoes that would then take them to the western ocean. But the Bitterroot Mountains were and are a formidable obstacle, and they still needed horses to transport their supplies. They had to find Indians.

SHOSHONE

Lewis and his three walked down into a "handsome valley" and waded across a rapid stream about ten yards wide. They followed the stream to the north for about four miles when they spotted two women, a man, and some dogs on a rise about a mile away. "They appeared to vew us with attention and two of them after a few minutes set down as if to wait our arrival," Lewis wrote.

He halted his men, unfurled the flag he carried on a pole, and advanced, leaving the three men behind. But as before, his caution failed him. The women disappeared and, when he got within a hundred yards, the man also vanished. The dogs didn't seem to mind the intruders and trotted up to investigate, but when Lewis tried to grab one so he could tie a few trinkets to its fur to convince its owners he was friendly, the dog yipped and skipped away.

Lewis called his men and they kept walking.

Within a mile, they "were so fortunate," writes Lewis, "as to meet with three female savages. the short and steep ravines which we passed concealed us from each other untill we arrived within 30 paces. a young woman immediately took flight, an Elderly woman and a girl of about 12 years old remained. I instantly laid by my gun and advanced towards them. they appeared much alarmed but saw that we were too near for them to escape by flight; they therefore seated themselves on the ground, holding down their heads as if reconciled to die." Lewis took the old woman by the hand and raised her up, showing her the white skin beneath his buckskin sleeve.

Lewis then gave the woman some beads, awls, pewter mirrors, and smeared some red paint on her cheeks, having heard, no doubt from Sacagawea, that for this tribe, red signified peace. The old woman called in the young girl who had run into the bushes and Lewis gave her beads and smeared paint on her cheeks.

They then set out down the valley with the Indians, making their way over dry, yellowish clay mixed with gravel—a poor soil, notes Lewis, that "produces little else but prickly pears, and bearded grass about 3 inches high."

They had walked about two miles, when 60 warriors "mounted on excellent horses" charged them. Once again, Lewis laid down his gun, took up his flag, and walked out alone, a remarkably courageous act in the face of galloping, armed warriors. The Indians reined in their horses in a cloud of dust and called out to the women, who "exultingly shewed the presents which had been given them." The lead warriors then dismounted, walked up and embraced Lewis, repeating, "*Ah-hi-e, ah-hi-e.*" Lewis's three men came up and they too were hugged. Other Indians dismounted with each one performing the one-armed hug. Lewis says, "we wer all caressed and besmeared with their grease and paint till I was heartily tired of the national hug."

When Lewis brought out his pipe and lit it, the Indians sat down in a circle, first removing their moccasins and insisting that Lewis and his men do the same. The smoking ceremony was, for virtually every tribe they encountered, a sacred ceremony. It was not merely a social or political ritual. De Smet noted the details of the ceremony when he first met the Shoshone in 1840: "Just as among the Cheyennes, we had first to go through all the ceremonies of the calumet. To begin, the chief made a circle on the ground, placed within it a small piece of burning dried cow-dung, and lit his pipe from it. Then he offered the pipe to the Great Spirit, to the sun, to the earth and the four cardinal points. All the others observed a most profound silence and sat motionless as statues. The calumet passed from hand to hand, and I noticed that each one had a different way of taking it. One turned the calumet around before putting the stem to his mouth; the next made a half-circle as he accepted it; another held the bowl in the air; a fourth lowered it to the ground, and so on." The smoke was a physical representation of their prayers, and their pointing the pipe to the six directions was a summary of their dependence on the spirits. One never dared lie during the ceremony of the calumet or break a promise, for promises made during this ritual were made as a covenant with the Great Spirit.

Lewis and Clark seem strangely irreligious for the times. Thomas Jefferson, who had sent them out, was a son of the Enlightenment, not of Puritanism or Protestantism and certainly not of Catholicism. Neither Lewis nor Clark comments that their expedition had any spiritual purpose whatsoever.

The Indians they met, in contrast, were all deeply religious. Perhaps this is why De Smet received such a consistently favorable response from the tribes he met; he spoke their spiritual language, even if his theology and rituals were different. Both Indians and Jesuits used sacred ceremonies where gesture, chant, and song expressed spiritual meanings, physical objects held sacramental value, a sacred calendar was associated with certain colors, and material things had transcendent meaning. Both sides also shared social values of "generosity, community, obedience, and respect for family," as historians Peterson and Peers point out.

For Lewis and Clark, the calumet ceremony was just a necessary and perhaps annoying prelude to their more important material concerns: food, tribal alliances, trade agreements, maps drawn in the dirt or sketched in charcoal on leather. The stamped medals and flags they handed to headmen must have had spiritual connotations for the Indians, but for the white men, they were emblems of practical, political alliance.

Through Drewyer, the one man in the advance party who knew sign language, Lewis communicated his mission. The Shoshone seemed to understand. After the calumet ceremony, the Indians led the four to their camp of willow brush huts, but the chief led them on to an old leather tepee, produced his personal pipe, a carved one of greenish stone, and led them in a second ceremonious smoke.

Contact was made. But the chief, Cameahwait, was hesitant to follow Lewis back over the pass to meet Clark and the men with the boats. Blackfeet had attacked these Shoshones in the spring and the village had lost 20 men, most of their horses, and all their tepees except the old one they were now sitting in. The Shoshones had not been able to hunt buffalo that summer for fear of their enemies, and they were barely subsisting on roots, berries, and an occasional antelope or salmon. That night the Indians entertained their visitors with singing and dancing around a bonfire. It seemed to Lewis the same wild, wavering songs, thumping rhythms, and clacking bone rattles that he had heard among the Mandan and Hidatsa. About midnight, Lewis grew sleepy and retired to rest, but the dancing and wailing went on in the clear mountain night, and several times Lewis awoke to the yells, "but was too much fortiegued to be deprived of a tolerable sound night's repose."

The next day the men had almost nothing to eat but the berries the Indians gave them. Lewis sent his two best hunters after antelope, but they returned that night with nothing.

The following morning, Lewis "arrose very early as hungry as a wolf." He ordered McNeal to divide in half the last two pounds of flour they carried and make a kind of pudding paste of flour and berries: half to be eaten for breakfast, half in the evening. The four men shared this with Cameahwait, who declared it the best thing he had tasted in a long time.

Lewis was anxious to leave. He tried again to persuade the chief to come with him, and Cameahwait explained that although some of his men thought the whites were decoys for the Blackfeet, trying to lure them all into a trap, he did not believe them and would go with Lewis. He was, he said, not afraid to die.

At first only a handful of warriors mounted up and joined them, but eventually almost the whole village trailed along, including a number of women. "They were now cheerfull and gay," wrote Lewis, "and two hours ago they looked as sirly as so many imps of satturn."

They walked and rode back up the narrow valley toward Lemhi Pass and encamped at a spring on the west side of the divide. Lewis and his men ate the last of the pudding paste. The Indians had nothing but roots and berries.

At sunup, as no one had anything to eat, Lewis sent Drewyer and Shields hunting. Lewis asked Cameahwait to keep his men back so they wouldn't frighten the game, but "so strongly were there suspicions exited by this measure that two parties of discovery immediately set out one on ech side of the valley to watch the hunters as I beleive to see whether they had not been sent to give information of their approach to an enemy that they still preswaided themselves were lying in wait for them."

Lewis and the two men who had not gone hunting mounted on Indian horses, doubling up in front of Indian riders. Suddenly, just as they were crossing over the pass, a young warrior came galloping back up the trail, whipping his horse. Lewis was startled, thinking maybe some Blackfeet had been spotted, in which case he and his men were in serious trouble. When the young messenger jerked his horse to a stop, he shouted something in Shoshone whereupon the band of warriors took off down the mountain at full speed. Lewis's horse was galloping wildly along with the rest, and Lewis, with no stirrups to support him and the Indian hanging on behind him, went bouncing down the trail in an almighty rush. Lewis finally reigned up the horse and reached back to stop his backrider "who had given [the horse] the lash at every jump for a mile." The Indian immediately leapt off and sprinted ahead.

Lewis followed on horseback. When he trotted the horse up to the gathered Indians, he discovered that Drewyer had killed a deer. The deer was lying in the willow brush where it must have made its last startled leap after catching the slug from Drewyer's heavy rifle, its head now laid back, its large dark eyes sightless, the skin along the haunch being pulled back by Drewyer's fist while his knife cut the tough white connective tissues between skin and muscle. The guts had been flopped in the grass nearby, a loose pink-grey pool of intestines and stomach, lungs and dark red liver. The Indians had jumped off their horses "and ran tumbling over each other like a parcel of famished dogs each seizing and tearing away a part of the intestens...some were eating the kidnies the melt and liver and the blood runing from the corners of their mouths, others were in a similar situation with the paunch and guts...one...had provided himself with about nine feet of the small guts one end of which he was chewing on while with his hands he was squeezing the contents out at the other."

That day and the next Lewis's hunters shot two more deer; Lewis reserved some of the venison and gave the rest to the Indians, which put them all in a good humor. Even so, the following morning most of the Indians were alarmed by something and departed, leaving about 30 Indians, including a few women, to accompany Lewis as they kept searching for Clark and his boatmen.

They walked their horses down the broad sagebrush valley but still failed to find Clark. The Indians eventually stopped and seemed unwilling to go on, suspecting a trap. Lewis handed his own gun to the chief and communicated to him that if this were a trap, the chief could shoot him. Cameahwait responded by draping Lewis with his own furs, a beautiful robe of otter and ermine, which Lewis took to be an attempt to make the whites look like Shoshones, though it seems just as likely that Cameahwait assumed Lewis was giving him his rifle and sought to return a gift as precious.

Lewis then put his own hat on Cameahwait, and Lewis's men then handed their guns over to Indians, which evidently gave them all some confidence. Through Drewyer's sign language, the men had communicated that with Clark was a Shoshone woman and a man whose skin was all black, and had short, curly hair. "This," says Lewis, "excited their curiossity very much. and they seemed quite as anxious to see this monster as they wer the merchandize which we had to barter for their horses."

Still not finding Clark and his men, Lewis felt he was in a desperate situation. If the Indians fled, he knew he would have virtually no chance of finding them and of obtaining the necessary horses. That night he slept badly.

***

It was a cold morning for late summer when Captain Clark and the boatmen rolled out of their blankets, 42 degrees by his thermometer. His men were stiff and sick to death of hauling the heavy canoes over rocks and through shallow rapids, but at seven in the morning, after eating, they returned to their struggles. They were American soldiers and obeyed orders. They had poled and pulled about a mile when Clark, walking on shore, saw at a distance several Indians on horseback. Sacagawea and her husband, some distance ahead, spotted them, too, and she began dancing up and down, making signs to Clark that these were her own people.

When Clark's party approached the Indians, he discovered that Drewyer was dressed like a Shoshone. Drewyer and the Indians met Clark with shouts of joy and the combined party walked up the river a couple of miles, the Indians singing songs all the way. There they met Lewis and 16 of the Indians sitting under a circular shade they had constructed out of willow branches. Lewis came forward with Chief Cameahwait, and they repeated the one-armed hug. Clark then took a seat on a white robe laid out in the enclosure. Cameahwait took six small shells resembling pearls and tied them in Clark's hair, after which they all sat down to smoke the ceremonial pipe, having, of course, first taken off their shoes and moccasins.

When the rest of the Corps arrived, the Indians soon noticed York's black skin. They were further astonished by tricks that Seaman, Clark's dog, performed—the animal seemed to understand human speech. They were fascinated by the canoes, clothing, rifles, and about everything else they saw of these strangers. Lewis brought up his air gun, fired it, and so shocked the Indians by its effect they thought it was the work of spirits.

At some point during the early introductions, a young Indian woman spotted Sacagawea. They ran to each other and embraced. The young woman's name was Jumping Fish. She and Sacagawea had been childhood companions. Both had been captured by the Hidatsas on the same day, but after several days in captivity, Jumping Fish was the girl who had escaped by leaping through a river, from which she had received her name. They were delighted to see each other safe.

Lewis and Clark then called Sacagawea to the willow shade enclosure to help translate. She sat down and began to interpret when suddenly she jumped up, ran to Cameahwait and embraced him, throwing her blanket over him and weeping. She had suddenly recognized her own brother. "The chief was himself moved," writes Biddle, one of the Corps, "though not in the same degree." She then resumed her place and began to relay messages in Shoshone to her husband Charbonneau, though she often broke down in tears.

Lewis and Clark told the Indians they needed to trade for horses and find a way to the west. Cameahwait expressed his friendship and said he would help them in any way he could. He was sorry, though, that they would not now trade for rifles, which the Shoshone very much needed to fight their enemies the Sioux and Blackfeet, who had already obtained rifles from British traders.

At the end of the discussion, Lewis gave Cameahwait a uniform coat, a pair of scarlet leggings, and a twist of tobacco, and handed out medals to other prominent leaders. He and Clark then decided that Clark should go ahead with eleven men, carrying axes and other tools to make dugout canoes. Lewis then had his men take a number of hides and weight them down in shallow pools to soak for the night. They would later cut them into rawhide straps and baggage sacks with which to load the hoped-for horses.

The next morning Clark and the eleven set out to cross the divide and find a navigable river. Meanwhile, as Lewis's men were preparing the soaked skins, and were engaged in sinking their canoes in a nearby pond to save them for the return trip, Lewis asked Cameahwait about possible passages west. The chief drew the rivers of Lemhi Valley in the dirt, but when he came to the river passage to the west, he piled up little heaps of sand and rock all along his drawing of the river. These, he said, "represented the vast mountains of rock eternally covered with snow through which the river passed. That the perpendicular and even jutting rocks so closely hemned in the river that there was no possibility of passing along the shore; that the bed of the river was obstructed by sharp pointed rocks and the rapidity of the stream such that the whole surface of the river was beat into perfect foam as far as the eye could reach. that the mountains were also inaccessible to man or horse."

This was dreadful news, and several days later, when Clark and his men returned, Lewis learned it was true. The river has since been called The River of No Return and is impossible to navigate in a dugout.

After entering into more discussions with Cameahwait and another old Indian, Lewis determined to follow the North Fork of the Salmon River up into the Bitterroots, and make his way over the mountains along a trail the Shoshone allies, the Nez Perce, used when travelling east for the annual buffalo hunts. The Corps first needed to barter for horses and a guide, and Lewis eventually traded for 29 horses, though over the course of several days, the Shoshones kept raising their prices. Near the end of negotiations, Clark had to trade his pistol and 100 rounds of ammunition plus a knife for a single horse. And the horses were not the best. After Clark took a close look at his little herd, he wrote that they were "nearly all Sore Backs several Pore, & young."

MANHOOD

After crossing Lemhi Pass and winding down the steep gravel road to the valley floor, Alex and I drive north up a valley of irrigated pastures backed by dry, stony hills and sagebrush. His throat is getting worse, which worries me. I don't have the money or the time to live in a motel for a week or two till he recovers, but I also don't want to put him in a sleeping bag in a chilly tent in the mountains while we hike the Lolo trail.

I worry about him. He has little idea of what he wants to do with his life. Doesn't know that life will cut you, sometimes with fine razors, and sometimes will split you with a claw hammer, and maybe you'll have a friend who can talk you through it, and maybe you won't. Doesn't yet know that the contradictions, losses, pain, the work you can barely stand, the slaps and hatreds life slings at you are worth it. Worth it if you can take it and if you know what you're pursuing. He told me once he wants to be wise, but he doesn't seem to be searching for wisdom in the obvious places. He doesn't read the old books that connect us to our past, what British philosopher Edmund Burke called "the collected reason of ages." He watches movies, some of which aren't bad, but not usually an exploration of ideas, values, and wisdom. I have found a need to walk and think my way through long novels and dramas and histories in order to see things from alternative angles. C. S. Lewis put it this way: "The only palliative [for the prejudices of our own age] is to keep the clean sea breeze of the centuries blowing through our minds, and this can be done only by reading old books." Books are, says George Highet, "minds alive on the shelves...So by opening one of these volumes, one can call into range a voice far distant in time and space, and hear it speaking, mind to mind, heart to heart." Meriwether Lewis, for example, or Pierre Jean De Smet.

Perhaps we should listen to De Smet and consider his faith, but many who practice Christianity don't really dig into theology and ancient practice to find what's really there. Sometimes I've thought that Christian communion should consist of a piece of dried biscuit that can break your teeth and a hard shot of whisky to alert you to the fact that you're walking in on a God who got whipped, cut up, gouged, bloodied, mocked, and hung up to dry, and if you read the Bible straight, it seems to take for granted you'll be getting the same treatment if you live the way you should.

***

A half hour later we drive into the town of Salmon and park near a café. Beyond, the mountains rise through humped and folded treeless pastures, up into high black forests that stand against a fading twilight sky. It seems we'll be driving up through the Bitterroots after dark, which will give Alex time to sleep. Maybe with more rest his sore throat will disappear.

The young waitress has a thin face, loose, light hair, wears glasses and a ready smile. She tells us her high school had two students. "I grew up in the only county in the United States that has no stoplights," she says. "We looked it up one day on the Internet, the only county. But I like having moved to Salmon. Now I've got two stoplights."

The Lemhi Valley is an isolated stretch of pastures and bottom land cut off by mountains on three sides. The Shoshones used its isolation as protection from their enemies, though in time it did not, of course, protect them from white settlers. The Shoshone chief, Tendoy, who took over leadership of his band some 60 years after Lewis and Clark passed through, kept his people from joining their age-old allies the Nez Perce to the north and the Bannocks to the south in their final, bloody conflicts with the whites. His commitment to the safety of white settlers earned the loyalty of local whites and kept the Lemhi Shoshones from losing the valley they loved during his lifetime. But the year he died, 1907, the government deported his people to the dry Fort Hall Reservation near Pocatello, Idaho, far from their mountain homeland.

It's a familiar tale.

Not only did the tribes try desperately to hold their lands, but young men saw war as one of the only paths to manhood and leadership. "War," wrote Francis Parkman, "is the breath of their nostrils. Against most of the neighboring tribes they cherish a rancorous hatred, transmitted from father to son, and inflamed by constant aggression and retaliation."

N. Scott Momaday says of his own ancestors the Kiowa: "War was their sacred business...a matter of disposition rather than survival."

Lewis and Clark, who were trying to pacify the tribes they met in order to establish safe trading routes, encountered not only a resistance to peace but also a strong cultural bias that peace would undercut the established customs of their people. One day, at Fort Mandan, Lewis was addressing some of the Hidatsa chiefs regarding the advantages of making peace with their enemies. The older chiefs, who, says Lewis, had already gathered the laurels of war and knew "those inconveniences attending a state of war," readily agreed with him, but a young Hidatsa warrior then asked him, "if they were in a state of peace with all their neighbors what the nation would do for Cheifs?, and added that the cheifs were now oald and must shortly die and that the nation could not exist without cheifs. taking as granted that there could be no other mode devised for making Cheifs but that which custom had established through the medium of warlike acievements."

My own sons have fought for prestige and independence. Not in war, but in the ways sanctioned (and not sanctioned) by our own society. A young man may play sports, as all my sons (and daughters) have. Alex's older brothers were state champions or medalists in running the half mile. They all played basketball. Alex has played football, basketball, league and travel-team baseball since he was seven.

On a cool day last March, he was playing third base for his high school team. As a freshman with a lot of travel-team experience, he had moved up from the freshman squad to varsity about halfway through his freshman season. He pitched, played shortstop, and second base. A skinny freshman, he won the first varsity game he pitched and pitched well the rest of the year. But his sophomore year, in the very first game of the season, he tore the labrum in his pitching shoulder after striking out sixteen batters. That injury put him on the bench for the rest of the season, though he continued to bat.

The following year we moved into a rural area where he attended a school known for its winning baseball teams. His shoulder had healed, but the new coach didn't let him try out for pitching his first year, so he played first base much of the year.

Then, on a cold, overcast day in March of his senior year, he was playing third base. Behind the backstop and beneath the announcer's booth was a concession stand. I'd taken up my usual post next to this concession stand so I could watch and join in on the moans and complaints at the umpire's calls. Heavy clouds were blowing over the forested hills. It was cold—a wind coming down from the north, twirling maple seeds through the late afternoon sun. Beside me stood the shortstop's father. I was listening to him talk about bloodhounds and beagles while keeping an eye on the game when an older man walked up to the concession stand, zipping up his black jacket.

"How you doin'?" he said to the woman behind the plywood counter.

"How are you?"

"Life is good," he said. "It's not always fair, but it's good." He paused. "Better than the alternative."

Our team was doing badly. Already eight to zip against us.

The man put his hands in his pockets and asked for coffee. The woman behind the counter said they hadn't made coffee.

"No? You guys are missing the boat. You could sell that for five dollars a cup this afternoon. I'd take it over to my wife and she'd give me a hug." He paused. "She might even give you a hug."

The bases were loaded. The batter bounced a slow dribbler toward third base; Alex charged, scooped it up, and flicked the ball to the catcher. The ball bounced out of the catcher's mitt and rolled to the backstop. The catcher, a tall, gangly boy, scrambled back, grabbed the ball and threw it to the pitcher, Michael Tatum, who was covering home. One run had already scored with the dropped ball, so Tatum caught the ball and slapped his glove down in the dirt as the second runner slid home. The boy's shoe slammed into the thumb on Tatum's pitching hand. Somehow, Tatum hung onto the ball, and the base runner was called out at the plate. Tatum stood up, tightly holding his wrist. There was a big bulge at the base of his thumb. Coach Abell walked over and called in a second pitcher.

After the roar of the crowd died down, the man in the black jacket turned back to the plywood counter and put down the dollars for two hot dogs with chili. He said, "My nephew. He got a part in his school play. So I ask him, 'What part you playin', Mike?' Well, he says he's playin' the husband in the family." The man paused. "So I say, 'Well, that's real good, Mikey. You keep workin' hard and some day they'll give you a speakin' part.'" He grinned, took a bite out of a hot chili dog and walked off to the bleachers.

The score climbed to 11 to 3. The bases were reloaded.

Coach Abell called for a timeout, walked onto the field, and told Alex he was pitching. After throwing a few warm-up pitches, Alex looked for the catcher's sign, went into his stretch, and let go a fast ball: a strike on the outside corner. The next pitch, a strike at the waist. Then a changeup bounced in the dirt in front of the plate and the catcher blocked it. The count was 1-2. Alex leaned forward for the sign, shook it off, nodded, then went into his stretch and threw a 12-6 curve ball that looped in for a called strike three.

He then struck out the next batter to end the inning.

Over the next two innings, he struck out four more and allowed one hit. His left fielder dropped a fly ball and one more run crossed the plate, but he got two ground ball outs to end the game.

Alex was suddenly the starting pitcher for his team. He helped win the next three games he pitched. Then came the mistake. One afternoon after practice he left his billfold on the dugout bench. The assistant coach, a young man with an earnest face, picked it up and shuffled through it to find out whose billfold it was. Inside he extracted a package of cigarette papers. These he gave to the school principal.

Alex was called to the principal's office where he explained to her that he used them for starting campfires, which, technically, was true—he had used them to start a campfire just weeks before.

The principal looked at him and said, "Alex, do you think I'm stupid?"

She then benched him for three games for carrying drug paraphernalia. He didn't pitch for the next three weeks of his senior year, and the coach, for some reason, didn't have him practice pitching all that time. When he returned to pitching after the suspension, he had lost the touch on his curve ball and lost that game—and the season was soon over.

What of the drug paraphernalia charge? He admitted to me he'd been smoking marijuana with some friends. One of their mothers was a weed hound and didn't mind if her boys smoked in her house.

We had a discussion. Alex said he didn't think it any worse than drinking beer. I admitted it might not be worse than beer, but I said that since it was illegal at the moment, he needed to obey the laws, especially since he could lose all his college student loans if he were arrested for possession. Given our financial condition, without loans he wasn't going to college.

He could see my point.

I made him promise to quit smoking.

He promised.

That was the first time I caught him lying. Twice more he made me promises to quit smoking weed. Twice more I found him out. The first two times I was upset and disappointed; the last time I was angry. We were sitting in the car next to our home. He admitted he'd lied to me again. I picked up his cell phone and snapped it in half, telling him he could buy his own phone with his nonexistent money.

Alex looked at me. "Dad, you just broke your own phone."

I looked down. Yes indeed. I then reached over and picked up his phone and snapped *it* in half. So we were both without phones for quite some time.

A boy wants to find his own way. I understand that. The Shoshone and the Sioux rarely if ever disciplined their sons, saying it broke their spirits and diminished their sense of independence and self-reliance needed to survive in the wilderness. However, my experience with teens affirms my belief that they need punishments of some sort, or they will soon discover disciplines from the state—which are harsher than mine. If you learn early to break rules, you are quite certain to pay a heavy price.

There were times I did not punish him when I should have. His junior year he attended a party at a friend's house. The parents were absent—though I had been assured they would be there. A crowd of high schoolers were drinking and smoking throughout the home. Suddenly police cars drove up to the porch. Kids began scrambling for hiding places. Alex and several boys ran up the stairs into the attic where two hid behind the door while Alex slipped under fiberglass insulation stuffed between ceiling joists. It's a wonder he didn't crash through the ceiling.

It was winter, the attic cold. A policeman walked up the stairs, opened the door, and shone a flashlight around the attic, grabbed the boys hiding behind the open door, and took them back downstairs where they were checking drivers' licenses, calling parents, and writing the tickets for underage drinking. A girl was crying, "I won't go to college now! I'll lose my scholarship!"

In the dark attic, Alex was freezing beneath a pad of itchy, dusty insulation. He finally crawled out, brushed the dust and fiberglass off his shirt and jeans, and made his way downstairs. He moved through the crowd, then down the hall, and into a back bedroom where he opened a window. He couldn't get the screen out. He needed to pee in the worst way, so he walked back up the hall and opened the bathroom door. A girl with black hair was draped over the toilet throwing up. He closed the door and moved back into the crowd, searching for an escape.

Just as he returned to the living room, he saw a boy slip out the front door. Alex edged through the crowd to follow him. A policeman was standing on the porch to prevent escapes. The boy walked to the opposite side of the porch, unzipped his pants and took a piss, then came back. Alex waited for the boy to step by him, then walked to the far edge of the porch, but he kept an eye on the policeman. When Alex unzipped, the policeman, perhaps out of modesty, glanced away, and Alex vaulted over the railing and disappeared around the house, sprinting to the back yard and on into a pasture, then dodged into the winter woods. He was miles from home and it was a cold, cold night. He pulled out his cell phone, arranged a ride with a friend who met him on a road next to the woods— and escaped without losing his place on the basketball team.

He did tell me that story, and I didn't punish him—partly because he had told me the truth, partly, I expect, because it was too good a story, and his cleverness and audacity won me over. That was my mistake. Perhaps if I had punished him, he would not have tried the marijuana, or driven too fast on a snowy day, flipping our Honda Civic.

Sports. Audacity. Lies. Drugs. Alcohol. Driving fast. They are for many young men ways of asserting their manhood and proclaiming a measure of independence. They take risks. Different risks than stealing horses or hunting grizzlies or charging into an enemy camp at dawn with a shield and lance, but risk seems to be in their blood.

THE BITTERROOTS

t's a long night drive up the winding, twisting highway through the Bitterroots. An occasional deer turns away from our headlights and leaps up a stiff slope or hobbles across the asphalt, its hooves slipping on the hard tarmac as we motor up towards Lost Trail Pass.

The Corps of Discovery was finding the weather cold that late August of 1805. On several mornings, water in their cooking pans froze while frost covered the mountain valleys, stiffening the dried summer grasses. But on August 31, the day was warm, and they began leading their horses up into the mountains, guided by an old Shoshone guide they named Toby, and Toby's son. They camped that evening in some old willow lodges near the place the path left the creek. That day the hunters killed one deer, a goose, and a prairie fowl. With their corn and flour nearly gone, they would now be depending almost wholly on their hunters. But service berries were ripe; they gathered them by the handful and ate as they walked.

That afternoon they noticed great white clouds of smoke rising from the valley behind. They asked Toby what was going on, and he told them it was a signal to the different bands scattered through the Lemhi Valley that it was time to cross the divide into the western buffalo country where they would join forces for safety.

By September 2, the trails ascending into the high country died away. Climbing along a rushing creek, they had to cut their way through thickets with axes and hatchets, struggling over rocky ridges while their horses were in constant danger of "Slipping to Ther certain distruction." Some horses, being pulled up difficult slopes tumbled over backwards, "which injured them very much," writes Clark. One horse was crippled and two were too exhausted and hoof sore to continue. The men suffered too. York's feet were so sore, he had to ride for a while. "With the greatest dificuelty risque &c. we made five miles." Clark mentions that the Indian ponies were remarkably adept at making their way over stones, but these steep slopes crowded with spruce trees and brush, broken by rock falls and fallen trees were dreadful. Horses balked and squealed, men cursed, and the dark mountains rose on every side beneath a leaden sky. All were hungry.

That night they camped in a stony bottom and slept as best they could.

The hunters, leaving early to find game along the route, shot some ducks and grouse and even one small black squirrel to throw into the soup, and they had a day's supply of dried salmon they'd bought from the Shoshone, but that, and service berries they picked in the creek bottoms, was too little to feed a party of more than thirty trying to scramble up steep forests. That afternoon a cold rain fell.

September 3. "A Cloudy morning, horses verry Stiff." The men ate the last of their salmon. "In the after part of the day the high mountains closed the Creek on each Side and obliged us to take on the Steep Sides of those Mountains...little to eate I killed 5 Pheasants [grouse] & The huntes 4 with a little Corn afforded us a kind of Supper, at dusk it began to Snow & rain...This day we passed over emence hils and Some of the worst roade that ever horses passed our horses frequently fell Snow about 2 inches deep when it began to rain which termonated in Sleet." Their carpenter, Patrick Gass, who almost never complained, calls this day's journey "fatiguing almost beyond description."

September 4. Another freezing morning in the miserable mountains: "every thing wet and fros[t]ed, we detained until 8 oClock to thaw the covering for the baggage &c. &c. groun covered with Snow." They chewed a few kernels of parched corn and set out.

Clark writes: "killed a Deer which we made use of." Gass is more effusive: "To our great joy, one of our hunters killed a fine deer. So we dined upon that." One deer was not much meat for a company of 34 men, a teenage woman and her baby, and a dog. Ordway says, "our guide and the young Indian who accompanied him eat the verry guts of the deer." (I expect the dog got some of the guts too.) After eating, they pressed on, forcing their way up a further mountain, following a difficult ridge for several miles, finally finding a little streamlet going down. They had passed the continental divide again.

Eventually, in a valley about a mile wide, they came upon a camp of the Salish Flathead: thirty-three lodges, about 80 men and 300 women and children, and 500 horses. One of the young Salish men later said he gazed up at the approaching party for some time, noting that none but their two guides wore robes, as Indians always did in cold weather. He thought the black man was an Indian painted for war. The Salish version of this encounter focuses largely on York, Clark's boyhood friend and slave. To the Indians, black skin might indicate bravery in a recent battle, or preparation for war. One Salish woman later said that a blackened face represented a coloring for the role of the blue jay (a clever bird) in a tribal ceremony. After the Corps made their way down into the high valley, they tried to communicate with the Salish through a relay of interpreters: Clark's English by way of a French speaker to

Charbonneau, who spoke Hidatsa to Sacagawea, who spoke Shoshone and could understand a good deal of Salish. Clark tried to explain that York's natural color was black, after which a number of the Indians wetted their fingers and tried to rub the coloring.

The Salish had heard of white fur traders to the north, but few, if any, had actually seen a white man. As usual, there were tremendous cultural misunderstandings. The Salish chief, Three Eagles, apparently told his men not to harm them and to bring them buffalo robes to sit upon. Instead of sitting on the robes, the men, who were cold, wrapped them around their shoulders. This mystified the Indians. The tribe later gave them robes and elk skins as gifts, but the Corps misunderstood and left the skins behind. By this time the clothes of the party were ragged and their hair was cut short—to the Indians a sure sign that they were in mourning. All that, plus the weak, downtrodden horses, led them to think the Corps were a band of ragged refugees who had recently been attacked, robbed, and were now freezing, poor, and hungry.

For Lewis and Clark, the meeting was a good one; the Corps was able to trade for eleven more horses and exchange seven of the weaker and crippled horses for better ones by offering merchandise. They were struck by how cheaply they could buy the Salish horses, but the Salish say they were not selling their horses and food cheaply; they were giving them as gifts, as acts of friendship, and were accepting the few trinkets from Clark and Lewis as return gifts.

The Corps stayed with the village through the following cloudy day, although the Indians had nothing to eat but cakes of dried berries. Their dogs were so hungry they devoured four or five pair of the Corps' moccasins that night. Clark wrote that the Corps' flour was now gone and they had but little corn left. The Corps' hunters managed to kill two grouse and Ordway mentions a deer, but what was that for 34 adults? After their exhausting climbs, they were not only famished, but also beginning to weaken. Clark, apparently, had the energy to form a liaison with one of the native women that night; some say she was a visiting Nez Perce. She later bore a son that the tribe recognized as

Clark's. Naturally, Clark fails to mention this in his journal.

The next morning, September 6, the wet moccasins that had not been eaten had frozen hard. It rained all morning long, so they waited in their tents till two in the afternoon for the rain to pass, then set out toward the valley below as the Indians broke camp to head over what is now Chief Joseph Pass to the southeast to join the Shoshones on their buffalo hunt. These Salish, or their descendants, were the very tribe De Smet would accompany 35 years later, founding his first mission here in the Bitterroot Valley. The young man who saw York and thought he was painted for war had, by De Smet's time, become Chief Victor.

That day, too, their hunters killed nothing. They chewed on kernels of corn and ate berries by the handful, then set off down the valley, a hungry, wet, and forlorn line of men, 40 horses, one woman and child, and one big, black dog.

September 7. "A Cloudy & rainie Day the greater Part of the Day dark & Drisley we proceeded on down the river thro a Valley" fording a number of rushing streams. Through the long hours, they would listen for the muffled pop of a shot in the distance, then hearing it, hope for hungry hours the hunter had not missed his mark. That afternoon the huntsmen brought in two deer, one goose, one crane, several grouse, and one hawk, to the loud congratulations of the men. Around the smoky campfires, they sat and sang and chewed on roast venison and birds.

September 8. "A Cloudy morning. Set out early and proceeded on." The wind was from the northwest and cold: "a hard rain all the eveningwe are all Cold and wet." Fortunately the hunters had better luck along the valley: an elk, a buck, a deer, and a prairie fowl.

By all accounts, Lewis and Clark, were very good friends. They made plans together, neither, apparently, asserting leadership over the other. During the long, rainy days in the Bitterroot, men must have complained while others despaired of ever making it over the mountains before them, but the two leaders managed this group of men effectively and without serious disagreements. Lewis, who had been President Jefferson's personal assistant in the White House, was the titular leader.

He had been given the rank of captain, while Clark was a lieutenant, yet they worked and planned as a team.

On the 9th of September, they camped on what is now Lolo Creek, a place they called Traveler's Rest. There they let their horses out to graze, hearing from the Shoshone guide Toby there was little grass along the high mountain trails and little game. They sent all the hunters out. One of them, Colter, surprised three Nez Perce who slapped arrows to their bows, preparing to fight. But Colter quickly laid down his rifle and walked toward them, his hands up. The Indians "were mounted on very fine horses," says Lewis, who saw them later when they rode into camp with Colter. Apparently they were chasing enemies who had stolen 23 of their horses. Lewis gave them some boiled venison and tried to talk them into serving as guides over the high Lolo Trail, but the three Nez Perce were intent on finding their horses and so, filed away.

Over the following days, the Corps forced their way up Lolo Creek, west into the high Bitterroots, passing the hot springs that are now Lolo Hot Springs, where Clark dipped his cold finger into the hot water and said at first he couldn't bear the heat for a second. He dipped a cup into the spring and sipped the water: "Not bad tasted," he announced.

Toby guided them on up over the continental divide, though Lewis and four men were left behind looking for horses that had wandered off. But after crossing the divide, Toby led them astray, climbing up into the timber on the left side of the creek, "an emencely bad road, rocks, Steep hill sides & fallen timber innumerable." Eventually they found a way back down and crossed a stream (now called the Lochsa River).

It rained, then hailed. Above them they could see snow whitening the peaks. After a long day's hike, they camped where a stream rushed in on their left which they called Colt Killed Creek, for here they were "compelled to kill a Colt for our men & Selves to eat for the want of meat." The trail had been difficult: "excessively bad & Thickly Strowed with falling timber...Steep & Stoney our men and horses much fatigued. The rain..." Here Clark stops writing. (Perhaps the colt was cooked and it was time to eat.)

LEWISTON

lex and I will begin our hike near Colt Killed Creek. But not
yet. My plan is to meet my boyhood friend Mark (the bee-fight
boy, now decades older), park our car and our canoe at his home,
and catch a ride with him back up to the Wendover Campground. This
is where the Corps of Discovery, following Old Toby, cut back north
toward the Lolo Trail. From there we will hike back into the mountains,
following a Forest Service map. Our plan is to hike eighty miles out to
the Weippe Prairie, call Mark, get a ride back to his place, load up the
canoe, and paddle the Clearwater and the Snake rivers, following Lewis
and Clark as they float toward the Pacific.

It probably won't work out that way. But I'm a hopeful soul.

For Alex and me, it's a long ride through the night in our white car.

After crossing Lost Trail Pass well before midnight, we pass the area where the Corps met the Salish camp at Ross' Hole on that miserable day in September, then drive on north through the night, ninety miles to the bright lights of the little town of Lolo, Montana. There we fill up with gas and turn west on Highway 12, driving up into the dark mountains, past Lolo Hot Springs and over the divide into Idaho, then down, winding along the Lochsa River past Colt Killed Creek, keeping an eye out for fallen rocks or sudden deer or moose.

Alex is awake, watching the twisting road. We can see nothing of the mountains on either side but the occasional granite cliff caught in the headlights.

I glance at him and ask, "How's your throat?"

He sighs and shakes his head. "Not getting any better."

"Better get some sleep."

"You okay, Dad?"

"Sure. If I get sleepy, I'll wake you up."

About three in the morning, I see the lights of the Nez Perce Tribal Casino on the right. It's the only place open, so I pull in to find sore throat medication for Alex. I return with some kind of dark, sweet syrup to soothe his throat. He unscrews the lid and takes a swallow.

Twenty minutes later, we turn into a motel parking lot. The lights of Lewiston, Idaho, lie along the river and sparkle across the hills to the south. It's a warm, dry night. We unload our packs and walk toward the motel. There's a big paper mill across the Clearwater River, smoke stacks rising into the night sky, a stench blowing our way. We check in and fall asleep about four in the morning.

Next morning I call Mark.

He's in Alaska.

"Okay," I respond on my cell phone, "Alaska. The *state* of Alaska?"

"Steve, I'm on a cruise with my father-in-law. I'll be back in a couple weeks."

I hadn't confirmed our plans in the last few months, and Mark, not hearing from me, had made new plans.

Now what?

It's Saturday morning. I decide that Alex and I will find a church Sunday morning and try to talk some of the good people into letting us park our car and canoe and give us and our backpacks a ride into the mountains. It's a lot to ask: give a couple of strangers a 150-mile ride up into the mountains, then turn around and drive 150 miles back to Lewiston. It seems overly optimistic. But I can't afford to wait in a motel for two weeks. Either in the mountains or somewhere in Lewiston, we'll be sleeping in a tent.

We drive across the Snake River into the state of Washington and check into a cheaper motel in Clarkston. The two great explorers have been memorialized in the adjacent cities: Lewiston in Idaho, Clarkston in Washington. The Snake River, flowing out of Hell's Canyon from the south, (the deepest gorge in the United States—deeper than The Grand Canyon), here runs straight into the Clearwater River, swallows it, takes a sharp left beneath high bluffs, then winds west toward the Columbia River.

It's a bright, clear morning. I leave Alex in the motel to sleep while I drive into downtown Lewiston to a little coffee shop called La Boheme. The mountains that rise across the river to the north are virtually treeless; blond grass covering high, rolling mountains scarred here and there by outcroppings of brown and black basalt six-to-twelve million years old. The layers of granite in these mountains are 80 million years old.

I step into the coffee shop, a small brick store in what they call Morgan's Alley. A young man behind the counter owns the place. I make my purchase and take my coffee and sandwich to a table outside. There's another young man sitting nearby at a table wearing a stained and broken felt hat, a hawk feather stuck in its leather hatband. He takes the hat off and runs his hand through mounds of blond hair, and keeps scribbling in some kind of a journal. He's a handsome young man with a deep tan.

"You a writer?" I ask.

He looks up. "Want to be."

"What kind of writing?"

"Poetry, travel writing."

He invites me over to sit and closes his little writing journal. His name is Simon and he smells of many days without washing. He says he's just back from a trip up Joseph's Creek that runs down out of the Wallowa National Forest into the Grand Ronde and thence into the Snake. He says he was carrying too much in his pack: 60 pounds of supplies—water, smoked salmon, batteries, wool pants, "just too much stuff."

Pickup trucks and cars sometimes beep or honk as they cruise by us. Simon responds without looking by raising and wiggling two fingers. He seems to know a lot of people.

"So I climb on up the trail. It's tough going with 60 pounds and I'm wearing out. After a while I sit down, lean back on my pack and just fall asleep. Don't know if it was a dream that woke me up or what, but I woke up suddenly, jumped up, picked up my backpack, and started off with a strange kind of energy. I should have been warned to sit back down, drink some water, maybe eat some food, wake up, but I didn't, just pushed on with this sudden energy and didn't see this snake in my path. Almost stepped on it. That should have been a warning, but I kept on moving—half awake, and suddenly this grouse bursts out of this big scrubby, shrubbery bush. Just runs right at me clucking, flapping its wings, and doing that snaky kind of dance they do. I stop. I mean, I'm surprised. Take a couple steps back, and man, that just encourages it. It charges, doing that fluffy, feathery, snaky kind of a dance thing—comes right at me. I step back, lean back, and overbalance, then catch myself, jerk forward and the weight of the backpack shoves me ahead and I fall down onto my hands and knees. Cut my hand, bashed my knee. Well, that finally scared the damn grouse and she runs away. So I look at my hand—not too bad; look at my knee—bleeding, but not too bad, but then I look at my water bottle. It's just chugging out water all over the ground. I grab it and drink the last of it, but, man, that was all my water! I see that bird down the trail and I slip out of the backpack, pick up a rock and throw it."

Someone driving by on the street shouts. Simon wiggles two fingers and keeps talking. "But then I thought: man, how ironic!" He takes off his bent hat and runs his fingers through his blond hair again. "How ironic! It's Goliath heaving rocks at little David! This little bird just smashed me: bleeding leg, broken water bottle, ended my trip, but what was I doing throwing rocks at a little bird!

"So I just pulled myself together and walked back the way I'd come."

I sip my coffee and smile. Later, I would think that if I'd had any sense, his story would have been a personal warning to me. I, too, was planning on heading up into the steep mountains with a 60-pound pack along a trail where water was said to be scarce. I would be packing batteries and extra clothes, and even carrying smoked salmon. But in the present I'm overconfident, and dismiss his story as just an entertaining anecdote.

"Man, wolves are the hot topic around here," Simon says. "This farmer I know up on the Wallowa must own 30,000 acres. He's mad about wolves, cannot stand 'em, says they're killing his cattle."

Someone honks. He raises a hand and waggles his fingers. "Says they're bigger wolves than the ones in the past. But man, these guys don't remember. Who remembers how big they were back around 1900 when they poisoned and shot 'em all? I've seen old photos of dead wolves killed back in the old days, lines of 'em hung up next to a cabin or storefront with men standing beside 'em. There were some big monster wolves back then, let me tell you. This farmer friend of mine's just worried about his cows."

In the next few weeks, Alex and I will see billboards along highways saying, "Stop Idaho's Biggest Poacher!" There'll be a picture of a wolf snarling at you, looking like he's ready to tear your face off. The sporting goods stores all have photos of wolves killing moose or deer, blood all over the snow. Stacks of locally produced newspapers are completely devoted to taking the wolf off the Federal Endangered Species List, arguing that wolves are not only decimating elk herds and endangering pets, but they'll also kill your children, and introduce some kind of Canadian tapeworm pandemic.

Simon says, "They say the wolves are killing off the elk. Do you know the elk are the most heavily managed species in the West? Tons of money going to manage elk, keep track of 'em, feed 'em in winter. They tried counting the herds from helicopters one winter. Flew above the herd and of course the elk take off running through the snow in all directions. Lots of 'em died. Pretty soon they were counting corpses. Found out in winter they need to conserve their energy. If they use up their energy running from helicopters, they won't have enough to run from wolves." He pulls out a cigarette, strikes a match, and lights it. Someone honks. Two-fingered waggle.

Simon and I talk about trying to save the salmon. The many dams along the Columbia River system have destroyed salmon populations.

"I have this friend up on the Yakima River," he says. "Member of the Yakima tribe. Been working for ten years to bring back the salmon. There were no more salmon in the Yakima—none. Zero. He found out that if you brought back the beaver, then the birds came back: the raptors: eagles, hawks, ospreys, and the pools help the salmon spawn. The beavers seem to be the critical thing." He takes a draw on his cigarette and taps an ash into a yellow ashtray.

I read later that Yellowstone scientists, comparing photos of rivers before 1900 with modern photos of the same rivers, noticed the earlier photos showed there were lots of beaver dams and willow brush and trees. The scientists argue that if you bring back the wolf, the packs will cut down the overpopulated elk herds that have denuded the streams and rivers of the willow brush and trees that provide food for the beavers. Cutting down on the elk will bring back the willows, which will bring the beavers back, which will then...you get the picture.

I wish Simon well on his writing and return to the motel. Alex is watching boxing. He's enthusiastic, punching the air, and says he's feeling okay, but his throat hurts and he can hardly swallow.

***

The next morning Alex's throat seems to be a little better, so we drive to the local Catholic Church to see what's up with De Smet's people these days and to try to arrange a ride into the mountains. The priest is Vietnamese and a bit hard to understand; I expect the Indians had the same problem understanding De Smet. I try to focus on the service, but I keep glancing around the crowd to see who I'm going to hit up for a ride, who's the likely Good Samaritan. I spot a Native American usher who has a real nice smile, seems to know everybody, so I decide to nab him after the service.

His name is Bill. He looks at me and frowns. Well, he doesn't know anybody that would be willing to do all that. He thinks about it. I give him my hopeful-eyed look. He shakes his head and looks down. But then he looks up. "Maybe the mayor. He'll know if anybody can help you guys out."

"The mayor goes to church here?"

Bill introduces us to Kevin Poole, a man of heavy proportions with a goatee framing a good smile. "Being mayor of Lewiston is my night job," he says. "I'm an engineer by day."

We shake hands. I fill him in on our dilemma. He gives it a thought, then says, "Well, I know some Nez Perce men who might be going up that way. They go up there every year for firewood after the winter snows have knocked trees across the roads. But if that doesn't work, I'll see what I can work out."

I give him my cell phone number; he gives me his. He says he's busy the next couple of days, but maybe on Wednesday we can get in touch.

***

Three days later Alex and I are in his pickup, tooling back up Highway 12. Kevin Poole couldn't get the Nez Perce to help him out at the moment, so he's taking time to run us up there himself. He has to stop in Orofino, 40 miles east of Lewiston, on business for a few minutes, but after that he has agreed to drive us all the way up to the Powell

Ranger Station. I'm much relieved—in more ways than one. After Alex's throat worsened Sunday night, I took him to a doctor on Monday. The doctor gave us a prescription for antibiotics, saying there was only a 20% chance the infection was bacterial. If it was bacterial, the antibiotics would help; if the infection was viral, we'd just have to wait it out. But the antibiotics did in fact help dramatically; his sore throat was now nearly gone, his fever definitely gone. I was also relieved to find a place where we could safely park our car and canoe: the mayor's house should be safe enough. The mayor also put us in touch with four old men whose lifelong fascination is the Lewis and Clark Expedition—a thoughtful bonus.

I met them on Monday morning at another coffee shop in Lewiston at a table on a deck in bright, mountain sunlight. Garry Bush is a tousled-haired man, his thick thatch of hair gone grey. He gives historical tours of the Lewis and Clark Trail, of Lewiston, and even a ghost tour I wish I had time to take. Chuck Raddon, a balding man with a grey goatee, used to be a Forest Service recreation specialist whose job included interpreting the Lewis and Clark Trail, though he's a stickler for details and objects to the use of the word *trail*. "What Lewis and Clark followed definitely was not a *trail*, yet this misconception pops up in all kinds of things." His point is that the Corps was more or less following the ridge lines used by the Nez Perce to get to buffalo country, but it wasn't a well worn trail. "How do you tell an Indian trail from an elk trail, anyway? It's kind of wishy washy." Raddon got into a discussion with the third man, a retired high school chemistry teacher from Lewiston named John Fisher, who has put together copies of the medical kits Lewis and Clark carried. The kits have 50 herbs and chemicals, along with medical instruments. Fisher said one of the only places we can be certain Lewis and Clark actually stood is at Traveler's Rest up near the town of Lolo. They've dug up the latrines and chemically analyzed the soil, finding traces of mercury that Lewis used to treat a variety of illnesses among the men, including venereal disease. (So the only ground on which we know the Corps actually stood was where they pissed.) The fourth old man named Barker walked in later, a lanky old man with a grim, leathery face, a faded baseball cap, and a grey moustache. From the looks of him, he could be the brother of the movie cowboy Sam Elliott. He runs boat trips up the Snake River into Hell's Canyon.

The four old men were not meeting here to give me advice. They'd scheduled this meeting to prepare for an expedition up the Snake, in which they planned to take people to the place Sergeant Ordway, a member of the Corps, took a few men to buy fish from the Nez Perce. Barker said he once tried to walk the route Ordway and his men took up across the hot grass prairie to the south of the Clearwater, but he didn't carry enough water and he nearly died of heat stroke. "I started hallucinating, getting the chills, had to sit down. Someone ran for water and ice cubes."

They warned me that since the Lolo Trail follows ridge lines, there will be little water up there. "You've got to carry enough along with you, unless there's still snow up there, which there probably is this time of year." They warned me that the "trail" is a long way from any place to get help. "A man got kicked by a mule up there and broke his leg; it took his companions three days to carry him out."

They also told me not to eat pink snow.

"Pink snow?"

"Yeah, it tastes like watermelon. But it'll make you sick and give you the shits." He said a film of pink on the snow is a sure sign of giardia, which was brought to our country from Europe back in the 1980s. It contaminates mountain streams all across the country now. He told me I had to buy a good water purifier (which I hadn't counted on, expecting high mountain springs and streams to run clean.)

They told me about a Nez Perce they called Slick Poo, Jr. who told them that during the 30s many Native Americans had lost their tribal identities and histories. Slick Poo's grandfather had told him stories about the trail, but as a boy he hadn't been interested in what the old man said. Then someone in The Forest Service took him up to the Lolo

Trail and showed him the path his ancestors had used. Seeing the trail made a deep impression on him. The Nez Perce have worked hard in recent decades to publish the history of their people, building a very good museum on the Clearwater just east of Lewiston, adding their voices to historical events.

The four got into a discussion about the massive trucks the oil companies want to take up Highway 12 to transport heavy equipment for processing oil from the Canadian tar sands. Normal semis weigh up to 80,000 pounds, legal weight. The huge trucks the oil companies need to transport their specialized machines weigh up to 500,000 pounds, and can be 24-feet wide; the legal limit being only 8 ½ feet. The oil companies are petitioning to close 150 miles of highway at night a number of times to haul the monster machine parts up that winding highway.

As they talked, I was watching a blackbird chase a falcon through a pale blue sky over the brick buildings along the main street. The day was already warming. Down in the Clearwater Valley the heat builds in summer, a dry, sunny heat. In time, I thanked the old explorers for their advice, and let them get on with their Ordway business.

***

Alex and I have stowed our packs in the back of the mayor's truck. I ask the mayor about the huge trucks the oil company wants to move up this highway. He tells me they actually hired him as an engineer to check all the curves along the highway to see if the trucks could even make it up to Missoula without rolling right off the mountain or crashing into a wall of granite. He says he did the measurements and the math and they can make the turns. He doesn't know what the legislature or highway department will decide about the whole issue. (The monster trucks have since begun rolling, though the Nez Perce tribal council opposed them, stood on the highway to block their passage, and were immediately arrested.)

The highway weaves up along the beautiful Clearwater River where Alex and I expect to canoe. As we drive, we're keeping an eye on all the rapids. There seem to be a lot of them, and some of them look vicious. I tell Poole that the water looks shallow. He says, "Don't be fooled. It's a lot deeper than it looks and you can see it's got a powerful current."

Past Orofino the blond, dry-grass mountains are collecting pines and fir trees, clothing the higher ridges. The rushing river below us picks up a clear green sheen from the passing trees and boils into patches of fleecy white where the river roars over ridges and swirls around massive boulders that have tumbled down the steep slopes.

This steep topography of bright streams that swirl and tumble out of the mountains is as beautiful a landscape as I have ever seen. It is the ancient homeland of the Nez Perce. Here they dug the rich camas root in spring, and netted the salmon and the steelhead in early summer. Here they followed the seasons into the high country, some of them riding their horses up the high ridgelines of the Lolo Trail east to kill buffalo, returning to build their reed-mat and hide lodges in the shelter of the deep canyons through the long winters. They have lived here for so many millennia that even their creation myths took physical form upon the land. The Heart of the Monster from whose blood their people sprang lies in a thicket of blackberries in a meadow near the Clearwater River. Coyote's fishing net lies on a mountain south of the Clearwater, and Bear, who annoyed Coyote one day, lies petrified to the north of the river where Coyote threw him.

The mayor tells us we won't get any cell phone service up in the mountains. "You get in trouble, you have to find your own way out." He asks if we have anything to stop the bears. I tell him I have a .357 magnum and a can of bear spray. He nods.

He tells us he grew up on a cattle ranch in the mountains, a 20,000-acre Forest Service allotment. He says that he hates horses.

"You grew up on a ranch and you hate horses?"

"They're refugees from an Alpo can as far as I'm concerned. I used to ride fence. We'd ride a week apart, so if one of us got hurt, we'd know somebody'd be along in about a week to haul us on out. But you'll find out horses have evil personalities. They'll skip out from under you if you give them half a chance. Riding fence was lonely. I used to spend the nights with Basque shepherds way back in the mountains. They keep big flocks of sheep in the mountain pastures all summer long. I took blocks of .22 shells and rolled-up *Playboy* magazines to trade for meals and shelter. Talk about lonely, those Basques were a long way from Spain."

Poole is proud of Lewiston. "We had the first telephone service in Idaho...President Taft visited us in 1911...Walt Disney married a Lewiston girl and introduced some of the first televisions here...The Curtiss Pusher airplane took off from the Lewiston-Clarkston Fair in 1910, just seven years after the Wright Brothers' first flight at Kitty Hawk." But being mayor has its difficulties. He's had to fire the former city manager for poor administration, and now the city manager's friends have organized a write-in campaign to oust Poole as mayor.

I ask him what the chances are they'll vote him out.

"Hard to say."

The Clearwater changes names after the Selway River joins it from the mountains to the south. Above the Selway the Clearwater becomes the Lochsa River: a clear, dashing mountain river, more turbulent and boulder-cluttered than the Clearwater. It's a bright day and I'm looking forward to canoeing, not so much to hiking these steep, wooded slopes that almost killed the Lewis and Clark expedition.

Hours later we finally pull into the Powell Ranger Station. There's a lovely log restaurant here called the Lochsa Lodge that overlooks the Lochsa Valley and river, a country store, a few little cabins. We step inside the restaurant. Our mayor has refused money to pay for his gas on the long trip, but allows me to buy him lunch. After hamburgers, salads, and blackberry cobbler with ice cream, he walks out and over to his truck, pulls out several wrapped packages of salmon he's bought from the Nez Perce and smoked at home in his own smoker. He hands them to us, takes our picture, and climbs back in his truck. I tell him we'll call him when we get back to Lewiston to pick up our car. He's a good advocate for his city, but more, he's a good human being. He'll get my vote every time.

WENDOVER RIDGE

We shoulder our 60-pound packs and set off down the highway. The packs are too heavy. Neither of us has prepared enough for this. Alex's thin self and my baggy-bellied self are in for trouble. After three long miles of striding down the highway, our shoulder muscles ache, and the straps are chafing Alex's skin.

Near a roadside campground, we drop our packs and tear through our supplies. We dump a third of our food (oatmeal, granola bars, a can of Spam) and most of our extra clothes into a dumpster. Having listened to the four old men, I know we can't get rid of the water, the heaviest single item we're carrying in canteens and camelbacks.

Near Whitehouse Pond, named after Lewis and Clark's man, we find a footpath winding through a brushy meadow and make our way north, away from the river, up through tall Douglas firs, spruce trees, grand firs that stretch their fingers of needles out as if to inspect their freshly grown green fingernails, ponderosa pines with their puzzle-piece bark and long, shaggy needles, and big cedar trees with flat, scale-like leaves of yellowish green, as if some mountain mother goddess took a rolling pin to them. The noon sun splinters down through high boughs of pine onto a mottled floor of orange needles and dirt as brown as old pecans. We're already sweating.

After a few minutes, the narrow trail begins switch-backing up a very steep slope. We climb and climb, stopping every 50 steps or so to lean over and pant. Alex moves on ahead of me, climbing hard. I'm trying to keep up without much success. He leans his pack against a ponderosa trunk and waits for me.

"This is going to be tough," he says.

"It's already tough," I gasp.

Over the next hour, we climb on, the switchbacks rising above the tops of 100- foot to 150-foot trees below us, descending layers of them. Stopping to rest for the hundredth time, we can see the fringed points of thousands of dark treetops below us flowing down to the thin line of the river running west. From up here the whitewater foam and rushing currents seem stationary, frozen in time like an old photograph. Looking on across the valley, the mountains still rise high above us, which means it's a very long way to the top of the mountain we're climbing.

Every fifteen minutes or so, I have to sit down again. We drop our packs and rest, sweating and panting and shrugging our sore shoulders. The little dirt trail angles up into shadow above us, on and on. We should have taken many fully loaded weekend hikes back home in Virginia to get in shape.

I tell Alex we'll camp early today, take it easy, let ourselves get in shape as we go. I tell him once we get to the ridge line, the going will level out, but I'm ignorant of what lies above us. Now, sprawled in the debris of sticks, yellowed pine needles, roots, twisted mushrooms, and scattered rocks, my heartbeat slows and steadies. But even after a rest of ten minutes, it takes a great act of the will to stand up again, shoulder the heavy pack, and take the next step up. Within ten steps I'm panting, spitting, leaning into the next step, forcing my body upwards.

After three of the toughest hours of my life, the narrow trail finally opens onto a Forest Service road of sandy gravel that curves away to right and left around forested peak. Which way now? They both head north around Wendover Ridge. We set down our packs and I pull out the map. Somewhere to the north lies the Lolo Motorway. It's not really a motorway; you need a four-wheel-drive vehicle to follow it and then you'd better carry a chain saw to cut fallen timber and shovels to dig through snow drifts. With its connecting roads, it runs about 200 miles along the ridge lines from the continental divide to the Weippe Prairie to the west. We're expecting to walk 80 miles of it. But we have miles and miles to go even to find the Lolo.

I opt to go right. Perhaps the downhill grade convinces me. We shuffle off down the road that snakes along the contour of the mountain, down, gradually down, toward a rushing stream we begin to hear far below us. Looking off to our right we see thick conifer forests standing on steep slopes as far as the eye can see. Along the road are bushes heavy with ivory-colored flowers with a strong, sweet, musky scent: flowers of the choke cherry.

It's been easier walking downhill, but every downhill requires, as we know, a further up-mountain hike thereafter. After an hour, we come to the shadowed stream that bounds down through mottled rocks, ferns, and young fir trees. The air turns suddenly cold as if we've trespassed into the shadowed domain of a forest spirit. The snow-melt stream pours through a culvert beneath our boots. The big pines and firs and cedars here are two to three feet in diameter and rise a hundred and fifty feet into the distant sky. Black mosses hang like beards from lower limbs, nourishing food for the elk. On one of his journeys, De Smet visited a village where the winter food supply was gone. The Indians boiled a block of this black moss. He said it tasted exactly like soap.

Turning down the road, we come upon a faded, key-lime-green

pickup parked off the side of the road. As we approach, a sunburned man walks out of the ferns and bracken. His name is Dennis and he's a forest biologist.

"How do we get to the Lolo Trail?" I ask him.

He frowns and thinks. "Not sure about that. It's quite a ways north."

This is bad news. Here's a forest biologist who rides these roads for a living and he doesn't know how to find the Lolo from here. He tells me the road we're walking curves back to Highway 12, so we need to turn around and go back.

I glance at Alex. Having walked an hour down that road, I expect it will take us three hours to walk back up. I look at the biologist. "Can you give us a ride? I don't mind hiking, but I hate to have to do it twice."

"Sure. Drop your packs in back there, and hop in."

Forest biologist is, for many environmentalists, an evil term, synonymous with despoiler of the wilderness. Forest biologists work for the Forest Service, which leases timber concessions to the lumber companies. Dennis is here to determine if a particular swath of mountain slope can be harvested.

"I'm not a protectionist," he admits as he backs onto the road and heads back up the road we just walked, crossing the stream and moving on up the mountain. "There are many natural disturbances: forest fires, avalanches, disease. No forest stays the same. We biologists examine the brush, the young growth, to see if it's time to cut timber. If you let too much of the white pine and fir grow up beneath the ponderosa pine, when a fire happens—and fires will naturally happen—the fires will be so intense they'll kill even the fire-resistant ponderosas. So we try to emulate the natural disturbances: a section here, a section there, giving the mountain time to regenerate."

"You guys are going to have fun," he says, "but stay on the Lolo. Don't go down Hungery Creek or some other creek. A guy did that and got lost for six days. I joined the search party. Me and my partner went right to where he'd left his backpacks. He'd walked away from the very supplies he needed to survive."

"Did you find him?"

"He made it. Managed to walk out living on nothing but berries. You don't want to do that."

"No."

He drops us where we'd left the steep footpath. "You guys give me a call when you get out." He hands me a slip of paper with his telephone number. "You get to Kamiah, give me a ring." He seems worried we don't know what we're doing.

Alex and I pull the backpacks from his truck bed, heave them onto our backs, and walk away around the other side of the mountain. The road here winds constantly upward, curving way back into the sides of the mountain, tall conifers rising high on our right, the slope so steep that on our left the tall trees drop quickly out of sight. We're crunching up the sand-gravel road, rutted here and there where four-wheelers once plowed through mud and around chunks of fallen rock. We're both panting again, leaning forward, our thumbs beneath our straps trying to relieve the constant pressure on our shoulders: city softies on a hard trail. The road swerves back out along a jutting peninsula of rock and forest, moving steadily upwards on a difficult incline. On a rare, short, downhill, I try whistling a melody from *The Bridge Over the River Kwai*. Alex has seen the Mel Brooks parody *Spaceballs*, that uses the same melody. He picks up the song and begins singing, "Dink dink, dink dink dink dink dink dink...Dink dink, dink..." He can't keep it up. The road bends upward and we're both breathing hard again.

Off to our left the slopes of intersecting valleys have been logged; sections are covered in green grass, others with half-grown trees, some with stumps and stands of black, burnt trunks where lightning fires have taken a slope: landscape plotted and pieced—fold, fallow, and saw. Far to the north the blue ridges still carry snowfields. For Lewis and Clark, this was another discouraging sight. These mountains, range after range of them, were a formidable barrier to the hoped-for trading routes between the Missouri River and the Columbia. No one, not even the Indians who had lived all their lives in this region, knew of an easier passage.

***

After breakfasting on the colt, which Patrick Gass says "appeared to me to be good eating," the Corps moved down the Lochsa River past an old Indian fishing camp on the riverbank. Toby turned them north, fording the river and guiding them up the mountain Alex and I are climbing. The old Nez Perce Trail climbed to the ridge line and followed those ridges up and down because it was impossible to follow the river, too deep and rapid to keep crossing, too hemmed in by steep rock slopes, and too densely wooded to follow down the mountains on horseback. But they could, in good weather, take horses through the thinner forests along those high ridgelines.

I can see them laboring up that steep slope, pulling on their horses' lead ropes, maneuvering around windfalls. One of the horses, while scrabbling up a sharp slope, fell over backwards and crashed into some trees. It took ten men to pull it to its feet. Another horse carrying Clark's desk and small trunk overbalanced and tumbled down a mountain for 40 yards and smashed into another tree, shattering their writing desk. The horse somehow managed to clamber out of the tree branches that had stopped its fall and clamber up the slope "but little hurt."

Four miles up the mountain, Clark found a spring and halted for the rear of the pack train to catch up, letting his horses rest and graze for about two hours. They were now on the ridgeline where the trees were fewer, but, as Alex and I were to find, the ridgeline itself keeps rising toward higher mountains beyond. At one point, Clark looked around: "From this mountain I could observe high ruged mountains in every direction as far as I could See.with the greatest exertion we Could only make 12 miles up this mountain and encamped on the top of the mountain near a Bank of old Snow about 3 feet deep."

There was no water, so they built fires and melted the patchy snow for drinking water. The evening was cloudy and frigid. Two of the horses had completely given out and would be left behind. That evening they made a soup of another colt, having shot nothing but two grouse.

***

Alex and I find a place where another forestry road from below joins ours. There we decide to camp. We set up our tent beneath two small ponderosa pines, pull out our sleeping bags and cooking pots, and Alex begins collecting rocks for a fire ring. I walk down the lower road till I find a cold, running spring, use my new water purifier to pump our water containers full, and walk the half mile back up to camp. On a high ridge to the north I spot an elk observing me over its shoulder. I stop to get a better look. It turns and walks away.

As the sun drops below the western peaks, we fry up Spam and eat it with cheese and bagels. Who knows what's in Spam? Maybe a little bit of colt.

As the orange light behind the jagged peaks in the west fades away, the cold rises from the snowmelt valleys. The evening is still. Not a bird nor a breeze to break the great silence.

I look at Alex, sprawled out next to the fire in his hooded sweatshirt, as exhausted as I am. The flames are licking quietly at the broken branches, going gold and red and yellow and blue, and sometimes hissing a little or snapping into lazy sparks that lift into the night. "So what do you think? Think we can do this?"

Alex stares into the fire and shakes his head. "I don't know, Dad. Why didn't you at least decide to take 4-wheelers so we could carry all our stuff?"

"Didn't want to scare the animals with engines."

"What animals?"

"I saw an elk already."

"It's a lot of work for one elk, and I didn't even see it."

"I like doing things the primitive way, I guess, like the old timers."

"The old timers used pack horses."

After a while the stars come out for a look at us. We crawl into our little domed tent and into our sleeping bags. I click on our hand-sized electric lantern, pull out the book we've chosen for the trip, *The Fellowship of the Ring*, and I begin reading aloud of hobbits. It has been years since I read him stories, but he rolls up his jeans for a pillow, settles back in his sleeping bag, and seems happy to hear me take up the story. And so I read the tale of those little people who loved "peace and quiet and good tilled earth: a well-ordered and well-farmed countryside. And the world being after all full of strange creatures beyond count, these little people seemed of very little importance." Alex and I, of very little importance to the great world, and very much alone on the side of this ancient mountain, are feeling a certain kinship with those little, hairy-footed folk who would soon set out on their own dangerous journey into the Misty Mountains.

Alex and I agreed to read Tolkien's book partly because he and I together watched all three *Lord of the Rings* movies as they appeared when Alex was growing up and partly because De Smet reminds me in some ways of Gandalf, the wise wizard who would guide and advise those little people of the Shire who were about to be overrun by a growing power from far away, by a people whose seemingly magical powers were so advanced that the indigenous tribes had little chance of withstanding the coming onslaught.

The Gandalf Alex and I saw in the movies was a tall, grizzled old man with watery eyes, long, unkempt beard, and a tall, pointy hat— rather opposite of short, thick, often clean-shaven Pierre Jean De Smet, though they both wore a long robe. Each had a sense of humor, though De Smet's jokes and laughter were much more a normal part of his personality, while the wizard of Middle Earth is serious, intense, some-times imperious. Of course De Smet too had his serious side, and like Gandalf, he carried a knowledge of ancient books, of several languages, of the histories of many peoples, and employed rituals and words of power. Both wanderers intrigued the people they met with their arcane wisdom, and each man came, in part, to warn the natives of the great peril that was coming.

The evil each "wizard" faced was self-serving power. In a letter, Tolkien writes, "The Enemy in successive forms is always 'naturally' concerned with sheer Domination, and so the Lord of magic and machines," but the problem, he continues, is that "the frightful evil can and does arise from an apparently good root, the desire to benefit the world and others," which directly refers to Tolkien's wicked Lord of Mordor, Sauron, who, long before the events described in Tolkien's trilogy, had hoped to use his powers to order and unite Middle Earth, considering, says Tolkien, "the (economic) well-being of other inhabitants of the Earth."

Tolkien's words are also a fair summary of the American development of technologies and machines. Already in De Smet's time steamboats were plowing up the Missouri River and it wouldn't be long before railroads and telegraphs cast long metal webs across the frontier, to be followed by tightly strung, parallel strands of barbed wire. And then there was gold, the great "Ring of Power" in the American West that attracted hordes of the worst kinds of men and the armies that followed, who, too soon, would overrun The Great Plains and Rocky Mountains. Gandalf and De Smet became wandering guides to "the little tribes," though Gandalf called for war while De Smet counseled peace and rational compromise. Of course, Gandalf's success (as might be expected from a work of fiction) was far greater than De Smet's.

THE LOLO

The Corps was almost out of food. Huddled around their evening fires, they passed around a few handfuls of corn, and Lewis still had some "portable soup." It was some kind of boiled down meat that had been reduced to a gel, then baked into hard slabs to get rid of moisture, then broken up into a powder and stored in tin canisters. It probably had the food value of bouillon cubes. On the Lochsa River, the men had tasted it and insisted they kill a colt instead of being forced to eat the nasty stuff. But here they had little else. Then, three hours before dawn, snow began to fall. They rose with first light, shook the snow from their blankets and buffalo robes and packed the horses, the snow still falling. Ordway mentions their fingers aching with the cold. They mounted up and pushed on. Fallen timber everywhere, forcing the long horse train to maneuver around and down the slick slopes, then up the next rise, forcing their way over snow-blanketed logs, slipping, knocking snow from the laden branches of fir trees. The climbing was "emencely Steep."

All that day the snow fell. Men and horses were soon soaked, cold, and famished. Clark writes: " I have been wet and as cold in every part as I ever was in my life, indeed I was at one time fearfull my feet would freeze in the thin mockersons which I wore." Ordway reports that the men without socks were now wrapping their feet in rags and stuffing them back in their soaked moccasins. The snow was falling so thick and the day was so dark they could see no farther than 200 yards. Ordway says it was as if they were walking in clouds.

None of the men who wrote journals mention Sacagawea here. She was carrying her infant in her arms or, more often, strapped to her back. Leading her horse up the precipitous slopes, gasping, wiping her nose, mounting again to wind along a ridge, leaning back as the horse stepped and slipped down another broken slope, she was, like the others, weakening in the constant, unremitting cold. On she went, her shoulders wet, steam coming off the flanks of her horse, her toes losing feeling, worrying about baby Pompy, his fussing and sniffling and moaning. Every jostled step the horse took led to another view of thick, falling snow, and nearby snowbound mountains. Her husband Charbonneau rode among the others, leaning over his horse, perhaps pulling on the lead rope of a pack horse, distracted.

After a short delay in the middle of the day, Clark took one man and moved ahead of the column through the gathering snow. He spotted four black-tailed deer and stopped to fire at a buck. Seven times the firing mechanism snapped without firing, then the buck bounded away. He inspected the mechanism and found his flint was loose. Clark and his man pushed on through the snow for six long miles to a small stream, halted in a thicket of spruce, pine, and firs, and built fires for the party "agains their arrival which was at Dusk verry cold and much fatigued." Patrick Gass writes that these were "the most terrible mountains I ever beheld." When the long, ragged pack train finally made its way down to the welcome fires, the snow had stopped, and the men untied the packs and unloaded the horses, set up the canvas tents, and tried to dry their moccasins and footrags around the fires. Ordway says a hunter chased a bear but couldn't kill it. They were, he says, "half Starved and very weak. Our horses feet gitting Sore...We hear wolves howl ahead." They killed another colt. The remaining horses had nothing to eat, moving away through the shadows, snuffling the snow for scent of grass, weak and famished.

Lying down on beds of cut spruce branches to keep their blankets off the snow, the men must have regretted their summer cabins in Virginia and Kentucky, the plowed fields, the homespun girls bringing bowls of hot-buttered grits and bacon. A hard, hard time they were having, with voices singing in their ears, "saying that this was all folly."

***

Nothing disturbs Alex and me through the night but trying to sleep without pillows on hard, rollout mats.

By the time we're packed up and ready to go in the morning, the sun is strong. It's early July. We heave up our packs and start up the long, winding road. In some places we can see for fifty miles to the west over ever bluer ridges. By noon we're sweating, stopping in shady spots for ten-minute rests. We seem to be making little progress: we push one mile behind us and face another one rising at a steeper grade. I expect we're still far from the Lolo. I check my compass; we're still heading generally north. Mile after mile the road climbs. Around every bend, the mountain ridge itself rises with the road, like some living beast unwilling to be overcome.

A few hours after noon, we're done in. We lean back against the high bank of the road and slide to sitting positions. Alex has stuffed his jacket and sweatshirt beneath his shoulder straps to prevent the constant chafing on his skin.

"I don't think we can do 80 miles of this," Alex says.

I slip out of my backpack and find the map again. I point out a road that leaves the Lolo about halfway along. "Maybe we can make it that far." But at our present rate, I know even this will take us several days—if we can find a road to the Lolo.

We help each other up and keep going.

Once, on a slight downgrade, Alex tries to pick up a song our family has always sung, "King of the Road." I try to join him, but we don't make it beyond the first verse before we're both huffing up another incline.

Late that afternoon we find a level place just off the road near the inner u-bend of the mountain and set up our camp. After raising the tent, we both walk on up the road without our packs to scout out what's beyond the next ridge. We pass the ridge. The road keeps winding up, always hugging the side of the everlasting mountain. Without the heavy packs, we begin noticing wildflowers: yellow, purple, orange, and white alongside the continuous road. A black squirrel chatters at us from a high limb. Alex swings his .22 up for a shot, but the squirrel is gone.

Three or four miles on, we finally surmount a last high ridge where the main Forest Service road starts winding down and another road slips over the other side of the mountain. Neither road looks to be going north. We gaze across the steep, forested valleys to the mountains beyond. To the west are endless ranges. Southwards we can see clear across the Lochsa River Valley to the distant, fading ridge lines beyond, to the north, range upon range: panoramas of isolation. The trees along the ridge to our right are more scattered than they are below, but every mountain is somewhere cut by a young stream and if we proceed, we will have to drop down into that valley and force our way up onto the next ridgeline.

I look at that long, steep, roadless valley yawning before us and at the steep climb up to the distant ridgeline beyond and wonder if somewhere out there we'll finally find the Lolo. I'm wondering if, when the valley's yawn passes, it will snap its granite teeth together and swallow us whole. Down there in dense thickets of brush and fern, of fallen timber and broken rock, we could in fact lose our way or turn an ankle or slip and fall. Where is the wizard Gandalf or Old Toby when we need them?

We take each other's pictures standing there with all those mountains behind us, then walk the three or four miles back to our little camp, entertaining ourselves with hungry talk of our supper to come: simmering chili (from freeze-dried packets) mixed with lots of cheese and summer sausage. As tired as we are, it's good to be together.

***

September 17, 1805. Their horses had scattered widely through the night looking to paw up a little grass from the snow, so the men had to follow the hoof prints and didn't get them rounded up and packed till one in the afternoon—a lot of energy spent with no progress made. The mare of the last colt they ate had led four horses all the way back to the noon camp of the day before, looking for her lost colt. The morning was cloudy, but by noon, Gass says it was a fine day with warm sunshine, "which melted the snow very fast on the south sides of the hills, and made the traveling very fatiguing and uncomfortable."

Clark writes that the pathway was still "excessively bad." They killed a few grouse "which was not Sufficient for our Supper which compelled us to kill Something.a coalt being the most useless part of our Stock he fell Prey to our appetites." That was the last colt they had. Two more horses had fallen and badly hurt themselves. Clark and Lewis had to be worried. Men and horses were weakening and they had little but bouillon portable soup and the remains of the recently killed colt. There was no telling how many mountains lay ahead.

***

Alex and I eat well. We have almost a two-weeks supply of food in our backpacks, so we are in little danger of starving—unless we lose our way. Having read the pamphlets, I had planned on a well-marked Forest Service road to the Lolo, but I'm beginning to think we've taken the wrong route into the mountains.

As the sun eases down over the western peaks, we sit by our campfire and read of Bilbo and Frodo Baggins's birthday party, which celebrated Frodo's coming of age and Bilbo's eleventy-first birthday. Alex will, within the next month, reach his nineteenth birthday. He will be going to college, which, increasingly, is the necessary rite of passage to adulthood for Americans, though about 50% of those who begin their college educations drop out for one reason or another. Alex is not looking forward to college, which worries me. He knows he should go, but he doesn't particularly want to. I myself dropped out of college after two years and it took me thirteen years of working jobs as a truck driver, carpet cleaner, roofer, grave vault maker, and carpenter to find my way back. By then, having a growing family to support, I had to work a nighttime paper route seven nights a week, 60 hours per week, plus another part-time job during daylight hours (while attending college classes) to finish off my college career—which almost finished me off. I don't want Alex to have to go through that.

I close the book and look at him. "I don't think we can carry these packs in the shape we're in. And I'm not sure where exactly the Lolo Trail is."

He glances up at me. His grey eyes are hopeful. He doesn't want to quit either, but he likes the idea of canoeing better than walking. "But how are we going to get out of the mountains? There's no phone service up here."

"We'll rest up here for a day, then hump it back down to Highway 12 and see if we can hitchhike out."

Alex is pleased with the plan. I'm both relieved and disappointed. I took a thousand-mile canoe trip with Alex's older brother Justin and we never quit. But we haven't found the trail and I'm wary of walking off road, straight north into that precipitous valley. Wilderness is a severe host, intensely judgmental of fools. Dennis the biologist warned us against leaving the roads, and I'll at least take that warning seriously.

The next morning we awake to a grey day and a patter of rain, so we stay in our tent and follow Frodo and his friends away from the Shire, fleeing the great power of Sauron the Dark Lord that is rising to the south and east. "That name," says Gandalf, "even you hobbits have heard of, like a shadow on the borders of old stories."

Similar stories had come to the Shoshones, the Salish, and the Nez Perce. A great power rising in the east, hordes of men with whitish skins and strange facial hair whose mystical powers harnessed the lightning and created thundersticks that killed at a distance, whose white-humped wagons rumbled on disks as round as a shield, whose winged ships flew over the great waters carrying treasures beyond description, whose foods included little cubes of white sand that dissolved in the mouth, sweeter than honey, whose flasks of strong water burned the throat like fire and drove men crazy, whose spiritual powers were contained in black books and were celebrated with candle lights and mysterious melodies, whose clothing was not that of bird or beast but was woven from unknown plants, who melted rocks into bright discs of silver and gold into which they pressed images of themselves. These were terrifying tales, yet every tribe wanted those rifles, black powder, and lead balls for hunting and war. Lewis and Clark told the tribes that the Great White Father now owned their lands. Indians were mystified and stories of the powerful invaders spread like a great shadow.

By noon, the clouds have cleared. Alex and I make lunch of freeze-dried mac and cheese and mix it in with powder of lasagna and hot water. We eat, then walk off to follow deer paths up the slope, hunt for elusive squirrels, and after a few hours, return to the fire to read again of wandering hobbits.

We look up from our book. Far down the mountain, a truck is climbing the mountain road. We watch the little silver pickup disappear behind the nearest outthrust of mountain. In time it rounds the ridge and moves up the road toward us.

There are four men in the crew-cab truck. The driver has shoulder-length silver hair. He stops opposite our tent and says, "You can't order Domino's up here."

Alex and I smile. "No, but we've got food."

"You guys walk up here?"

"Yeah."

"Cool."

"You know exactly where we're at?" I ask.

"Idaho," says one of the men in back.

"You have a map?" asks the silver-haired driver.

"Yeah, but it doesn't seem to be that accurate."

The driver nods his head and says, "That's true."

"It doesn't give all the switchbacks and curves, so it's easy to lose track of where we're at," I add. I ask them what they're up to and they tell me they're just up here messing around and looking for firewood. They drive on.

I'm wondering if our mayor Kevin Poole has sent them to check up on our welfare.

When they return, hours later, their pickup bed is full of tree stumps. The Forest Service cuts up trees that have fallen across the roads during the winter and moves them aside. These men are picking up the pieces. They wave and drive on down the mountain.

We return to our book and read the hobbit walking song: "Still round the corner there may wait/ A new road or a secret gate...Home is behind, the world ahead,/ And there are many paths to tread/ Through shadows to the edge of night,/ Until the stars are all alight."

As the sun slides below the western ridges, we eat again. Poole's smoked salmon is the tastiest salmon I've ever eaten.

Bright stars above the dark mountains gather around us in the great silence as the fire subsides into red, pulsing coals while we read of dangers from Black Riders and of fortunate meetings with passing elves.

***

September 18, 1805. "A cold, fair morning." They ate the last of the colt for breakfast, then Clark set out, this time with six men, to find food. Lewis would follow "as much as the abilities of our horses would permit." One of the men had not kept track of a horse which had strayed in the night, so Lewis sent him back to find it, while Lewis set out with the main party. About four in the afternoon the man caught up with the pack train. He had not found the horse. Lewis's party made eighteen miles that day and encamped on a steep mountain side, no place for tents. "We suffered for water this day passing one rivulet only; we wer fortunate in finding water in a steep ravine about ½ maile from our camp." That night his men "dined & supped on a skant proportion of portable soupe, a few canesters of which, a little bear's oil and about 20 lbs. of candles form our stock of provision, the only recources being our guns & packhorses." Chewing on candles made of tallow was a last resort.

Meanwhile, Clark and his six men out ahead made 32 miles, a prodigious hike through these mountains, even with the help of horses. They saw a few deer tracks, but no deer. The ridges were like the ones before: heavy treefalls and difficult going. They camped near his aptly named but misspelled "Hungery Creek." They carried no food. He called a nearby creek Doubt, which tells us something of his assessment of the situation that night.

September 19. A little after sunrise, Lewis and his pack train, far behind Clark, set out along a forested ridge for six miles. Where the ridge sloped down, they caught sight of a large tract of prairie estimated to be 40-60 miles away. "The appearance of this country, our only hope for subsistance greatly revived the sperits of the party already reduced and much weakened for the want of food." The ridge they walked "was excessively dangerous" along a creek, "being a narrow rockey path generally on the side of steep precipice, from which in many places if ether man or horse were precipitated they would inevitably be dashed in pieces. Fraziers horse fell from this road in the evening, and roled with his load near a hundred yards down into the Creek." They all expected the horse was killed, but to their astonishment when men picked their way down an almost perpendicular slope "broken by large irregular and broken rocks" to the half-submerged horse, the horse stood up and shook its head. Twenty minutes later, says Lewis, "he preceeded with his load. This was the most wonderfull escape I ever witnessed."

Gass reports they made seventeen miles that day. "Having nothing from our hunters, we again supped upon some of our portable soup. The men are becoming lean and debilitated, on account of the scarcity and poor quality of the provisions on which we subsist: our horses' feet are also becoming sore."

They encamped beside Hungery Creek and "retired to rest much fatiegued." Lewis noticed that several men had dysentery. Skin rashes and boils had become a common affliction. Yet there's no evidence they considered retreat.

Meanwhile, Clark and his men, ahead of the main party, came upon a skinny horse in the forest. Not having eaten anything the night before nor for breakfast, the men begged permission to shoot it. They shot it, skinned it, and roasted parts of it, "which we thought fine." They hung the rest of the horse up in a tree for Lewis and his men. Then they forged on up Hungery Creek, over windfalls, and along rocky precipices, still hunting, but managed to shoot only two grouse, not much of a meal for seven men.

***

The morning is cold as Alex and I roll up the tent and stuff our sleeping bags into their sacks. We're not yet hungry, so we lift our packs and start down the mountain without eating. I'm upset with myself for allowing us to retreat. Going down, we take longer strides and don't have to stop every fifteen minutes to catch our breath.

Once, a little bird scampers across the road in front of us then flaps awkwardly into the bushes on our left where it jumps from limb to limb flapping too-short wings. We stop, wondering, when we hear a hiss and a distinct growl right behind us. We whirl around just as a mother grouse charges us. Like Simon of the coffee shop before us, we're so caught by surprise we stagger backwards. She's fearless. She shakes her feathers at us and jumps about, making a low, flurried sound that we had taken for a growl. Then she ducks into the bushes and zigzags up the slope looking for her baby.

"Wow! Scared the crap out of me," says Alex.

"Me too. I thought we had a bear after us."

We pass our earlier campsite and take a side road down the mountain. Hours later, we stop for lunch. We're walking beneath towering cedars, and Badger Creek is rushing down through thick brush and ferns where we stop for a half hour to fish the bounding, swerving little stream, but Alex feels no nibbles on the flies he casts. We move on down the road, back to Highway 12.

That afternoon we reach the highway just a few miles below the place where, four days ago, we hiked into the mountains. We move down the highway a few miles, cars rushing by us, an occasional sixteen-wheeler blowing by. Eventually we find a stand of young pine trees, firs, and older cedars, with the Lochsa River rushing by beyond the grove. Picking up dead branches and sticks, kicking away mounds of pine needles and dirt, we find a space between the trees to place our tent. It's a rough place to camp, dead sticks poking out from tree trunks, fallen logs mossy and rotting, twisted roots. Nobody camps here.

Alex wants to fish the Lochsa. We have no waders, so he steps out into the powerful snowmelt current in his shorts till he's knee-deep. He begins learning how to cast a fly rod. I watch him, worried he'll slip and get carried down the surging river, but he manages to keep his balance a few yards from shore and, as the sun declines, he begins to get the hang of the rapid, repetitive motion that will send his fly up and across the swirling currents. He loses two flies on the back swing, caught in brush or branches, so he has to stagger out of the current to tie on new ones. He has none of the specialized gear of the well-equipped fly fisherman: the vest with pockets, the khaki hat with flies attached, the old-fashioned basket hung from a shoulder strap, the glove for the casting hand. We're novices, members of that uncoordinated category of men Norman Maclean says should not be allowed to disgrace a fish by catching it.

After another retreat to rescue a snagged fly, Alex steps carefully back into the strong current, slipping, stepping, the icy water rushing against his shins, the weight of the current heavier with every step. And then he straightens up, rather precariously, and begins his motion: back and forth, a motion Maclean describes as a four-count rhythm, and the line and leader and almost invisible fly shoot out over the clear green waters, disappearing into the running swirl and boil and pull. The tip of his rod and his head turn slowly with the current as he watches the fly bob down the current.

Grey clouds are crowding the nearby peaks and I turn away to build our fire and boil water to pour into our freeze-dried packages of portable beef stew. I worry about him standing in that cold, powerful current. How quickly he could slip and be sucked into a surging hole or bashed against a boulder. The danger is clear and present, yet the early explorers took such risks for granted and refused to hold back. Life itself is a mortal journey. We can only delay, not avoid our end, and caution can dilute our lives. How many Americans secure themselves behind doors and locks, observing the roar and rage of a mountain river on a flat television screen, but never experiencing it?

I gather sticks for the campfire and ignite the dry pine needles that fire the small sticks that flame the larger limbs. I walk back to the river with our cooking pan. Alex is a few steps farther from shore. I scoop up the cold water and return to the fire. As I watch the water in the pan begin to boil, it starts to rain, a soft whispering through pine needles, a light patter on our tent. I leave the water to boil and return to the river. Alex is a third of the way across the foaming river, maybe thirty feet out, thigh deep, and the rain is coming down; his khaki hat has wilted around his ears, his shorts and T-shirt are soaked. I yell that the food is almost ready, but he can't hear me in the roar of white water beyond. He makes another cast, then takes a few precarious steps, slips, and almost goes down. I move upcurrent along the bank over fallen logs and rocks, wave at him and finally get his attention. I make motions for him to return. He shakes his head no. I make motions of spooning food into my mouth. He nods his head, but turns to make another cast. I stand there watching, the steady rain slanting down across the river, fading the steep, blue-green of the forest beyond. Alex seems unconcerned, reeling in his line and whipping his pole back and forth into another cast...and another. I'm somewhat protected from the rain by the big cedar trees above me, but he is soaked top to bottom. I squat down to watch and listen: the harsh waters chanting their wild ancestral songs, the rain falling soft over ancient forest, and out there, within the chaos of competing currents and jumbled boulders, a boy stands alone.

And what will become of young Alex? He has as open and caring a heart as anyone I know, angering only when he hears criticism of those he loves (including himself). His future, like the disappearing mountains beyond him, is incomprehensible. We can only walk our way, talk our way, read our way, think our way through this single day. Tomorrow will worry about itself.

After a few more minutes, he finally gives up and turns for shore: slipping, staggering sideways, stepping ahead through the shoving currents, swinging his pole for balance, at last stepping onto the bank. I reach out, grab his icy hand, and pull him up.

"Looks dangerous out there. I don't think you should go out that far."

"It's not so bad."

"Looks bad to me. You're soaked and freezing. Not too smart after just getting over a sore throat."

"The throat's fine, Dad."

"Get any bites?"

He's shivering, his teeth chattering. "No, but it was still a lot of fun. I think I'm getting the feel for it. The first movie I'm going to watch when I get home is *A River Runs Through It*."

We make our way back to the fire where he crawls into the tent and digs out some dry clothes, changes and puts on his rain jacket, then joins me by the fire, sitting on a wet log, holding cold hands to the fire. The water's boiling, the flames are hissing at the rain. I pull out a handkerchief and take the handle of the pan. One at a time, Alex holds open the aluminized bags of dried beef stew, anchored between his feet, and I carefully pour in the boiling water. We let the bags sit for a few minutes as the rain comes down, steadily rustling through the trees. After a few minutes, we stir up the stew and devour it.

***

Inside our little hump of a tent, bundled up in his sleeping bag, Alex is slowly warming. I open our book and read of the hobbits' journey into the Old Forest where all the trees seem alive, whispering to each other, "passing news and plots along in an unintelligible language," the branches swaying and groping. As we read, the crowded currents of the Lochsa River keep up their conspiratorial conversations, and all night long the rain falls steadily through the high trees upon our thin little dome.

THE NEZ PERCE

September 20, 1805. As hungry as they were, Lewis and Clark kept track of the birds. Clark noticed a blue jay, a small white-headed hawk, crows and ravens and larger hawks. The first thing Lewis noted on the morning of September 20 was "a species of bird which I had not seen before." He gave a detailed description of the little bird that was "reather larger than a robbin" that was feeding on the red berries of the mountain ash. He then described the Steller's jay (new to science) whose note, he says, is "cha-ah, cha-ah," and another jay whose call resembled the mewing of a cat. He had time to study birds because, once again, he was waiting on his men to round up wandering horses.

Lewis's party set out about ten in the morning and within two miles came upon the horse Clark had dressed and hung up for them. They cut the carcass down and loaded the meat on the horses. At one o'clock "we halted and made a hearty meal on our horse beef much to the comfort of our hungry stomachs." Here Lewis learned that while they had stopped to load the horse meat, another pack horse had disappeared into the bushes. He sent Baptiste Lapage, who had been responsible for the horse, in pursuit. Lapage returned that afternoon without the lost horse and its pack. "The load of the horse was of considerable value," writes Lewis, "consisting of merchandize and all my stock of winter cloathing. I therefore dispatched two of my best woodsmen in surch of him, and proceeded on with the party."

Night came on before they got off the long, winding, timber-strewn ridge, and they camped with little grass for the horses and some way from water. The cedars here were immense, some as much as six feet in diameter. That night they ate more of the skinny horse. The two woodsmen had not returned.

Clark and his six advance men had set out early that morning over a rugged mountain and up the forks of a large creek. They climbed the creek for two miles, then scaled a steep mountain, followed its ridge some twelve miles, and finally descended into level pine country to a small plain where they spotted Indian lodges, (the pole and reedmat lodges used in summer). When they approached to within a mile of the lodges, three Indian boys spotted them and took off running, then dropped down in the tall grass of the meadow to hide. Strangers were often enemies.

Clark dismounted, handed his gun to one of the men, and went in search of the boys. When he found two of them lying flat in the grass, he held up ribbons and walked slowly toward them. The other boy remained hidden.

I can see their frightened eyes as they slowly stand up, knowing they've been caught. Clark holds out the colorful ribbons, talking to them calmly in a language they've never heard. At last one boy steps forward and reaches out to take the beautiful ribbons and sees the strangely bearded man motioning for them to go on to their village. They turn and sprint through the tall grass the bright ribbons fluttering behind.

In time Clark and his men caught sight of a man approaching with great caution, but he soon vanished, then, suddenly reappeared and stood to meet them. After exchanged greetings, he led them to a "large Spacious Lodge which he told me (by Signs) was the Lodge of his great Chief who had Set out 3 days previous with all the Warriors of the nation to war on a South West derection & would return in 15 or 18 days." The few men who remained in the village were old, but there were crowds of women and children who had been busy harvesting camas roots, the blue-flowered plant that covered large, wet stretches of this plain. At first they all seemed afraid of the newcomers, but in time they calmed down and offered the men a small piece of dried buffalo, some dried salmon and berries, as well as bread made of the baked camas, which Clark says tasted sweet. The half-starved men ate and ate, then accompanied one of the Indians two miles across the thick-grass meadows to another encampment. Along the way they saw great piles of the little camas bulbs that the women had been prying up from the wet ground with pointed sticks. At the new village, Clark watched women dig three-foot holes in the turf where they would steam the bulbs for hours on layers of coals, hot stones, and grass.

By evening Clark was sick "from eateing the fish & roots too freely." He sent out his hunters, but they returned with nothing. They spent the night with the Indians and began awaiting Lewis's arrival.

September 21. Lewis was again delayed, waiting till 11 o'clock to find more of his wandering horses and the two men who had gone in search of the one from the day before. Everyone was famished, men and horses alike. Sacagawea, having to nurse her child, was terribly hungry. Lewis did manage to shoot a coyote, which, with some crayfish they caught in the cold stream, a duck, and two grouse gave them one more meal. "Not knowing where the next was to be found...I find myself growing weak for the want of food and most of the men complain of a similar deficiency and have fallen off very much."

It was another dreadful day. Gass says they passed along the ridge "with great difficulty and fatigue, our march being much impeded by the fallen timber. A great portion of the timber through which we passed along this ridge is dead, and a considerable part fallen; and our horses are weak and much jaded. One of them got into a small swamp, and wet a bale of merchandize." That night Lewis ordered his men to hobble the horses so they could not wander off.

Meanwhile, Clark, feeling sick in the Indian camp, had sent his hunters out again, but again they killed nothing. Game in the area had been driven away, so it was most fortunate they had met this tribe willing to feed them. Clark traded for a horse-load of camas roots and three dried salmon and sent it with Reuben Fields to find and feed Lewis and his men. Clark then set out with a guide and his other five men across the camas prairie where the blue flowers of the camas were so thick they sometimes looked like lakes of water. They followed a stream that drops 2000 feet to the Clearwater River.

There they found a small camp of five women, a boy, and two children. The old man of the camp was across the river fishing. Clark's Nez Perce guide, whom he'd hired for a handkerchief, called the man over. The fisherman was about 65 years old, cheerful, and willing to help. His name was Twisted Hair. As usual, Clark gave Twisted Hair a medal. They sat and smoked together beside the river, but Clark was still sick and the temperature here in the steep valley enclosed by high mountains was very warm, which didn't help. Clark threw up, then lay down in the shade and fell asleep.

September 22. Again, one of the men in Lewis's party failed to hobble some of the horses, and Lewis was delayed till almost noon—extremely frustrating when they were all starving. About an hour after setting out, they were met by Reuben Fields with the three dried salmon and the bags of cooked roots and berries. They halted and filled themselves for the first time in many days. Gass says the cooked camas tasted something like pumpkin bread. The camas, a major food source for the Nez Perce is rich in energy, with 1700 calories per pound, and therefore an excellent winter food supply. However, after having lived on a little meat and powdered soup for days, Lewis's group suffered the same stomach upsets as Clark.

The two trackers Lewis had sent out two days earlier to find the horse carrying his clothes and supplies finally struggled in. They were carrying the important lost packs. They had found the horse with Lewis's gear, but again lost it in the night. Thus, they had loaded Lewis's supplies on their own backs and trooped upstream and down and over the rough ridges till they caught up with the party—a rather heroic effort considering their weakened condition.

After the meal of camas and salmon, they all followed Fields across the meadows to the Indian lodges. And so at last, they had come down into a temperate valley, wet, below the snow line, smelling of vegetation, with the voices of women and children and the barking of dogs. For all of them, it was a great relief, tempered only by the knowledge that they would have to ascend those same mountains the next spring on their return journey. Nevertheless, Lewis remarks that he felt a distinct pleasure in finally "having triumphed over the rocky Mountains."

As Lewis's party approached the little village of rush-mat lodges, the Indian women and children mounted horses and fled to the nearby woods. However, the old men "seemed little concerned" and walked out to greet them unarmed.

Meanwhile, Clark left his five men down on the Clearwater camp and climbed, with Twisted Hair and another Indian, back up the long, steep incline to the camas prairie to find Lewis. Clark's horse proved skittish and threw him, hurting his hip, but he finally reached the village, suffering now from a hurt hip as well as an upset stomach. Lewis and his men were waiting. Clark warned them about eating too much of the camas and berries, but it was too late. By the next day, virtually the whole crew was sick. Lewis was so ill he stopped writing in his journal for weeks. Clark says that Lewis was scarcely able to ride a gentle horse that the chief lent him, and that several men were so unwell that they had to dismount and lie beside the trail for some time. Others could not walk, "nearly all Complaining of their bowels."

Clark treated them with Rush's Pills, a potent blend of mercury and jalap intended as a laxative to clean them out. It took several days for the crew to recover from their change in diet, and Lewis wasn't able to walk till October 4, twelve days later.

On September 23, they made camp down on the Clearwater near Twisted Hair's little campsite. In the days following, they proceeded down the river with Twisted Hair and a younger chief named Tetoharsky, who had agreed to accompany them through Nez Perce country. They camped near what is now Orofino, Idaho, where they found pines or cedars large enough to make into dugout canoes. At Orofino, with the ready help of the Nez Perce, who drew them maps of the rivers ahead and provided the Corps with more food, they made plans to float westward to the Columbia River, and then on to the Pacific.

SLEEPY BEAR AND CRAZY BEAR

n our forested camp beside the Lochsa, the next morning is damp, cloudy, and cold. Alex and I stuff everything into our packs and try to disguise Alex's rifle with a jacket. I expect people won't be anxious to pick up two men who carry a rifle. We shoulder our packs, cross the highway, and start walking down the blacktop westward. I tell Alex we've got maybe 80 miles to go to reach the little town of Kooskia where we can buy food if we need it. If no one picks us up, we've got plenty of food to make it that far. That's not very encouraging news to Alex, pacing along under his heavy pack, and he's unusually silent.

We keep walking, turning around and holding out our thumbs whenever we hear a car humming down the highway or a semi-truck whooshing around a bend. It's still raining a little, but we're pretty well

SLEEPY BEAR AND CRAZY BEAR

bundled up and the walking keeps us warm.

We've carried our packs a mile when a silver pickup pulls over. I can't believe our good luck. We walk-jog beneath our heavy packs to the truck. A man rolls down his window as we approach and says, "Get in the back. Don't step on the fly rod."

We unshoulder our packs and heave them over the tailgate into the bed next to a cooler. The truckbed is full of duffels, tires, tackle boxes, and I walk around, expecting he'll let us in the cab where it's warm, but the engine revs up and the truck starts moving forward. A thought flashes through my mind that he's going to drive away and steal our backpacks, but the truck stops and he motions for us to get in back.

Alex climbs in and finds a place to sit down between packs of gear. There's little room, so I put my butt on the tailgate and hang on for dear life as the truck roars out onto the highway.

Alex has been quiet all morning, not saying much as we ate our breakfast of bagels and pepperoni. Not saying anything as we walked down the highway. But now he's smiling into the wind. Maybe he was worried we'd never catch a ride.

There's a cold wind and a little rain is spitting in our faces. I'm a bit angry the man hasn't let us ride in the warm cab, but a hitchhiker doesn't have much leverage to negotiate. At least we're not walking, and the steep, forested slopes are flying by.

Just ten or twelve miles down the road, the truck swings into a roadside parking lot. He can't be stopping already, I think. We've got another 70 miles to go to Kooskia and 120 or more to Lewiston. But stop he does. He opens his door and steps out. He's a short, thick man wearing brown sunglasses, and a khaki hat. He looks like a well-fed Hungarian peasant.

He wants to talk. In my experience, most people who pick you up hitchhiking want to talk, a few want money for gasoline, and occasionally, once in ever so long, someone picks you up just to help you out.

"I've got an appointment with Fred," he announces. "Fred, Henry, and Jerry."

All right. I climb out, lean over the tailgate and grab my backpack. "So who's Fred?"

"Fred's a nineteen-inch rainbow trout. I've met him before, just down there." He points to the river.

"You think you'll catch the same fish again?"

"Just might. I catch and release."

I struggle to hoist my pack out of the truck as Alex, standing up in the bed, lifts his pack out and drops it next to the truck. Looking up, I notice the man is wearing a necklace of large, yellowed teeth. I've never seen a necklace like that before. "So what's with the teeth?"

He smiles. I've hit on a subject he loves. "Elk teeth," he says. "The front ivories of nine elk. Killed one with a rifle, eight with a bow."

"So you hunt elk with a bow?"

He talks for fifteen minutes about his bow, strung to 84 pounds of pull, about how exactly to set its sights, about being able to pick off a daisy in the grass at 50 yards, about the finely honed arrowheads. In his brown Polaroids, he somehow reminds me of a sleepy brown bear.

I'm anxious to get moving, so I lift my pack and slide my arms through the straps. But he doesn't take the hint. He tells me he "blew through an elk" with an arrow at 70 yards. He tells us about adventures way back in the mountains where he once shot an elk, skinned it out, and carried 70 pounds of meat for miles. Interesting stories, but after 20 minutes I'm ready to walk. I begin taking a few steps toward the highway. Alex shoulders his pack and joins me.

The fisherman reels us back with his words. He tells us he once walked 26 miles through the mountains in a single day. Says he prepared for this by taking 22-mile walks. "The motivation's up here," he says, tapping his forehead. He describes the neighborhood where he lives, the route he takes on his walks, the names of streets I've never seen.

"Well, got to get going. Good luck with Fred and Jerry."

He jerks back on his verbal fly rod and we don't get five feet. I don't want to be impolite to a man who gave us a ride, so I let the pack slide off my shoulders and thump to my feet. He's going on about hiking, shooting, hunting—about carrying elk heads with antlers attached, about taxidermy, about towns I've never heard of, about hunting buddies I've never met.

Alex drops his pack and looks at me. After ten minutes, I wish the man good luck again, but he jerks us back again with a rambling monologue about his relatives who live in Helena, Missoula, Boise, Billings, and Pocatello. "But I won't visit the one in Pocatello. I hate that part of Idaho." For being a believer in catch and release, he's not much for letting us go.

Finally, we lift our packs, wave, and just walk away against the drag of his long, long line of words. I feel suddenly sorry for this solitary man who will now find himself alone again with his necklace of teeth, fishing for friends.

***

I'm expecting a day of walking, but within a half mile, a damaged Saturn swerves over and we're jog-walking down the highway hoping he won't pull away before we get there.

A burly young man in a bright blue T-shirt steps out and opens his trunk. As we drop our packs into the trunk, he asks us how far we're going.

"Lewiston," I tell him.

"Where's that?"

"Straight down this highway, maybe 100 miles," I say. "Where you headed?"

"Bonney Lake, near Seattle."

"That's great. Lewiston's on the way."

Alex climbs in the back seat, and I slide into the front. His name is Tyler Lamere and he's Native American. I ask what tribe and he tells me his mother told him he's Ojibwa, Cree, Assiniboine, and Sioux, all tribes that used to live in Canada, Montana, and the Dakotas. All were dread enemies of the Salish, Shoshone, and Nez Perce who lived in these mountains. He pulls onto the highway and steps on the gas. As with Lewis and Clark, an Indian has helped us on our way.

We're moving fast down the mountain and he soon overtakes a car, but it's impossible to pass with the highway constantly curving in and out around the mountains, so he keeps his bumper almost attached to the car ahead and awaits his opportunity, swerving out occasionally to weigh the risks.

He is a risk taker, a UFC amateur cage fighter trying to work his way into the professional ranks. Says his record so far is 7-0. He's wrestled all through high school and now trains at a gym with a trainer "who knows what he's doing." He's had a fight with a 253-pound heavy weight who was introduced by the announcer as being six-feet-eleven. Tyler's about a foot shorter but strong in the shoulders. When the announcer called out Tyler's 205 pounds, the big fighter just rolled his eyes in disgust. "Wouldn't even shake my hand...I knocked him out in 57 seconds." He tells us stories of his fights, a longer tussle with a gigantic Samoan, about his training regimens: two mile runs at dawn and two more miles after practice in the evenings. As we rush down the mountains, he occasionally darts into the passing lane and floors it to roar around a car or pickup. He talks about the danger of getting kneed if you come in for a double-leg takedown in a cage fight. About how amateurs aren't allowed to use their elbows. About how he wants to move to California where he can get noticed.

I ask him where he's coming from today. He's been to see his father who lives in Montana. His mother, with whom he lives near Seattle, left her husband when Tyler was eight. He didn't see his father again till he was seventeen. During that visit, his father got drunk and threatened to break the noses of his new wife and her daughter, so Tyler walked away. He had tried again to visit his father this past weekend, driving some ten hours one way to see him over the Fourth of July, but once again his father started drinking, and Tyler drove away.

"So how do you make ends meet?"

"I'm a manager at Pizza Hut, but, man, I never want to take another job in food service. Customers are terrible. They try any excuse to get a free pizza. There's this guy comes in a lot. Eats the pizza then tells us he's been given the wrong crust and wants it free. He's done it so many times we've put him on a list. No more free pizza. We've got a list of quite a few thieves.

"But once I was delivering a pizza and we were so busy I was late and delivered a cold pizza to this older woman. I saw she'd given me enough money, but I didn't count it because I figured she was mad I was late and she wouldn't give me a tip. After I drove away, I counted the money and saw she'd given me an eighteen-dollar tip. So I drove back to the house, knocked on the door and said, 'Lady, did you realize you had a ten and a five in those bills you gave me?' She said yes, she *did* know. Man, that made my day!"

Alex leans over the seat and asks Tyler if, as a cage fighter, he has a fighter's nickname. Tyler says no, but he's thought about it. "Maybe Crazy Bear," he says.

Alex asks him about the tattoos in Chinese characters on his forearm. Tyler says they stand for "God, Family, Loyalty." "*Loyalty* was so close to my wrist the Marines wouldn't take me when I tried to sign up. It can't show under a long-sleeved shirt."

"Crazy Bear," says Alex. "So you do anything else that's crazy besides cage fighting?"

"Sky diving. I've jumped from 13,500 feet."

"Really? How did that feel?"

"It's a rush, man. You should try it."

He tells us of street racing with his friends, of how he once smashed into his buddy's car trying to speed past him on an entry ramp to a highway, which is the reason the driver's door of his Saturn is the color of grey primer and there's a crack in the windshield.

On we go, speeding down the mountain, swerving around cars, hot-footing it on straight-aways, gunning it past tractor-trailers. We're making very good time. The clouds are gone, the trees on the mountains are disappearing; it's a warm, bright, blue-sky day.

He talks us all the way to the Motel 6 in Clarkston where we stayed before meeting the mayor of Lewiston. He's been good company and a big help, so I buy him lunch at Tomato Brothers' Italian Restaurant next to the motel; we take pictures, and off he goes, a fatherless boy working hard to make his way.

MARK AND SON

lex and I spend a few days walking the streets of Lewiston and Clarkston waiting for my friend Mark's return from Alaska. On Sunday, we walk to church hoping to meet the mayor and retrieve our car from his house. He hasn't been answering his phone. We find out he's on a camping expedition with a church group, but a lady in the church gives us a ride back to our motel and that evening we're able to contact the mayor by cell phone. Monday he picks us up and takes us to his house where he introduces us to his wife and gives us iced tea, as well as more of his most excellent and delicious smoked salmon. We thank him again. Sometimes saying "Thanks" is a damned small return for extraordinary help.

In time, my boyhood friend Mark returns and leads us out to his home south of Lewiston, a relatively new ranch house isolated on a gentle hill from which we can see fifty miles in every direction. He used to raise cattle on the place, but after a woodcutting accident, when the trunk of a pine tree swung down and shattered his knee, and after his little daughter slipped under the fence where the bulls were corralled, he's settled on raising hay.

The house and large metal barn are enclosed by a chain-link fence. He drives up to it, punches in his code on the box next to a phone, and the gate slides open. We drive on in behind him. He gets out of his car and leads the way, hobbling a bit on his bad leg, opens his front door and invites us into his beautiful home. He seats us in the large living room that lies open to the kitchen and brings us each a beer. His hair is still dark after all these years, and despite the injury to his knee, he's in good shape. He's always been a sportsman—hunting deer, elk, and cougar, fishing for smallmouth bass. He once won a state competition in bass fishing because he carefully scouted and mapped the nearby rivers. He even participated in the national competition in Arkansas that year.

His second wife died just a year and a half ago and their grown daughter has moved away, so he lives alone on this hilltop, hunting elk and deer and grouse in the fall with bow and arrow or pistol, traveling occasionally to his mountain cabin 90 miles away. He spent years as an airplane mechanic in the Seattle area, eventually becoming a partner in an aeronautics firm that made parts for Boeing. His first wife was a grade school principal north of Seattle. They had two children, a boy, Michael, and a girl, Christine. One morning, after 20 years of marriage, this wife turned to him and said, "I'm not in love with you anymore. I want a divorce."

Mark sits in his wide living room across from us and sips his beer. "I was shocked," he says. "I'll admit I didn't handle it well. She poisoned the minds of my kids against me and I finally crossed some kind of a line. I just couldn't fight it anymore. It turns out she had fallen in love with some lawyer she met at the school. I had no clue it was happening. After I crossed that line, I left them all. Disappeared. Didn't see any of them for fourteen years. Had no contact with my two children. I'm not proud of that, but that's what happened.

"Then, just four years ago, someone picks up the phone out there by the gate and says, 'Happy Father's Day!' I say, kind of gruff, 'Who is this?' A voice says, 'It's Michael, your son.'"

That afternoon we meet Michael. He arrives with his good friend Andy, bringing three big pizzas Mark has ordered from Papa Murphy's. Michael is a strong young man in his twenties now, a square jaw like his father's. He picks up the story where his father left off:

"I was living up north of Seattle with my mom and sister. In some ways things were going good; I was a good soccer player and the national Olympic team had recruited me to play on their team for developing young players. But for some reason, I got sick of traveling around playing soccer. We even went to Europe and played there. Let me tell you, those Europeans play from the time they're three years old, have special schools where that's what they focus on. They were unreal soccer players.

"When I got back from Europe, I just walked away from soccer, got into an argument with the coach and walked away from the team. Got into drugs. Spent time in jail. Got my third conviction, but the judge had some sympathy and sent me to a six-month bootcamp to reduce the penalty to a misdemeanor, otherwise it was three strikes and you're out. By that time I knew I had to kick the habit. When I got out of jail, I left the state and drove east to Montana to a friend's house to get away from my druggy friends in Seattle. I felt this gap in my life and I missed my dad. I had no idea where he'd gone.

"Then a strange thing happened. One day I get a phone call in Montana from a friend of my sister's boyfriend. He's working for a phone company, taking complaints, helping people work out problems with their phone systems. He calls me and says, 'Michael, guess who called me today?' And of course I didn't have a clue. 'Your dad. I know more or less where he's living.' He's not supposed to divulge this information, but he tells me that my father lives somewhere south of Lewiston, but there's no actual address listed."

Michael and his friend Andy are sitting in the living room in T-shirts and basketball shorts sipping their beers. Mark walks in from the kitchen and offers us all more pizza, then sits down and joins us.

Michael continues: "I needed my father. I felt this. When I took that call, I looked at the calendar and saw that Father's Day was just ahead. I piled into my car and headed for Lewiston. I didn't have an address, so after hours and hours on the highway, I drove into Lewiston and camped out at Hell's Gate Park. I started asking around for anyone who knew where my father lived. He wasn't in the phone book. Some people had heard of him, but didn't know where exactly he lived. Some guy said he thought he lived south of town somewhere in the countryside.

"So, I was driving around out there and I saw these people in a front yard talking. I pulled over and asked them if they knew. Two of them were real estate agents; their last name was Prophet. They offered to lead me to his house.

"So, on Father's Day, led by the Prophets, I drive up this long, winding drive, pick up the phone at the locked gate, and call."

Father and son had a long talk that day. Michael said he needed to change. He wanted a last chance to change. Mark asked him what he wanted to do. Michael said he might like to be an electrician. Mark told him there was a second house on his property just a quarter mile away where he could stay if he agreed to take classes at the local college and work toward his electrician's license.

Michael now works for an electrician, has just finished his four years of classes, and is studying for his electrician's certificates for the states of Idaho and Washington. He and Andy, also an electrician, have started their own rap band and have recorded CDs. This impresses Alex, who wants their CD. What impresses us both is this extraordinary story of a son finding his father after fourteen years. It's clear they have a good relationship now. Mark is making arrangements to let Michael and Andy take his four-wheelers up to his mountain cabin for a few days of trout fishing. Father and son trust each other. I think of Tyler Lamere, whose journeys from north of Seattle to Montana to visit his father ended twice with finding a drunken dad.

The gold sun has gone west into an evening sky of intense, burning orange, and we all move out to the deck on the south side of the house where hay fields fall steeply into a narrow, shadowed valley of brush and trees where, far away, a yellow light glows from a farmhouse window. Mark and I fall to reminiscing. The evening is cool and we can still see a ridge of mountains to the south as this wide sky of the West is slowly scattering stars. I recall that when Mark was young, he and his older brother Bob had a pet skunk. Mark sits back and smiles.

"Bobby and I were biking back home from Wildcat Creek where we'd caught crawdads and were carrying them home in an old blue suitcase. We spotted this mother skunk and her six babies running across the gravel road and down into a culvert. You know that culvert on the road to Wildcat Creek, after you cross the railroad tracks?"

I nod.

"Well, Bobby and I..."

"How old were you?" I interrupt.

"I don't know, maybe I was six and Bobby was nine? Anyway, we decided to capture a couple baby skunks for pets. So we crawled into the culvert after them. The mother blasted us, and then, as we got closer, the babies let us have it. It was a humongous stink, but that didn't stop us. The mother got away and took off with two of her babies, but we managed to grab four of the six and get them into this blue suitcase we were carrying on the bike. Inside the suitcase were the crawdads. So the babies got locked in there with the crawdads pinching at them and the skunks blasted the last of their reserves into the suitcase.

"When we pedaled up to our house, we called for our mom. She came out on the deck and we yelled, 'Look what we've got, Mom!' She cried out, 'Oh, no you don't! You take off those clothes this minute and take them to the farm pond,' which was half a mile away, 'and bury them. Then you come back and hose each other off.'

"So that's what we did. Came walking back across the pastures stark naked, then hosed each other off."

Alex asks, "What happened to the skunks?"

Mark leans back in his deck chair and smiles again. "We kept them."

"You kept them? How could you?"

"My dad drove them over to Kansas State University and had them de-scented. They agreed to do this for free if we let them keep two of the babies. So Bobby and I both had a pet skunk. The first one died two days later, but the other one lived for months and months, used to run all over that basement where our bedrooms were."

"What'd you feed it?"

"Milk in a bottle at first, but they'll eat almost anything."

The air is clean, the stars, so bright, the sky wide and full of memories. It's good to see my boyhood friend again. We talk long into the night of remembered escapades: of coyotes shot, of black snakes picked up and swung around the head like a whip, of gigging for bullfrogs and frying up the legs for breakfast, of snapping turtles decapitated and cooked, carp caught, and wind-driven sail boats capsized.

We sit back in our chairs and gaze along the high star path of the Milky Way, and I hear Mark say, "It's beautiful."

He gets up and shows us the guest bedrooms, and promises he'll take us up the Snake River tomorrow in his jet boat before driving us back into the mountains for our canoe trip.

MURDER AND PETROGLYPHS

By early afternoon Alex and I are on the Snake River with Mark: Mark at the wheel, Michael, Andy, a boy named Lane, Alex, and I are watching the high, treeless mountains slide by. Strange rock formations: vertical segments of volcanic rock that look as if prehistoric bears have clawed deep lines into the rock, horizontal ledges that layer the mountains, humped mounds of rock that pick up colors of ochre and orange in the sunlight, and steep slopes everywhere shaded green and blond under the summer sun. Along bush-crowded, rock-strewn banks, we spot two mountain sheep grazing. They hardly look up, unconcerned.

Jet boats can navigate the Snake because they have an inboard motor that sucks in the water and kicks it out the stern, thus avoiding propellers bent or broken by rocks in the many rapids that interrupt the flow of the river out of Hell's Canyon. It's the deepest canyon in America, though the sloping mountains that hem the twisting river don't have the precipitous drama of the Grand Canyon. Still, the history of this canyon has its drama.

On June 16, 1887, someone found a body floating down the Snake. A judge named Joseph Vincent took a look: "about 5 feet 6 inches high, 4 very large teeth, 2 above standing out, 2 below standing out and down. He had on clothes, a leather belt around his waist, shot in the back just below right shoulder blade, 2 cuts in back of head, one on each side done with an axe."

A second floating body was naked: "shot in the breast, just below the heart, head very much cut and chopped."

A third body had two bullet wounds "in small of back near back bone, head off as though chopped...he was lodged in a large drift pile when found. Some recognized him as Ah Yow [a Chinese gold miner]." (How this particular headless body could be recognized is not mentioned.) Other bodies began appearing, caught in rocks, washed up on gravel bars, bobbing in back eddies, some of them just bleached, gristled skeletons that had been picked by the buzzards. "It was the most cold-blooded cowardly treachery I have ever heard tell of on this coast," wrote Judge Vincent, "and I am a 49er. Every one was shot, cut up and stripped and thrown in the river."

A rancher named George Craig and his son who lived near the river said, "We couldn't imagine how so many men had been killed without our hearing about it."

All the victims were Chinese gold miners; 34 of them. They had set up a camp in Hell's Canyon near Dead Line Creek and had been panning for gold for about six months. It's a rough, rocky area, the gravel along the river fist-sized and difficult to walk. Apparently a gang of young men led by a rancher and horse thief named Blue Evans, who lived on the Oregon side of the Snake, had ambushed the Chinese near the end of May, shot ten of them near Dead Line Creek, more at a sand bar a few miles away, and more on down the river. The bodies were badly hacked, perhaps as an incentive for the survivors to divulge where they'd hidden their gold.

As in the Rock Springs riot, the Chinese embassy appealed for an investigation. One Chinese man even paid Judge Vincent to ride up the river and find out exactly what had happened. According to a magazine article written by Gerald Tucker, Vincent crossed the Snake River just below Dead Line Creek and disguised himself as a gold miner in order to make friends with a group of white men camped on the Oregon side. They appeared to be keeping a close watch on him. "Vincent set about panning gold and visiting the camp occasionally. He made friends with two young fellows whom he entertained with tales...of a fabulously rich vein of gold which he knew about, but needed assistance to develop. Meanwhile, he asked innocent questions and picked up a lot of information." Judge Vincent even poisoned their dog so he could sneak up to the camp at night and listen in on the gang's conversations.

Whatever Judge Vincent found out, the case was not pursued from Lewiston, where Vincent lived. Blue Evans, the gang leader, was arrested in late May, but not for murder, and not in Lewiston but in Wallowa County in Oregon. He was jailed for altering the brands on horses and then stealing them. This was just days before the bodies were found floating down the Snake. Before Evans could be tried, and while being held in the county jail, he arranged for someone to leave two loaded pistols in the outhouse and a horse saddled and tied nearby. He was no doubt rather anxious to escape before the bodies were found. That night Evans told the deputy he needed to take a leak. He soon returned with both pistols pointed at the deputy and told him to take a walk. The deputy did take a walk. Evans then ran to the horse, mounted up, and took off at a dead run.

He and two other men who were later accused of the murders soon left the area. Some school boys who were apparently a part of the murders accused only the men who had escaped, and the boys were all acquitted.

Five years later, after his son Robert's death at the age of sixteen, one of the boys' father, Hugh McMillan, published an account of his son's confession:

"...my son and Bruce Evans, J. T. Canfield, Mat LaRue, Frank Vaughan, Hiram Maynard, and Carl Hughes were stopping in a cattle camp four miles from Snake river. My son and Evans, Canfield, LaRue, and Vaughan went to the Chinese camp on the Snake River. Canfield and LaRue went above the camp and Evans and Vaughan remained below. There were thirteen Chinese in the camp and they were fired on. Twelve Chinese were instantly killed and one other caught afterwards and his brains beaten out. The party got that evening five thousand dollars in gold dust. Next day, eight more Chinese came to the camp in a boat. They were all killed and their bodies thrown into the river. The party then took a boat and went to another Chinese camp four miles distance where thirteen Chinese were working on a river bar. These were all killed and their bodies thrown into the river. The camp was robbed..."

Historian R. Gregory Nokes, who has written a book on the incident, questions some of the details of this confession, but agrees that between 31 and 34 Chinese gold miners were shot and hacked to death for their gold, and that the trial which followed convicted no one, largely because of anti-Chinese sentiment in the West at the time and because the pioneer settlers of the Wallowa wanted to protect their children. This massacre followed the Rock Springs killings by less than a year. It was a hard time for Chinese immigrants, and frontier justice paid little heed to the Declaration of Independence's affirmation that "all men are created equal."

***

Before spending a good part of our afternoon fishing for smallmouth bass, Mark brings his jet boat ashore on the Idaho side near some large boulders and slabs of rock called Buffalo Eddy. The sun is high and hot. We climb down from the boat and follow Mark through dried grass and thistles, past thorny locust trees and dying apricot trees, following a path around the tall grey rocks and then into a place where ancient natives pounded figures into the volcanic boulders: mountain sheep and human figures with strange horns that look like antennae. The place is still considered sacred to the Nez Perce. In the branches of a nearby apricot tree, someone has hung beads, bells, and feathers. Mark turns and says, "You can feel the magic in this place."

It is a beautiful place: a cluster of large grey and dark brown boulders tinged with black, ochre, and orange, crevices and lines broken vertically and horizontally, some of the rock shattered into chunks, the clear waters of the Snake swirling around the outcropping and past a white sand beach, hackberry trees and locust trees painting a yellow-green border to the river, and tall mountains of dry grass and layers of brown basalt rising up both sides of an intersecting valley into a pale blue sky.

Who made these figures on the dark, flat surfaces of ancient stones? What did they mean? Were they records of conquests? A cry for protection? Were the mountain sheep pictured an appeal to the gods for material security, for food in time of famine? A boasting of kills? There are hundreds of figures on both sides of the river: humans, deer, snakes, concentric circles. The mass of rocks protrudes into the river sending the currents swirling round a reportedly deep and dangerous place for boats.

That bearded wanderer Edward Abbey went ashore once to examine petroglyphs. He imagines a village where the women ground corn with mortar and pestle and the naked men "convened in sacred committee meetings down in the kivas, smoking their sacred joints, and the swarms of children romped in the river, climbed the stony walls, chased lizards, and tormented the village dogs...And then one day they all left. Departed. *Vanished.* The world dissolves around us, hour by hour. Whole ranges of mountains come and go, mumbling of tectonic vertigo. Nothing endures, everything changes, and all remains the same."

THE SELWAY

The next morning Mark drives Alex and me and our canoe, Clueless, over a hundred miles up the Clearwater, past Orofino, Kamiah, and Kooskia, to Three Rivers, where the westward flowing Lochsa joins the Selway to become the Clearwater that rushes off to the Snake and thence to the Pacific. At Three Rivers, which is a shady arrangement of cabins, a café and a country store, he turns up the winding gravel road to the south, following the Selway for about ten or twelve miles, where he drops us off with our gear, takes a few pictures as we load the canoe and embark, then leaves us to our adventure.

It is a bright day, full of rushing water, steep green mountains of fir and cedar, spruce and pine. Great slabs of granite and broken moraines of lesser rocks line the banks. In the clean, clear water, we can see rocks of ochre and brown six or ten feet below us. In the deeper torrents, the water darkens to a shadowed forest green. We have no spray skirt to keep out the crashing waves of the rapids, so within the first miles our canoe fills, and we barely get young, green Clueless paddled to shore, the icy water sloshing around our ankles and shins. Having forgotten to bring cut gallon jugs with which to bail out the water, we end up spending a half hour bailing water with coffee cups till we can tip the water-laden canoe enough to dump the water onto the sand and gravel.

We stop a few times on riverside boulders to fish, but catch nothing.

On we go, swerving over submerged boulders that lift and slam us down, cutting between foaming rocks, twisting right and left, and slipping over roaring ledges. It's a wild, exhilarating ride, the icy snowmelt is in a great hurry to get down out of the mountains, currents slewing around huge boulders, dancing, babbling over shallow rocks in the sunlight, subsiding into deep, reflective pools swirling back into eddies.

Between the roar of the many rapids, we coast along quiet, limpid pools, the warm sun soaking us, a summer breeze blowing in our faces. A day to be alive!

Once, toward evening, a doe and her fawn stand in the shadows and watch us, then the doe fades into deeper shadows as her fawn kicks its gangly back legs and awkwardly follows.

Once or twice more, we stop to bail and fish. In a deep pool that turns in front of a long gravel bar and swings into rough rapids, we see steelheads two-and-a-half feet long swimming beneath us, slowly swaying along against the current. We stop and try different flies: dry ones, wet ones, any ones, but the huge fish are absolutely uninterested, dismissing our efforts with a slight turn, then sinking into deeper, darker waters.

About sundown, we pull Clueless onto a wide gravel bar scattered with young willows and smelling of fresh mint. We've reached the conjunction of the Selway, the Lochsa, and the Clearwater. There on the east bank are the cabins and the Three Rivers Café. After setting our tent and unloading our packs to let them dry in the evening breeze, we paddle the empty canoe across one of several channels to the eastern shore, tie it up, then climb the steep bank through tall green grass and weeds, entering the café just as they're closing. But they let us eat: salads, hamburgers, and fries. Coffee for me; iced tea for Alex.

The sun has set by the time we walk into the cool mountain twilight and slide down the grassy bank to our canoe, push off, and cross to our tent site where we haul Clueless onto the gravel and flip him upside down, then crawl into the tent and into our sleeping bags with the sound of many waters running all around us.

Alex wants a story, so I click on the light and we read of Frodo's flight from the Black Riders, his dangerous crossing of the river: "Frodo heard the splash of water. It foamed about his feet. He felt the quick heave and surge as the horse left the river and struggled up the stony path." The black horses behind him "were filled with madness, and leaping forward in terror they bore their riders into the rushing flood. Their piercing cries drowned in the roaring of the river as it carried them away. Then Frodo felt himself falling, and the roaring and confusion seemed to rise and engulf him..."

THE CLEARWATER

The night smells of mint and goose excrement. The Canadian geese that graze on this gravel bar are apparently fond of mint leaves. Setting up the tent at dusk, we hadn't noticed the droppings scattered through the knee-high willow brush. By morning the tent reeks of mint-flavored excrement.

It's a bright clear morning, a perfect day to ride the strong, living back of the great, green serpent. We repack our bags, load the canoe, and shove off, finding a shallow channel that feeds into the rushing Clearwater. A powerful current; we must be moving along at a five- or six-mile-per-hour clip, skimming over the multicolored rocks beneath us, avoiding the occasional rise and rush of the river as it humps over and sweeps around large boulders. We both dispense with our life preservers and peel off our T-shirts as the morning warms in the rising sun.

We can hear the coming rapids long before we see them. When the white water appears, we start plotting a course, looking always for the darker, deeper channels. Within minutes the fast water is racing, pouring us down the chutes and troughs with Alex fending off boulders and me ruddering hard left or right. All around us the river roars, waves slap heavily into the canoe, and the water sloshes around our ankles, and then, as suddenly, the danger is behind us and the river calms and smiles slyly at the sun.

It is as beautiful a river as I've ever seen, with the wooded mountains rising rapidly on either hand, the morning sun following behind, rising high into clear air. For a time we paddle steadily, taking in the day, living in the moment. "Where is he," says Thoreau, "who can excite in us a pure morning joy?" Give me the Clearwater on a summer morning.

"The overwhelming majority," says whisky-soaked adventurer Abbey, "seem condemned to the role of spectators...dependent consumers." But "a journey on foot into the uninhabited interior; a voyage down the river of no return" offers Americans "our ancient and rightful liberty. All that is needed is normal health, the will to do it, and a modicum of courage."

Then we hear the far shouting of rapids, "the fine white noise of troubled waters," and I feel the tension tighten, for there's no guarantee we'll slide down the next set of rapids as we have the last. I'm wishing I'd invested in a spray skirt snapped down on both sides of Clueless to keep the waves out.

The shouting builds and deepens to the roar of a great crowd and we see that this set of rapids extends all across the river—no easy passage here. There's a fine bank of gold-white sand on our left and another farther down on our right, but between these two havens, the rocks have raised a broken ridge of leaping, slashing waters that goes by the name of Three Devils.

The river picks up speed and sweeps us down, bouncing us over and through the waves. We slide a bit sideways, and a big wave falls heavily into the canoe, then another. We're suddenly slogging awkwardly through shoving waves, pulling hard with our paddles. The water pours in and young Clueless is drowning. I shout to Alex to swim for shore. Once, with his older brother Justin, I stayed too long with a capsized canoe and came very, very close to being swept over a dam. I grab the bag that holds the tent and tip myself into the icy water, plunging into the shocking rush, and come up gasping, my heart racing against the terrible cold of the surging waters. I see Clueless bobbing along the white-water current with Alex's head next to a gunwale, his hands hanging on. I hope desperately that he won't be sucked into another rapid before he can swim ashore.

Meanwhile, with my right arm I'm stroking strongly for shore, my left clutching the tent bag I'm using as a floatation device. But I seem to be paddling in place. I've escaped the waves and currents of the rapids and am swimming through what looks like calmer waters, but a powerful eddy is driving me up current and somehow holding me in place; I can't seem to make any progress toward shore. I'm panting for air and after a while my leg kicks and arm action begin to slow. It's a tough swim for a 60-year-old man. I turn onto my back and float for a few seconds, trying to get my wind, then turn and search downstream for Alex. Far down the river I see him leg kicking Clueless to shore; meanwhile my tent bag is filling with water and losing its buoyancy. The grey rocks along shore are no closer.

An old, shirtless man, sun-browned, with a tall walking stick and a long, scraggly beard appears on the sandbar downstream between Alex and me like some old mountain man emerging from a primeval forest. He seems to peer at us from the corners of his eyes, never looking directly at us. A wolf-like dog trots out beside him. I keep kicking, gasping, and stroking for all I'm worth, wondering what river spell has fastened me in place; everything is on the move but me. Exhausted, I glance into the pale sky and seriously wonder if these are my last seconds. The tent bag is beginning to sink. I'm about to drop it and try for shore with both weakened arms when I slip out of the strong undercurrent and am suddenly making progress. The roar of the rapids is constant, the water, liquid ice, the sharp ripples and waves leap and sparkle in the sun. My heart is drumming and breaths tear out of me in quick, ragged gasps as I reach repeatedly with one heavy arm for the broken rocks and weeds along shore. Finally I find the rocky bottom with my toes and drag myself gasping up a weathered boulder. I drop the soaked tent bag and sit panting in the sun, my eyes searching downstream for Alex.

The mountain man and his dog have vanished, but in the far shadows beyond the sand bank I see Alex. He's pulled Clueless to shore and is standing waist deep watching me. I wave and lean over to pant again. Alex is safe. Even Clueless is still with us; Alex has played the smarter part by staying with the canoe and thereby has saved both himself and our supplies, thus saving the rest of our trip. The Three Devils almost sucked us down and squeezed the air out of me, but we're alive.

In time I catch my breath and pick my way over rocks and down the sand beach to where Alex has pulled the canoe to shore. We check for lost supplies. One canteen gone. Two paddles gone. Unfortunately for me, we have only one spare paddle. This is good fortune for Alex because it means I get to do all the paddling while he learns to fly fish from the prow.

The evening before, we bought gallon jugs of milk at the Three Rivers Country Store, emptied and cut them open, and tied them to the front and back thwarts, so it doesn't take long now to bail. By the time we finish, the sun has warmed and dried us.

I tell Alex about the difficult swim. He says, "When I got the canoe out of the current, I looked back and couldn't see you. I thought you were gone."

* * *

We shove off again, still not putting on our life preservers (we never learn) but placing them beneath bungi cords where we can grab them if needed. Some people are constitutionally opposed to risk, though most of them drive cars. Edward Abbey again: "A venturesome minority will always be eager to set off on their own, and no obstacles should be placed in their path; let them take risks, for Godsake, let them get lost, sunburnt, stranded, drowned, eaten by bears, buried alive under avalanches—that is the right and privilege of any free American." After our near drowning in snowmelt currents, I am shirtless and already working on my next sunburn.

Off we go, searching the shorelines and reedy shallows for our lost paddles. In time Alex pulls out his fly rod and starts working on his casting skills. On we go, paddling down the winding river as he learns to whip the fly rod back and forth and to cast effectively from a sitting position, finally catching one little trout on a dry fly. It's his first trout ever and we're both ecstatic. Much joy in a small fish. It's too small to eat, and after careful examination, he releases it. We never do find our lost paddles.

The Clearwater River is, as its name states, crystalline because it flows out of granite mountains, not picking up the sediments of lime-stone and sandstone. Slopes of blue-green firs and yellow-green cedars come right down to the shoreline. Broken boulders break the current here and there and dead trees have washed into shallows or collected on obstructions. We maneuver left and right. Sometimes the current roils along dark and deep, then again it spreads into wide, sunny shallows that murmur and ripple and glitter and bubble around weedy little islands of round rocks, sand and willow brush.

We're always looking for the least volatile passage. Once, coming upon a low, gravel island thickly planted with young willows, I decide too late to take the channel to our right. We're caught in a fast, shallow current that pulls us backwards. We can't fight it. Stroking hard through six or seven inches of water, we can't catch a deep enough purchase on the water to fight the sliding current that sweeps us backwards, so we swerve the prow around and run with it, swirling down the sparkling river, not knowing what dangers lie around the bend, knocked about a little with the occasional wave slapping over the gunwales, but all in all it's a joyous ride through the clear mountain morning, on into a blue-sky afternoon.

***

By September 27, 1805, Lewis and many of the men were still sick, but they had work to do. Clark writes: "Set about building 5 canoes. day very warm." These canoes were chipped and burnt from large trees, in this case probably ponderosa pines. They built a row of small fires to burn out some of the wood from the center section, and then used their axes and carpentry tools to chop, chip, and scrape out the smoldering contents, a process they learned from the Nez Perce.

It didn't help their upset stomachs that the days were hot. Then, on the first of October, a cool breeze blew down from the mountains. They kept hacking away at the wood, carving out their dugouts, but they had little to eat, just a little dried fish which worked on them much like the powerful laxatives Lewis had been giving them. Ordway says, "the party so weak that we git along Slow with the canoes." One of the men killed a coyote, but after boiling it to broth, the tough, skinny animal provided no more than a few chewy, stringy mouthfuls for each member of the party of 34, so they killed another horse to make soup for the sick.

Day followed day. Lewis was still unable to write or walk.

SPARKY AND SMOKY VS. THE FEDS

About midafternoon, Alex and I have worked up a heated thirst. We've used up the water in our canteens and need to stop to refill them by pumping water through our purifier into the water bottles and canteens. I expect the water is clean enough to drink, but why take a chance? I'm sure Lewis and Clark were glad to get the cold, clear waters of this river after a year of drinking Missouri River silt.

Highway 12 lies beside the river like a great black snake sunning itself next to its more lively green companion. Above the right bank and across the highway, we spot a home with a small sign in the window that advertises a coffee shop. Thinking we can purchase cold sodas, we slip into shore, tie Clueless to a tree, climb the steep bank, cross the highway and make our way along a knee-high wall of grey and white

173

river rock to an immaculate home set among spruce trees. Behind a trimmed yard is an old, repainted schoolhouse with broad pastures beyond where two horses graze beneath the steep slopes of a grassy mountain scattered with trees.

We step through the front door into a little gift shop selling cards and knickknacks. A trim, pretty woman named Mary Park walks in from her kitchen and greets us. While drinking iced Pepsi and Squirt, we fall into conversation.

For two decades Mary and her husband raised German shorthair hunting dogs behind their home, using the old schoolhouse as a school for dogs. Their dog Sparky was a seven-time national champion. Sparky's father, Smoky, was a six-time national champion.

"He missed being national champ a seventh time," she says, "by one point, so to me he's a seven-time champ, just like Sparky." She tells us that when the local forest rangers went on vacation or needed to travel for meetings, they'd drop their dogs off here at her kennels and the Parks would board them. The former District Forest Ranger boarded his dogs with them off and on for eighteen years.

"Then we got a new District Forest Ranger, a woman from Vermont."

Mary tells us that this District Ranger let it be known that she would enforce the laws on "scenic easements," whereby the Forest Service decides what can and cannot be done within so many yards of the Clearwater River. An old couple up the river needed to cut down a dead tree that threatened to fall on their home, but the new District Forest Ranger forbad it. The insurance company would not cover the house unless the tree was cut down. The couple didn't have the money to fight the Forest Service in court, so they sold their home in this beautiful valley and moved away.

The Forest Service then required the Parks to take down their signs advertising their coffee and gift shop and dog kennels. They would not be allowed to run a dog kennel, even though the grounds were perfectly kept and the dog kennels were well back of the house. (Alex and I hadn't seen or heard a single dog when we walked up to the house.) Even the small OPEN sign behind the glass of their home's front window was a problem for the woman from Vermont.

The Parks thought this unjust. They loved their dogs and their work and this valley, so they decided to fight the Forest Service in court. They hired a good lawyer, but they lost the first court case in the local court where the judge had often supported the Forest Service. They appealed to District Court, got their state congressman and senators behind them, and kept fighting. Legal bills mounted, even though the Parks' lawyer gave them a cut rate because she believed in their case.

"I'm a bookkeeper," Mary says. "I kept every communication the District Ranger sent us. I published them in the newspaper." Public sympathy grew for Mary and her husband.

The legal process took ten years and about $100,000. The Parks finally won their case, but because the Federal Government, unlike private corporations, is not required to pay the legal fees of people unjustly prosecuted, the Parks were unable to sue the Forest Service to reimburse their legal fees.

"Why did you keep fighting when you couldn't possibly make enough money raising dogs to pay the legal fees?" I asked.

"Because it was the right thing to do. Somebody has to stand up for what's right. Someone's got to stand up to them. They had no right to take our business away after they had allowed it for so many years. If no one fights for justice, what will become of our country?"

"So you're still paying off the lawyers?"

"Yes. It's been years, but the lawyers have been very patient with us. We keep making payments, but it wasn't just the money. It was ten years of anxiety. Always worrying about what would happen next. Would we lose our house? Would we lose our business?"

"Was it worth it?"

She is adamant. "Yes, it was worth it!"

There were other casualties. The local District Attorney who had hoped to make a name for himself by prosecuting the Parks, lost the next election, and the District Forest Ranger from Vermont lost her job. "Last I heard, she was washing cars," Mary says.

We finish our iced sodas and bid Mary and her lovely home and gift shop and kennel of champion dogs goodbye. Her case reminds me of a garbage man in tiny Alma, Kansas, who took his case all the way to the United States Supreme Court, arguing that he had the legal right to compete with the local garbage service that was supported by town and county government. He won, too, though it must have cost him and his supporters a hefty amount of money. I'm proud of these little folk who are willing to take on the hydra-headed government and keep whacking away with their homemade weapons till they drive the monster back. Sometimes they win. I expect most of the time they cannot afford to win. But then again, where else in the world can a single dog trainer or garbage man fight his or her way to the higher courts and win? Sometimes, perhaps not often, government of the people, by the people, and for the people still works.

TO JUMP OR NOT TO JUMP

Back on the river, a summer wind is blowing up the river valley from the west. The forested mountains on our right are giving way to tall slopes of blowing blond grass with forested ravines that cut their way down from the high prairie above. The mountains on either side rise a thousand feet above the riverbed, but the forests of willow and hackberry and pine still cling to the banks. The current is strong and we're skimming the deep green waters and swinging around boulder-bent swirls, gliding over sun-struck floors of golden cobbles, knifing through green-glazed sheets of liquid glass. Alex keeps fishing and I keep paddling.

After passing under a bridge, we see rapids to our right and I guide Clueless to center where the water seems flat. Suddenly we spot a drop-off. A ledge runs across all but the far left side of the river. Directly in front of us the current swims smoothly over and crashes into the water below. Alex shouts a warning as I jab my paddle down and backpaddle hard on my left. Alex is helpless, not having a paddle, but Clueless slowly swings broadside to the crashing waters. I paddle hard toward the far shore, but the current sweeps us toward a ledge that is broken in several places by strange, volcanic rocks that look like clumps of broken, petrified clay. The current is strong and I see we're not going to make it the fifty yards to our left where the ledge finally slides below the surface. I shout, "I'm going right!" Alex grips his fly rod and watches as I backpaddle on my right, straightening Clueless just in time for us to run straight over the ledge. Alex in the prow slides into thin air and then crashes down. We take the two-foot drop and rock sideways, just avoiding a three-foot swell that would have sunk us. We ship a little water but rock through waves and roaring whitewater and escape, cruising into calm.

"That was close!" I call out.

Alex shakes his head and takes a deep breath.

**

Late that afternoon, we paddle to shore across from the little town of Kooskia, a place rich in history. This was a favorite campsite for Chief Looking Glass's band of the Nez Perce, and just up the South Fork of the Clearwater which enters the Middle Fork here, a two-day battle took place between the U. S. army and the Nez Perce.

We set up our tent on a weedy, sandy beach on the north side of the river, near the concrete bridge that takes Highway 13 over the river and then up the intersecting valley. As we unload our packs, we notice boys on the far side of the river standing on one of the concrete bridge piers. All we can see are the feet and legs of three boys standing beneath the deck of the highway where five-foot-high I-beams cross the river on concrete piers. Suddenly one of the boys whoops and jumps, dropping fifteen feet into the cold Clearwater below. He bobs to the surface and shouts, then swims rapidly to the far shore.

After a few minutes the second boy yells and jumps.

The two boys, one skinny, the other big and chunky, climb out of the water and turn to wait for the third.

And wait. The minutes must be moving slowly for the boy in black shorts still standing on the pier.

Skinny and Chunky call up encouragements. After a few minutes of impatience, they rail and laugh and make fun: "Yellow! Come on, just do it!" they shout. And wait. The minutes tick slowly by. Alex and I set up our tent, put our packs out to dry in the sun and are thinking about walking into town to buy paddles and find a place to eat.

The skinny boy gives up, puts on sunglasses, and climbs the bank and walks away.

Chunky, in red shorts, pulls on a T-shirt and calls out more encouragements to his friend on the pier. To no avail. Finally he, too, gives up and climbs the bank beneath the highway and leaves.

The last boy in the black shorts waits. Alex and I can feel his need to jump. To prove his courage. To allay the mockery of boys who know him and will publicize his cowardice.

Alex and I sit down together on the sand and watch his white legs and feet, three-quarters of the way across the river. Still standing. Somehow trying to summon a quick flash of courage so important to a boy his age.

Finally, we see the feet disappear—but not into the river. He's making his way along the steel beams that hold the highway, shuffling along beneath the highway deck till he can climb down to the bank. Then he does what I did not expect. He walks down into the cold river and submerges himself. Then he leaves the water and climbs the bank to follow his friends.

Alex and I look at each other.

"He's going to tell his friends he jumped," I say.

Alex grins. "Sure is. He couldn't jump, but he's going to tell them he did."

How does a young man demonstrate manhood in the 21st Century? Getting an A or a B on a Biology test, hitting a double or single in a game of baseball, finding a job, even going to college, seem pale accomplishments compared to the courage expected of Sioux or Blackfeet or Nez Perce boys. Boys crave excitements not offered by our staid society, so they devise their own adventures.

A summer evening on a bridge over Soldier Creek, ten miles north of Topeka, Kansas. The concrete bridge spans two wooded banks that drop steeply into a stream 40 feet below. The brown water eases around a bend from the west and washes over a sloping layer of limestone. Having passed under the bridge, the flat, brown water pools. Boys from Silver Creek and Topeka have checked its depth and decided it's deep enough to break the fall of a boy leaping off the four-story-high bridge.

Alex and his friends have jumped from the Huxman Bridge several times. They plummet 40 feet and plunge deep into dark water. It's an adrenaline rush.

One summer evening he and his friend Cory went to the bridge. A black fisherman on the far bank watched as they climbed the footpath through weeds and shrubs up to the high deck of the bridge. They walked the roadway to the center and Cory volunteered to jump first.

He sat down on the knee-high concrete guardrail and swung his legs over to face the stream, peering down at the dark current so far below. The sun was down and the western sky was fading from orange to mauve. Swallows skimmed the surface below and a silver quarter moon stood high above the bankside cottonwoods, maples, and walnut trees.

"Ready?" Alex asked.

Cory nodded and Alex counted him down: "Three, two, one..."

Cory jumped, dropping feet first, dropping free, arms flailing the air to keep his balance, hitting the water hard with a sudden clap and disappearing.

Alex leaned over the rail and waited for his friend to resurface. Cory's head and shoulders burst from the surface and the boy swam for shore.

"You all right?" Alex yelled.

"I'm okay, you ready?"

Down the stream, the fisherman had turned his attention from his red-and-white bobber to the remaining boy on the high bridge.

"You ready?" Cory shouted up again as he found his footing and stood up in shallow water.

Twilight was deepening, and far away they could hear a train approaching on the tracks that parallel the stream. Above the dark trees, the moon was undergoing the alchemy of evening, exchanging silver for gold. The air was warm. The swallows were gone to their clay huts under the bridge, and bats were dodging and flicking along the stream. Alex sat down on the concrete guardrail and looked down. The evening shadows had dyed the water black. He turned about and faced the roadway, his hands gripping the knee-high guardrail, his bare toes on the deck.

A car approached from his right, its headlights picking up the shirtless boy at the edge of the bridge. The driver slowed down. Alex grinned fiercely and gave the man the thumbs up. The train was coming, a heavy rumble shaking the air. The car pulled away and rolled over the tracks just before the red lights began flashing and the striped crossbar swung down to the metallic ding, ding, ding of the warning bell. Alex heard the coming diesel horn call out its warning.

A phrase from a movie comedy was running through Alex's head: "Do something every day that scares you...Do something every day that scares you." Awful advice for teenage boys.

"You ready, Alex?" came another shout from below.

He nodded and took a breath.

"Three...two...one . . !"

He stood fixed to the concrete guardrail.

"Come on, dude!" Cory called. They had done this many times before. Why was Alex holding up? He was a black silhouette forty feet up against the western sky. The diesel horn sounded nearer, blasting three times across the corn fields and forest groves. There was the sharp, persistent ding, ding, ding, of the crossing bell, the red lights flashing.

Cory called out, "Three...two...one!"

Alex pushed off, leaning backwards into empty air. He bent his knees and pushed his legs hard off the concrete deck. His stiff body began pivoting backwards down the night, head under heels: one turn, a second turn, trying for a double back flip, but he already knew he wouldn't complete the second flip, he closed his eyes tight and stiffened as his horizontal body slammed down onto black water. Water surged around him, then the pain rushed up from the muddy depths and flooded him. He was kicking for the faintest light, his face surfaced, he gasped for air and found himself already stroking for shore. His hands, then his feet found mud and gravel and he tried to stand. Bent double, he waded a few steps, then pulled himself onto a limestone slab and collapsed.

Cory sloshed over and climbed the rock beside him. "You all right?" He leaned over Alex who pushed himself to his hands and knees.

"You all right? Geez! I didn't know you were going to do that!"

Alex coughed and red blood sprayed his forearm.

"Dude, you all right?"

He hung his head and coughed again, spitting up another glob of blood. There was a sharp pain in his chest. His bones ached. The skin on his back burned like a prairie fire.

The train was rumbling by, shaking the night. Alex tried to breathe through his pain.

Cory leaned over him and said, "You're the craziest sonofabitch I've ever seen! I don't know *anybody* that would do that."

Alex stared at the bloodied rock and smiled.

From the gathering darkness downstream, they heard the fisherman call out, "You guys crazy!"

Which about sums it up.

LIBERTY BELL

t's after 9:00 in the evening when we walk across the bridge into Kooskia. The only place open is a Chinese restaurant. Alex orders lemon chicken and I take the sweet-and-sour. Good food after a long day both on and in the water. Alex asks for iced Coke with lemon and gets into a conversation with the Chinese proprietor who tells him she loves boiled Coke as a drink. I've tried it since: to my taste it's remarkably like hot black sugar water—with no fizz. But we're hungry and the food is good. Afterwards, we walk back together through the night, taking in the scents of summer flowers, stopping on the bridge to watch the black waters rolling down from the mountains, the stars rising into infinite night.

***

After sleeping once again on our hard, inch-thick, roll-out mats, we get up and return to town for pancakes and bacon, biscuits and sausage at a café, then walk over to the grocery store and ask about a place to buy canoe paddles. A woman at the register picks up a phone and calls a place called Tom Cat's. She tells us they have raft paddles, but not canoe paddles. I figure we can make a raft paddle work and we set off walking the half mile to Tom Cat's.

We pass a health food store and step in—long counters with local herbs and roots: Osha Root: $58.80 a pound. Oregon Grape Root: $23.80 a pound. Orris Root, Olive Leaf, Orange Peel, Oatstraw Green Tops—and that's just the O's. I wonder if Nettle Root Powder will sting the tongue like nettle leaves sting the skin. The store must have carried camas root, but at the time I didn't think to look for it. I would have paid for the experience of eating what made Lewis and Clark so wretchedly sick. Such are the pleasures of risk takers. Instead, we buy smoothies made of wild cherry and Oregon blackberry and move on, sipping our way around a bend and on up the blacktop.

A white car pulls over and a woman with lovely large eyes and a thin face offers us a ride to Tom Cat's. This is a surprise; we weren't even hitchiking. It turns out she was standing in the grocery store when she heard us asking about paddles. Her name is Shari and she's a California girl recently transplanted to little Kooskia. She's written a cookbook called *Grazing on Pasta*: healthy recipes for the modern cook. She takes us up the road and drops us off.

Getting out and waving goodbye, Alex says, "We rely on the kindness of strangers," which is often a necessary component of risky travels.

The raft paddle we find consists of a hollow, black-plastic bar that screws onto thin yellow paddles at either end. It's better than nothing. I make the purchase and we walk back through morning sunlight, cross the bridge and make our way down towards our tent. Beneath the bridge we find seven or eight children playing in the water beside a pickup pulling a flatbed trailer lined with square hay bales that enclose a huge bronze liberty bell.

What's this?

Two young men are watching their children play in the sunlight. Their names are Cedar and Grady. They tell us this particular Liberty Bell was forged in 1857. A homemade sign painted in large letters on the trailer reads: Fighting for Liberty.

Cedar is a short man with blond hair and clear blue eyes. Grady has dark blond hair and a scruffy beard. They are furniture makers, fabricating elkhorn furniture: lamps, chairs, tables, couches. Cedar looks at us and says, "It used to be the states were sovereign, and the people were the state. Now the Federal government has taken over. It's just the reverse of what used to be." In Idaho we keep encountering individuals who feel a chasm deepening between themselves and a Federal government they believe too distant and tax hungry to represent their needs.

Cedar and Grady have come from displaying their Liberty Bell in a parade through a nearby town. They've painted American flags on plywood on either side of the flatbed and the bell hangs on a wooden device that allows it to swing. I ask if they can ring it.

Grady walks over and gives the heavy bell a push: it swings back and the clapper hits hard, ringing four times through western Idaho, the reverberations humming down the river. We smile and nod. The children turn to look, then wade back into the running Clearwater.

***

It's eight river miles to the little town of Kamiah (pronounced Kam-ee-ai). Ospreys float the air currents as we float the wide, sparkling water currents. A young golden eagle perches in a pine and watches us move by, a doe breaks from riverside brush and stops for a moment, her long face framed in front of a flat, reddish boulder. The sun is hot, but it only takes a brief scoop of the hand to slap the face and hair with fresh, cold water.

An hour or two later, we disembark beneath the highway bridge that crosses into Kamiah and walk the hot streets to find lunch and look for canoe paddles. Alex is using half the raft paddle and it works, but he's already snapped off one thin paddle fighting through a set of rapids, and we don't expect the other half to last. But we find no paddles in Kamiah. I forget to call Dennis, the forest biologist from Kamiah who had given us a ride in the mountains and seemed genuinely concerned for our welfare.

We return to Clueless and move on down the river between high bluffs and steeper canyons of grey basalt, dark pines, and yellow-green brush. Sometimes the river spreads wide, slipping its shallow way over a bed 300 yards wide, and then the mountains shoulder in on either hand, squeezing it into a deep, corrugated current no more than 30 or 40 yards wide where massive grey cliffs of stone plunge steeply into the jade-green waters. In these deep waters, ominous swells erupt from beneath and everywhere through the narrower channels strange currents curl and twist and hump and tear the surface as the pace picks up, speeding us toward the next bend. I tell Alex to keep his life preserver handy.

Our ears listen for the roar. Since our capsizing, rapids make me edgy. Soon enough we hear it. "Alex! We'd better put on the life jackets!"

He lays down his paddle and reaches for his life jacket. By the time we've snapped them on, we can see the churning waves snarling over rocks, heaving around boulders, sucking, swirling, bursting onto a long succession of rocks. I swerve left to clear the chaos but within seconds the prow bounces up and slaps down, waves shove us left then right, pitching, bucking and throwing us forward. A few minutes more and the danger passes—the current calms and the banks recede. Risk is worth the trouble, though it's always a matter of balance. How much is too much? Courage lies somewhere between the coward and the fool.

On we go. Huge ponderosa pines stand among boulders or climb the broken draws into the higher, treeless elevations. Occasionally a deer scrambles up a steep slope of brush and gravel or a raven croaks from a high dead limb.

As the westering sun slips over the mountains, we begin looking for a sand beach and find one formed of fine dry sand sloping up into thorn trees and pines.

While I'm setting up the tent and kindling the fire, Alex drags in dry wood, singing, "Don't you, forget about me! Don't you, forget about me!"

I look up and smile.

"This is the most beautiful country yet," he says, dropping an armful of limbs and sticks. "Remember those three words Mark kept using?"

"What words?

"He kept saying things were 'humongous,' 'phenomenal,' and 'beautiful.' He's right."

"Yes, he is."

Alex picks up his fly rod and heads for a boulder the size of a shed at water's edge while I walk the perimeter of the sand beach and chase a king snake into a tree. Our Lewiston mayor, Kevin Poole, told us king snakes keep the rattlers away, so I'm pleased to find this neighbor, though I've given him a rude welcome.

Towards dark, Alex returns with his apparently useless fishing pole to eat a supper of simmered beef stew. We watch the coals burn down and speak of many things. The stars have appeared and a soft breeze fans the coals. The river murmurs peacefully along as if it hasn't tried several times to kill us. Alex sits beside me in his boxer shorts and a T-shirt, staring at the red coals and wincing when smoke swirls into his eyes.

I tell him this vast country needs a strong federal government, strictly limited in many ways so that the citizens will take up needed responsibilities.

He looks up in the light of the fire and says, "But you said you agreed with Cedar and Grady back there at the bridge."

"I do with their call to take responsibility, with the need to assert states' rights, county rights, city rights. Local rights should often take precedence over the distant rule of Washington, but the states can't be totally sovereign. What would have happened if the South had won the Civil War? Would we be two countries today? Three? More? Would we be a continent of competing countries like Europe was through the twentieth century? That's why Jefferson made the Louisiana Purchase and sent Lewis and Clark down this river. He wanted a united country. And that was going to be hard to do. Back then, the fastest way to move across country was by horse. Jefferson and others back east thought Lewis and Clark had died when they didn't hear from them for almost two years. Even with Jefferson's hopes, it was going to be a difficult, chancy thing to keep this country united."

Alex leans back with his hands in the sand, watching the fire.

"There were people in Jefferson's time," I continue, "who were making plans to make the land from the Appalachians to the Mississippi River a separate country. You know the guy who shot Hamilton in that duel? I forget his name. He went west and conspired to found a new country west of the Appalachians. There was a lot of anger then in the West against a government in the East making rules for them, but I've always agreed with Hamilton's arguments against Jefferson's: that national unity requires a strong enough federal government to keep us working together."

Alex, who has just reached voting age, looks out into the night.

ONION MAN AND KNIFE LADIES

The next morning we rise just after dawn and pack up. I expect we're several miles from Orofino, the place Lewis and Clark built their dugout canoes, and where the North Fork of the Clearwater joins the Middle Branch. It's Sunday, and I'm wondering if we'll make it to Orofino in time for church services—if they'll accept a couple of grubby, smoke-scented refugees whose only bath has been an unintended plunge into the Clearwater. We skip breakfast, hoping for coffee and doughnuts before or after a church service, and push Clueless into clear water.

The sun is still a long way from appearing over the mountains and the air is pine-scented and cool. Deer keep bounding away from us into the tree line. Two does walk a fawn into the brush and stop to stare.

We swing around a 90-degree lefthand turn in the river as a

kingfisher swoops from riverside trees and wings along the surface, giving its skittery call. Slowed by a strong back eddy, we pull back into the running current in time for the river to swerve 90 degrees back to the right and carry us on into Orofino. We tie Clueless to a pine tree beneath the city water intake, put on shoes, and walk into a Best Western Motel to ask directions.

Several blocks later, we walk into St. Theresa's Church, two minutes before the 10:30 service begins. Perfect timing. The priest is a black man from Swaziland. He has a fine British accent. The sermon involves the story of the Good Samaritan, a parable dear to the hearts of traveling refugees. It responds to the question: Who is my neighbor?

The priest recounts an incident when he, with many of his countrymen, were trying to make their way through a border crossing into South Africa. The white Afrikaner border guards serviced one short line for whites and diplomats, another, much longer line for blacks. The blacks were often subjected to much closer scrutiny and often to contempt. "I had to change myself and learn to care for those guards," he says.

After mass, the Good Samaritans of St. Theresa's are indeed serving coffee and doughnuts. In the basement, we sit down with our Styrofoam cups of hot brew and begin wolfing down doughnuts. A man in his fifties, slightly balding, sits down across the table with his coffee and asks us if we're new in town. His name is Bill Shamion, "pronounced like *onion*," he says. "It's Polish. It used to have a complicated spelling, but when my people landed in Chicago, they simplified the spelling."

I ask him what he does for a living.

"Run a body shop. Used to replace a lot of large plate glass for the government when they were building the Dworshak Dam [the massive concrete dam across the North Fork of the Clearwater]. When they were dynamiting out the granite, the blasts would crack glass windows and sometimes the rocks would rain down and break windshields. Now our main income comes from deer crashes."

He had worked for his father when he was young, logging the forests. "But I didn't like being bossed around, so I went to work for a body shop. Now I own my own place. Maybe it's a good thing I got out of logging. My father was killed in a logging accident." He takes a sip of his coffee. "That was a long time ago."

Alex asks, "Who's the pretty girl who was talking to you?"

"That's my granddaughter. We raised two boys and a girl. Now we're raising three grandkids." Good Samaritans still at work.

***

We walk the streets of Orofino like hunter gatherers, seeking more food. We find a Mexican restaurant and eat well. While Spain plays for the World Cup soccer championship on an overhead television screen, a Mexican cook keeps darting out of the kitchen to ask if we need more water, which gives him the chance to catch a few more seconds of the game. The water in our glasses never drops an inch before he's pouring them full again.

We ask which team he's for. He gives us a sheepish smile and says, "España."

He's a happy man when Spain beats the Netherlands in the last four minutes of extra time, 1-0. We finish eating and walk back into the hot mountain sunlight. Hearing music, we stroll down the sunny street to a gas station. A bank registers the temperature at 93.

A boy in a black fedora is sitting beneath a camouflage-colored tent awning pounding out music on a battered electronic keyboard—"Don't Stop Believin':" "Just a city boy, born and raised in south Detroit/ Took the midnight train to anywhere..." The music rolls off his fingers, his head bobs to the rhythm. "Crazy Train:" "I've listened to preachers/ I've listened to fools,/ I've watched all the dropouts,/ Who make their own rules..."

We stand in the sun and listen. The boy's name is Jedidiah. His mother, a tall redhead in a tie-dyed hippie dress stands behind a counter arranged with an assortment of maybe 100 knives: jackknives, switchblades, elkhorn hunting knives, fishing knives, staff swords.

"We've been married 22 years," she says. "Got nine kids. If we have any more, we'll have to get us a longer bus." She points across an alley to an old GMC school bus painted blue. "That's where we live while we're on the road. We've been on the road for eleven years now. We park it, set up the booth in a town like this, and the kids scatter. They find lawns to mow, or a musician they can learn from, whatever interests them." A freckled redhead boy with pale blue eyes stands next to his mother. His name is Malachi. "I'm trying to play the guitar," he says.

Meanwhile, Jedidiah, at the keyboard in the shade behind them, is pounding out Elton John's "Rocket Man:" "Mars ain't the kind of place to raise your kids,/ In fact it's cold as hell,/ And there's no one there to raise them if you did,/ And all this science I don't understand..."

"We chose this lifestyle," says the tie-dyed mother. "My parents have Jaguars in the driveway. But my husband and I live with the kids 5000 feet up in the mountains when we're not traveling. We usually have to walk six miles from the blue bus to get to our house. We see more snow in the winter than a resort sees. We've been running from the county law."

Alex and I look up from the knives we've been examining.

"My husband was a Marine and was sheriff of a county. He made the big mistake of arresting the county circuit judge for growing marijuana. That man was the biggest marijuana grower in the county, but when a kid would get arrested for possession, the judge would slap him in jail and give him a stiff penalty with jail terms to prove to the population he was tough on crime. Well, you can't fight the local judge."

A young boy with pale, blond hair runs around the corner of the gas station and joins Jedidiah and Malachi beneath the tent awning. "This is Joshua," says his mother.

"All these Biblical names," I say.

As if to dispute this, she says, "I've got two girls named Echo and Crystal."

Behind her, Jedidiah is banging out a song from *The Lion King:* "There's a calm surrender to the rush of day/ When the heat of the rolling world can be turned away..."

Alex and I walk away down the overheated sidewalks, making our way back toward the Best Western and its air conditioning. The song follows us: "An enchanted moment.../ It's enough for this restless warrior just to be with you,/ And can you feel the love tonight,/ It is where we are./ It's enough for this wide-eyed wanderer/ That we got this far..."

The clerk in the motel thinks we've rented a room and offers us cookies and iced tea. We eat and drink and somehow fail to mention we're living on the river.

About the middle of the afternoon, we return to Clueless and push off into the running river. It's a bright, lazy, Sunday afternoon, so I tell Alex he can fish while I paddle. On his second cast he hooks a 12-inch trout. He's thrilled. We both examine the shining, beautiful fish: "polished and muscular and torsional," as Cormac McCarthy says. I pull out a stringer, attach it, and drop the fish to swim along with us.

The massive Dworshak Dam just above town releases the North Fork water into the Middle Fork. As we pass the mouth of the river, the air turns suddenly cool. Reaching into the water we can feel that the water released from the depths of the dam is much colder than the already cold water we've been traveling. Bill Shamion had commented on this: "They say that the reason for this dam that has kept all kinds of salmon from making their way up the North Fork is to cool down the water of the Clearwater, make it a better environment for the fish in the hatcheries." He snorted. "Cool off the Clearwater! That's like spitting in a bathtub!"

The river swirls and bubbles and turns. Two boys are fishing from the left bank, a family from the right. Alex keeps casting, but the fish have stopped biting.

***

Lewis and Clark made arrangements with Twisted Hair for his young men to care for their 38 horses while the Corps was away. They cut the forelocks from between their horses' ears and branded their rumps with a branding iron, a branding iron recently found along the river.

Then, on October 7, though Clark was feeling terrible again, having
eaten more camas root, the party loaded and launched their five new
canoes. On the third set of rapids, Clark's canoe, in the lead, crashed
into rocks and sprang a quick leak, but they managed to patch it and
maneuver through seven more "danjerous" rapids that day.

October 8th started with a cloudy morning. They passed fifteen
rapids and four islands, moving by little fishing camps of the Nez Perce
who were terrifically curious about this party of strangers. Twisted Hair
and Tetoharsky did their best to explain.

Because it was fall, water levels had dropped, so the currents were
calmer, but in low water more rocks were exposed. Patrick Gass (steering
one of the canoes) smashed into some rocks that split open his canoe
and rapidly sank it in the surging rapids. The men who could not swim
clung to the canoe in the numbing waters, waiting for help. Clark
directed the fleet to shore, quickly emptied one canoe, and with the help
of nearby Nez Perce in one of their native dugouts, managed to unload
the stranded log canoe and save the men. The river is deceptively deep.
The sunlight flashing off the rocks below looks to be no more than four
or five feet down, but you can easily see down twenty feet on a bright
day. Let go of that hollow canoe and you could find yourself bumping
along fifteen or twenty feet below the surface.

The Nez Perce, wrote Clark, "appeared disposed to give us every
assistance in their power dureing our distress." The men laid the
soaked goods out to dry and tended to Thompson, who was hurt in
the accident.

Waiting through the afternoon for their supplies to dry, the men
joked and laughed and tried to converse with the curious Nez Perce.
One of the men began playing his fiddle. A woman Clark thought was
mad, or pretending to be mad, started handing out her bracelets and
little gifts of camas root while singing native songs. She glided among
the men, chanting and lisping and swaying to the fiddle music, passing
out bits of food. One of the men refused her gift. She seemed suddenly
angry and threw the remaining trinkets into the fire, grabbed a sharp

flint stone from her husband and began slicing her arms; blood gushed out. Scraping the blood from her arms into her hands, she then ate her own blood. This went on for about a half hour till the woman fainted and collapsed into seizures. The Indians then poured water on her, which awakened her.

The men of the Corps didn't know what to make of all this, but the Indians seemed to accept her behavior. Perhaps refusing food was more of an insult than the Corps understood.

By this time, "the wet articles not sufficiently dried to pack up obliged us to delay another night." At dark someone reported that he had seen Old Toby and his son, their Shoshone guides, galloping back towards the mountains on two horses. Clark wanted the Nez Perce to send horsemen to tell Toby to return and receive his promised pay, but the Nez Perce advised Clark to let them go. The party never saw them again. The father and son carried nothing back up the long, hard trail but two horses and their stories—which are often a journey's best reward.

***

That evening we beach Clueless on a broad sweep of sand backed by locust trees and, higher up, by a bluff of grey rock and more pine trees. We'd accidentally left our cooking grill at the last camp, so we have to fry the trout in a small pan. There isn't much food in the little fish, but it's mild and tasty. Alex fishes from a large boulder, catches his lure on a rock and falls neck deep in the cold river trying to retrieve it. He returns to the campfire soaked through.

After he changes into dry clothes, we sit beside the smoldering coals and watch the dusk cast drifts of shadows along the river and leach the color from the surrounding mountains. Far up the darkening slopes, one prominence holds the gold-red rays of the setting sun.

WIND

The next morning is clear and warm. A breeze is blowing up the river valley as we paddle west. High bluffs stand in the river on both sides and the river runs dark and deep, swirling and boiling up from the depths. Occasionally the bluffs back away and the river spreads, and we find ourselves bouncing through more rapids.

By afternoon the wind is hot and strong, rushing up the valley at 40 to 50 miles an hour, thrashing through the willows and locust trees, twisting off limbs, singing through pine branches, cutting the current into choppy, wind-slapped waves. We try to keep to the side least affected by the wind, but can't fight it. About 1 p.m., we tie up behind a pile of boulders on the left bank and try to rest.

I locate a shady spot beneath some ponderosa pines. The wind pours through the long pine needles above me. I fold up my life preserver for a pillow and try to sleep, but almost immediately feel a sharp bite on my shin. I brush off a big black-and-red ant; it's almost an inch long. Then another bite, then a third. I sit up to see a swarm pouring out of the long, dried pine needles beneath me, running up my t-shirt, stopping to latch onto its cotton fabric. As I yank their bodies off, their big pincered heads stay attached to the fabric. Their bites are hard and painful.

I walk down the shore, still wearing my newly decorated T-shirt, to some boulders where Alex is resting. I ask him if he wants to walk the highway to see if we can find a place to eat. We climb the steep bank to the road and begin walking. The hot, dry wind whips meadow grasses and wildflowers on our left and the riverside trees on our right. We lean into the wind and pull our hats low over our eyes to keep them on our heads. A mile or two down the road we find the Thunderbird Convenience Store, a fortunate find given the scarcity of stores along this 40-mile stretch of highway. Apparently the Vermont Forest Ranger missed this one. We purchase German sausages smothered in chili. The wind and sun have dried us out, so I buy an iced huckleberry slush and Alex fills up a large Styrofoam cup with some pink soda. We sit down at a table inside to eat and drink (convenience store food, true enough, but more appetizing than boiled coyote and camas root) and wait for the wind to die down.

But it doesn't. After eating, I buy a cigar, and we sit outside at a table in the lee of the building and watch the wind scouring the surface of the river. The pines standing up the slopes look like a gathering of Indian titans, throwing their great heads one way, bowing, and beating the air with massive arms while the deciduous hackberries and locust trees below dance to the same caustic chant like the women of the tribe, their robes flying one way, then the other with a wild tossing and flowing of their hair. The temperature is in the low nineties, a hot dry wind. I smoke slowly through the cigar and wait.

A group of high schoolers on bicycles blow up the highway and stop at the store, buy drinks, then mount their bikes and sail away. They're on the first leg of a coast-to-coast bike ride.

After a while, the wind begins to calm. We need to find a camping place before dusk, so we walk back up the highway to where Clueless awaits, rocking among the grey and black boulders. We step into our places and lift our paddles, but the wind is still too strong, driving us sideways and back to shore.

We walk back to the Thunderbird and order up hamburgers and chicken sandwiches for dinner. A new clerk has started his shift. He tells us that one recent winter, three boys drove their car to the river down the steep ramp near the store. There was ice on the road, and the car slid out onto the river ice, then broke through. The three boys managed to scramble out the windows before the car sank. Two of them swam to shore, but the third was losing coordination in the brutally cold water. One friend who had made it to shore dove in after him but got sucked under the ice by the current. "They found his body three months later," says the clerk.

"Did the boy he tried to save make it to shore?"

"Yeah, I think he did. It's a dangerous river. In the spring when the water's up, fishermen who don't know what they're doing drive up from the cities and motorboat up form Lewiston, then throw out an anchor. The anchor catches in the rocks and the current tips the boat over and swamps it. Lost quite a few city folk that way," he says.

About six in the evening, we walk back to Clueless and shove off. It's still rough going, fighting a steady but diminishing wind. The current helps carry us along, pulling us through rough waters between steep bluffs. Around a bend or two in the river, we find a small clearing of grass and a rubble of rocks surrounded on three sides by thick willow brush, where it seems we'll have to set up our tent.

We've already eaten, so we sit around our campfire and watch the flames heel over, casting a red glimmer that burns on rough water. Distant stars begin to appear above the partially forested slopes. On the far side of the river, red taillights of cars pass down Highway 12.

The river holds the evening light as long as it can and then releases it.

Late that night, I awake to the sound of something wading along the river a few feet from our tent. The night is perfectly still; the energetic winds of the afternoon have exhausted themselves and fallen asleep. I take the big pistol from under my pillow, unzip the tent and peer out. Nothing out there visible but a sky full of stars above the black shoulders of the nearby mountains. Alex wakes up and crawls over to look out too.

"Thought I heard something in the water," I say. "Wanted to know if it was a bear."

Alex nods and turns back to his sleeping bag, turns over, and sleeps.

***

Having heard the clerk's stories of multiple drownings on the Clearwater, I'm watching the river closely: the dark creases of water, the sudden surface eruptions, the boil and swirl of a living thing. As we work the paddles, we listen for the roar of troubled waters.

We're fortunate, always finding a green sluice to one side or another where we can avoid most of the white water; but once, flowing around rocky islands of willows and brush, the current takes a sharp bend to the left. Almost instantly, Clueless swings 180 degrees before we can jab our paddles in and lever free of a huge whirlpool.

"Keep your life preserver handy!"

"I think a whirlpool like that would suck us down even with a life jacket," he calls.

"Maybe so, maybe so."

***

We stop once to walk an island, relaxing in the sunlight, trying to absorb the loveliness of this world of gravel and sand, willow brush, cottonwood, and locust trees, noting the hoofprints of deer, the delicate handprints of a passing raccoon.

Choosing one of the several currents that weave their way around islands of tall cottonwoods and pines, we start passing occasional riverside homes. By midafternoon, we see the tall towers of Lewiston's paper mill ahead. The current has been carrying us more swiftly than I thought. The mountains on either side are almost treeless, covered by dried summer grasses. Paddling past the monstrous paper mill, Alex's second raft paddle snaps. We need to find real canoe paddles to continue our voyage.

**

Clark writes in his journal of October 10: "a fine Morning loaded and Set out at 7 oClock...haveing passed 2 Islands and two bad rapids...at 8 ½ miles lower we arrived at the heade of a verry bad riffle at which place we landed near 8 Lodges of Indians." This was near Lapwai Creek where Henry Spalding, one of the first Protestant missionaries to settle among the Nez Perce, would set up his mission 30 years later, the first white settlement in Idaho.

Here another Corps canoe caught on the rocks and it took the men an hour to pry it off. Meanwhile from the Indians they bought fish and dogs, both of which they cooked and ate. Clark, whose pet Newfoundland still accompanied them, could not bring himself to eat dog. Clark writes, "All the Party have greatly the advantage of me, in as much as they all relish the flesh of the dogs." After the men ate their lunch of fish and canine, they pushed on, finally arriving at "a large Southerly fork." This was the Snake River, though they named it Lewis's River at the time, thinking it the same river they had found in the Lemhi Valley and had been unable to follow. This was an excellent guess, for the Salmon (sometimes called The River of No Return in its upper reaches) does indeed flow into the Snake, about 50 miles upstream from where they were.

While camped near or on the present site of Lewiston, Clark remarked that the Nez Perce, whose scattered fishing lodges they kept passing, "are Stout likely men, handsom women, and verry dressey in their way, the dress of the men are a white Buffalow robe or Elk Skin dressed with Beeds which are generally white, Sea Shells—i e Mother of

Perl hung to ther hair & on a pice of otter Skin about their necks hair
Cewed in two parsels hanging forward over their Sholders, feathers, and
different Coloured Paints which they find in their Countrey Generally
white, Green & light Blue." He goes on to say the Nez Perce expect
to be paid for every service they render or for any food they offer. The
Corps was running out of trading supplies, so they had become stingy
traders, handing over a few ribbons or beads for fish and dogs. Their
stomachs seemed to be recovering at last from the diet of camas root.

*****

Alex and I need to trade for food, but we also need paddles. We tie
Clueless to a rock at the base of the stone-rubble dike that surrounds
this side of Lewiston. We climb the dike, cross the railroad tracks, and
make our way into the downtown area to the Army-Navy store, looking
for paddles. They have no paddles.

We follow the tracks that lie between the stores and the river, Alex
is making a game of walking the rails without losing his balance. It
takes me back to my childhood when my friend Mark and I used to do
the same thing while out hunting for squirrels and coyotes, quail and
rabbits. Alex manages to tightrope a rail for almost 50 crossties before
finally tipping off. I can manage six or seven crossties before my old
body sways and slips.

Walking across a parking lot, we come upon a tall, balding man
hoisting a bicycle into the back of his SUV. He's strong and lean and
has a good tan.

Alex asks him how far he rode today.

"Just to Hell's Gate and back today."

I'm thinking, *Hell's Gate and back? Now there's a journey worthy of
Dante*. "Where's Hell's Gate?" I ask.

He points through Lewiston. "Just a few miles up the Snake. I'm
a County Commissioner in charge of Health Services, so I guess I'd
better stay healthy."

I tell him we've been canoeing for six days and have lost two paddles and need to buy replacements to continue our trip.

"Do you know the Black Sheep Sporting Goods store?" he asks.

We don't, so he offers us a ride. He drops us off in front of the store and says he'll wait for us to buy the paddles, then take us back to our canoe. His name is Don Davis, the second exceptionally helpful official we've found in Lewiston, Idaho.

After returning to Clueless with our new paddles, we bid Davis goodbye and paddle beyond Lewiston's shops and cross the wide Snake River. The sun is setting beyond Clarkston as Alex and I pull for the western shore. We're not sure where to camp, but food—what Don Quixote's companion Sancho Panza called "belly munitions"—is now the priority, so we tie up to a small tree on the bank and walk to a Pizza Hut: good, heavy calories for this small corps of discovery.

ALIENS

It's 10:30 and the lights of Lewiston across the Snake twinkle as we board Clueless and shove off to circle the north shore of Clarkston; we've heard of a marina with a campground. The far stars glimmer in the deepening night as we use our new paddles to push out into the current. But the river here is very shallow and we run into sand just below the surface of the dark water. It takes us several minutes to lean on our paddles and pole Clueless into deeper water, but it's a fine summer night with a light breeze.

We don't really know where we're going, and canoeing after dark is almost always hazardous, but we paddle on. The city glitters on our left with a thousand lights. We pass some kind of loading facility and what appears to be an anchored excursion boat, then move past some grain silos silhouetted against the lights of the city. The breeze is in our face, so we don't pick up the stench of the paper mill, though we catch the city smells of sawdust and diesel fumes.

On we go, paddling quietly toward a tall black curve of a bridge that carries a road over the river. Off to our left in the dark waters, we hear the falsetto honks of alarmed geese, moving out of our way. Then quietness again, with the traffic hum of the city drifting across the water. Far above us a plane blinks green and red among the stars.

Canoeing is quiet, a way of walking the world with all the senses alive. Driving shuts out the feel of a landscape, the passing scents of the honeysuckle flower and the juniper tree, the delicate details of river waves changing color and texture even at night, and sounds...Suddenly, a strange, hideous cry from hundreds of voices arises all around us. We can't see them. They seem to be staying just beyond our visual circumference, the black waves picking up streaked reflections of the city lights but not the sources of this terrible wailing.

"What's that?" Alex asks.

"Never heard it before."

"Ducks?"

"I doubt it. Too many of them for this time of year."

"Weird."

We paddle on and leave the alien cries behind, but then, as we pass beneath the tall highway bridge, the strange cries rise all around us again. Desperate wails, alien calls. The water is suddenly very shallow, our paddles hitting gravel and mud. We push away and steer for deeper water and the awful cries move invisibly before us.

"It sounds like those aliens in Vin Diesel's movie *Pitch Black*," says Alex. He starts whooping like the aliens in the movie, aliens that are always just beyond the circle of lights the humans are carrying, waiting for the humans to lose their lights so they can attack. Alex can perfectly copy those movie aliens, but these invisible beings out in the black water are impossible to imitate. Hearing Alex, they redouble their cries and the hideous howling builds in intensity all around us.

We follow the shoreline into a bay glimmering with dock lights and gradually leave the dark callers behind. We turn left toward some glaring pole lights and begin passing anchored sailboats and motorboats. Surely we've found the marina. But in the darkness, we have little chance of finding a campground, so we move along the shoreline hoping for sand, not mud. It's past midnight.

We finally find a strip of sand maybe three feet wide backed by head-high weeds and some farther trees black against the lights that follow a highway beyond. Clueless scrapes onto sand and Alex steps out to pull him ashore.

I step into knee-deep water and scout the shore for a place to set up the tent. A little footpath leads back through weeds into the trees and I make my way up to a little clearing where a pickup camper is parked. My main concern is that we're on somebody's private property, but I'm willing to take a chance and camp rather than paddle night waters. Stepping up to the camper, I hear someone inside snoring heavily. I move around the camper and see no one else parked in what appears to be a small, shaded turnoff from the highway. There seems to be no place to set up a tent.

Returning to Alex, I tell him we'll set up the tent next to Clueless. "Keep it quiet. There's someone sleeping in a pickup camper up there; I don't want him investigating strange noises and coming out the door with a pistol."

We stomp down the weeds far enough back to set up our little tent on a rooty, stalky surface, then unload our packs and set up the tent by feel in the dark. When we finally settle down, our sleeping bags and thin pads aren't enough to protect us from the roots and rocks and stalks beneath us. It's hot in the tent, but Alex still wants a bedtime story, so I fish *The Fellowship of the Ring* from a pack, click on the LED light and read of conflicts with orcish hordes.

The students whom I teach want to write of wizards, vampires, aliens, and zombies. Occasionally I find a gifted writer who can create a visually and culturally vivid world of alien beings, but often they have learned too little of this real, fantastical, planet on which we live to create an alternative world of mystery and mayhem. Tolkien suffered through the trench warfare of World War I, which gave him devastating memories from which to create the land of Mordor. He had walked the heaths and forests of England, so his Old Forest grows thick and real. He had read in detail the stories of the Bible and studied Norse legends, so he could write of bright mysteries in forest dwellings and dark, rooted evil in The Old Forest, of the shadow of Dol Guldur that had fallen on the forest of Mirkwood, so that men began to call it *Taur-nu-Fuin* and *Taur-e-Ndaedelos,* the forest of great fear. It is by close contact and real immersion in this extravagant world we live in that we obtain the ability to write imagined mysteries. "I wish I could convey the perfection," says novelist Yann Martel, "of a seal slipping into water or a spider monkey swinging from point to point or a lion merely turning its head...I spent more hours than I can count a quiet witness to the highly mannered, manifold expressions of life that grace our planet. It is something so bright, loud, weird and delicate as to stupefy the senses."

This old Earth and its transcendent mysteries is a kaleidoscopic menagerie, and we have scarcely begun to sort out the astounding complexities of its most intelligent and perhaps misguided beings: us. Novelist and essayist Marilynn Robinson writes that "there are more neurons in the human brain than there are stars in the Milky Way...If we are to consider the heavens, how much more are we to consider the magnificent energies of consciousness that make whomever we pass on the street a far grander marvel than our galaxy? So," she writes, "I have spent my life watching, not to see beyond the world, merely to see, great mystery, what is plainly before my eyes."

I spent my early youth in Sudan in east Africa, where my friends told of spirits who spoke to them in the night, of black dwarfs that rose out of the ground and visited them, of turtles that talked and ravens that accurately foretold the future. Scientists have raised a mental, though not material, wall against all such experience. With their scientific belief in strict materialism, they have tried not only to kill the world of demons, but also to shoot down the better angels of our nature. Scientists are, as a rule, to quote Yann Martel again, "a friendly, atheistic, hard-working, beer-drinking lot whose minds are preoccupied with sex, chess and baseball when they are not preoccupied with science." Many will not allow for supernatural mysteries, though somehow scientists have misplaced about 80 percent of that material cosmos and have had to label it Dark Energy and Dark Matter. Physics itself is an astonishing set of mysteries: quasars, quarks, and quantum behavior that misbehaves in seemingly incomprehensible ways. And all the while, this beautiful planet whirls along on its law-abiding path around the sun, leaving us room and time to map the stars and measure the oceans, and ponder the meaning of things.

I will find out the following day that the hideous cries that surrounded us this dark, quiet night were nothing more than flocks of migrating seagulls of a species I had not yet encountered. But why am I so dismissive of seagulls? What marvelous beings are these grey-and-white feathered folk, so gifted in flight, so sharp-eyed in the hunt, so socially cantankerous, so geographically sophisticated that they can reliably migrate a thousand miles to the bay where they were eggs. And what of those migrating salmon that wander across thousands of miles of the deep Pacific and return two or three years later to find the very streamlet where they were spawned? And what of us, for good or ill? We're the most complex beings science has ever studied.

***

Lewis and Clark's carpenter, Patrick Gass, looks up from their camp somewhere around here and writes: "The country on both sides is high dry prairie plains without a stick of timber. There is no wood of any kind to be seen except a few small willows along the shore; so that it is with difficulty we can get enough to cook with....We set out early in a fine morning; proceeded on about 6 miles, and halted at some lodges of the natives, where we got fish and several dogs."

The morning sun drives Alex and me from our tent. Our snoring pickup companion is long gone. I walk several miles to a Wal-Mart to buy pillows (rolled up jeans as pillows are hard to get used to) and fluid for Alex's contacts. When I return, Alex is feeding ducks. He's offended by a mother mallard that steals bread from her only duckling. "Maybe it's because I'm the youngest," he says. "But it makes me mad when that big mother dodges in front of her baby and gobbles up every piece of bread I throw at the little guy."

We pack up and shove off into midafternoon heat. The river is wide and there seems to be no current. Downstream, a reservoir, or rather a series of reservoirs, has blocked the current and smothered the rapids that endangered the Corps' journey. It's no longer a pleasure to skim along the clear water. We have entered a land of dry prairie mountains, intense heat, and few trees. Across the wide river, a distant motorboat drones along, dragging a single skier. Our steadily dipping paddles seem to move us very slowly toward a bluff of grey basalt and dead grass far ahead.

Six or eight miles of this brings us to a tree-covered island where we hope for a concession stand. It's some kind of state park once inhabited by chief Timothy's band of the Nez Perce. There are no concessions.

We do enjoy the shade. Walking the island we see several white rabbits nibbling grass, domestic transplants from somewhere else. A robin keeps clucking a warning that alerts us to an owl resting high in a cottonwood tree. The owl must make a good living on tender, white rabbits.

There's the usual state park fee for camping, so Alex and I shove off and follow a northward bend in the broad river where we find, near sundown, a gravel bar grown thick with brush on the eastern shore. There's a ranch house maybe a mile away near the foot of the treeless, prairie mountains with a semi-circular barn of aged, grey wood. We set up our tent in tall, dry grass and dead thistles beyond the thin band of greenery beside the river and build a fire near shore on gravel as far as we can get from the tinder-dry grass. Dark green locust trees and willow shrubs closely follow the shoreline, but walk five or ten yards from the river and the knee-high grass is a fire hazard. We cook our supper of canned tamales and hear the cries of what I take to be prairie chickens or grouse. Lewis and Clark were able to shoot several of what was for them a new species of grouse along here—larger than the mountain grouse, smaller than a turkey—giving them a relished break from salmon, roots, and dogs.

Alex takes the canoe out fishing while I clean up. Within minutes, he's back asking for the camera; he's spotted a beaver swimming. We take the canoe out and snap a few shots of it before it slaps its way under water.

In the night a river barge chugs by, blinking its way south, and a train rumbles near and away. I awake hours later to the yips and yells of a pack of coyotes.

CRAWDAD MAN AND
A NERVOUS HOUDINI

The basalt-ridged and high humped prairie mountains rise 2000 feet on either side as we paddle. It's very hot, very still. We're losing enthusiasm for this leg of our journey. Hundreds of carp slowly sway through the warming water, surfacing, then sinking from sight. Alex takes the .22 and pops off a few shots at the lethargic fish, but the shots always angle off just to one side or the other. Lewis and Clark's men tried shooting salmon and trout in the streams with as much success.

About noon, we find on the western bank the shade of a solitary apricot tree heavy with its yellow-orange fruit. We pick the fruit and eat—a little dry, but tasty. Alex then straddles a log of driftwood, puts his life preserver beneath his cheek and tries to sleep through the heat of the day in the shade of the little tree. I munch apricots and walk the shore. Plums are ripe and I add them to my diet. A raspberry bush has already dropped its dried fruit. I find the carcass of a fawn that must have fallen from a high ridge above. Some bushes carry yellow berries, others white, but I can't identify them and leave them alone.

The heat is strong. I return to the patch of shade beneath the apricot tree, drink warm water from a canteen, and watch the empty lake spread out dark and glittering to the pale grass-and-rock mountains beyond.

Alex can't sleep for long on the driftwood log, and we soon push off and keep paddling. About midafternoon we spot a young coyote pacing over a jumble of rocks along the western shore. We paddle quite close, within 20 or 30 yards, but the coyote seems uninterested in anything out on the water and doesn't slow its pace, picking its way over rocks, through brush, and on. Many of the mountain tribes told stories around winter fires of Coyote, a humanized animal who had much to do with their creation myths. The Nez Perce had a story of Coyote being swallowed by a huge, devouring monster. Coyote managed to cut out the monster's heart: wherever the blood was sprinkled, a tribe grew up. The Nez Perce arose from where the huge heart fell (now a rock in a meadow near Kamiah). In Salish lore too, Coyote was swallowed by the monster. Leaping high inside the monster, Coyote stabbed its heart with his flint knife, killing the beast. As the monster collapsed, all the animals that it had devoured big and small, fled, the smaller ones out its anus (a canyon in the Bitterroot), the larger ones out its mouth. Ants, among the last to escape, were squished by the sphincter muscles—thus the shape of their little bodies.

An hour later we see some blue and pink Styrofoam floats in the water near a little inlet shaded by willows and locust shrubs. We paddle over to investigate. I slow the canoe beside one of the floats and Alex reaches into the water and pulls up a long line that holds a cage within which resides a single crawfish.

"A crawdad trap!" I remark, stating the obvious. Alex takes a close look at the one, mud-brown, five-inch crawfish lurking on the wire mesh bottom and takes a sniff of the rotting pieces of fish used as bait, then drops the cage back in the water. We paddle over to the other float and haul it up to see what it's caught. Nothing. We let it slip back to the bottom, and paddle on.

Within seconds of dropping the second trap, a motor boat roars out of reeds and rocks just ahead. Ambushed by the Crawdad Man!

"It's a good thing you didn't steal my crawdads!" he yells as he slows his boat near us, the wake rushing over to knock us around. "That'll get you arrested around here."

"Really? We were just curious."

"Curious will get you arrested around here. It's not legal to touch a trap."

"Sorry. Didn't know the rules. We're from out of state."

He shakes his head, "Not knowing the rules will get you..." and lays on the throttle, roaring away, the sound diminishing into a distant drone.

We paddle on.

The sun is high and fierce, and the journey insufferably slow. Where the 1500 to 2000-foot mountains approach the river, the rock falls clutter the steep slopes and shore. Dried grass and a few shrubs cling to more horizontal surfaces or thatch the gullies between towering summits. The rest of the surface consists of brown soil and gravel. Inexplicably, we spot another desiccated body of a fawn lying on some gravel beneath a bluff.

Keeping to the western bank, we spot a troop of birds hustling single file along a five-foot bank, dodging between tufts of grass, stopping to peck the occasional seed.

"Quail," I tell Alex. "Western quail. In Kansas they don't have that little floppy top-knot."

Alex ships his paddle and reaches for the .22. He's missed a number of slow moving carp, and I doubt his ability to hit a scurrying quail, so I let him give it a try. He leans into his aim and pulls the trigger. One black-headed, top-knotted quail takes off straight up into the air eight or ten feet, wings whirring loudly, then plunges straight down into the riverside dirt. Two or three females that were following him stop and stare, then make their quiet way on through the brush.

"I got him!" Alex turns and smiles.

"Amazing. Let's go find him."

Beaching the canoe among rocks, we climb out and soon find the quail—a mere handful of white, brown, and grey feathers. Its head has been completely blown away, yet headless, it managed to fly maybe twenty feet. I show Alex how to gut it, then I toss it into Clueless.

Late afternoon. We see a shelter roof of some sort near the eastern shore behind a patch of brush. We need a break from the terrible heat and slow struggle of lake paddle (the downstream dam has widened the river and killed the current), so we pull over and climb out.

We walk to the shelter, which is no more than a flat roof on poles with a picnic table beneath. We meet a thin, blonde woman with two dogs. She steps up and introduces herself. She's Tammy Montgomery and she gives us each a strong handshake. She's here to throw Frisbees into the river and let her dogs retrieve them. She has an ice cooler in the shade and offers us a cold, one-liter bottle of water, which is just about the best thing anyone could do for us at the time. Alex and I sit and trade swigs of cold, cold water.

Tammy introduces us to the first dog, Kona Houdini Anderson Montgomery, a pitbull-boxer mix with nervous eyes and a high whine.

"He's a rescue," she tells us. "I don't think he'd been treated right. He doesn't know how to play well."

The other dog is a happy, tongue-lolling black lab named Cleopatra Arial Montgomery, obviously a part of the family. Cleo keeps bouncing around and barking. Tammy says she's seven years old, "And she will not shut up." Tammy takes a bottle of citronella and sprays it in Cleo's nose telling her to "be quiet!" Cleo snorts and bounds away to bark again. Cleopatra is a willful queen.

Tammy follows Cleo down through willow brush to the water and sends her Frisbee sailing across the water. The black lab splashes in and swims hard for the green plastic disc, returning with it so Tammy can throw it again. Kona Houdini, the nervous pitbull, stands beside Tammy, whining, rolling his eyes, looking back at us.

After a few minutes, Tammy returns. We've finished the cold water but aren't ready to leave the shade, so she sits down and begins sharing her stories: "My father has dementia. His wife doesn't want me around him, so I had to go to court for four days to try to gain custody, but it isn't going well." She looks off into the dry mountains and shakes her head. "At least I've got visiting rights. He still recognizes me when I visit, though it takes him a second."

She loves animals and wanted badly to be a vet, but her grades didn't allow her into vet school. So now she works as a veterinarian's technician and takes college classes.

Kona Houdini stands next to her knee and rolls his eyes at Alex and me, whining and groaning, then gives a sharp bark.

"Quiet, Kona, quiet!" She threatens him with the citronella. He moans and backs off, keeping anxious eyes upon us.

"I've got a seventeen-year-old cocker spaniel at home."

"That's an old dog."

"Too old to bring her out here in the sun. Cleo here got out of the house the other night. When she came back to the house, she had a swollen eye and smelled really bad of skunk. So I tried to remain calm. Okay, I said, get the hydrogen peroxide and the baking soda. I poured the stuff all over her, washed her off in the tub, but she still had this terrible stench, so she had to sleep on the deck for a few days."

Kona Houdini whines and paws the gravel and gives a sharp yip.

"Quiet, Kona!"

He groans and we decide not to press our luck with an anxious dog. We wish Tammy well and return to direct sunlight.

***

No clouds. Heat. Slow paddling. Carp by the hundreds. Thick, yellowing algae floating the surfaces near shore as if the water itself were congealing and rotting. We come upon teenagers leaping twenty feet off of a huge boulder into the river. Shouts. Squeals. Splashes.

We paddle on.

After the sun falls behind the western mountains, we stop to set up the tent. I step knee-deep into the brown water to get clear of the worst of the algae-ridden shallows and pump water with our purifier to fill our canteens. There's so much gunk that the filter soon clogs, but I've pumped enough water for the night. We gather driftwood and get the fire going, boil water, and pour it into a tinfoil bag of chili mac and cheese and another of beef stew.

We pluck the feathers from the quail and roast its little body on a green stick—just a couple of bites for each of us, but with a little salt, quite tasty. We take our spoons and eat the chili mac and the beef stew while watching a skier on the far side of the river skipping along behind a powerful motorboat and doing complete overhead flips on his skies. The dammed river, the motorboats, the algae and carp, the occasional car or pickup following the nearby blacktop all conspire to distance us from Lewis and Clark.

I had hoped to follow the Snake all the way to the Columbia River, but the map tells me there are a series of dams, which means a series of placid, algae-ridden lakes, heat, and no current to carry us down, so I'm beginning once again to question my plans.

DAMMED

The next morning we set out into a headwind. Choppy lake waters. Cooler, but difficult going. From the map Mark loaned us, we seem to be about six miles from the first dam. On we go, rocking up and down against the wind. A few ducks try to out-swim us, then slap-run the water and burst into flight. Coming at last around a slow lefthand turn that bends the river westward, we spot the huge, concrete obstruction that is the Lower Granite Dam. We've been told we can lock through and continue our voyage, so we head for what looks like a lock about a third of the way from the south side of the dam.

It's hard going through the wind, but after an hour, we finally approach the lock, and slide up to a sign with instructions to pull a rope. Alex reaches up and pulls. Within minutes, the voice of a man named

Brian squawks from the speaker, asking us what we want. He tells us to wait an hour for the lock to open.

We paddle up to the boulder-made dam and tie up, clamber onto the vast jumble of rocks, and to the high roadway that crosses the dam. We walk across the pavement and look down the other side. It's a long drop to the ferocious outlet below, where leaping whitewater pours from the bottom of the dam. The lock to our left opens onto a quieter section of the river. Just then, a white pickup pulls up beside us and a uniformed man leans out his window. "What are you guys up to?"

"We're waiting to lock through the dam."

"You got a motor on that boat?"

"No. We're paddling a canoe."

"Then you can't lock through."

"What?"

"You can't lock through."

"Look, I've locked through all kinds of Mississippi River dams," I tell him.

"This isn't the Mississippi. You can't be standing on this dam. You can't be tied up down there, and you can't lock through."

"Where do we portage around this dam, then?"

"I don't know. I'm not from around here."

What can you say to a man in uniform? A uniform trumps any rational argument.

We pick our way down the boulders of the dam to Clueless and shove off, paddling back to the message cord. I yank on it. After a while, Brian squawks.

I call out, "The security guard told us we can't lock through. Is that true?"

"Yes. I told him to find you and pass that message. I thought you were a 20-foot motorboat."

"But we know the routine of locking through. We've done it many times on the Mississippi."

"I'm sorry."

"Not as sorry as we are. Where do we start the portage?"

Brian directs us to a dock a half mile east of the dam.

As we paddle away, Alex says he's always wanted to portage.

"Do you have any idea how difficult it is? Two trips for our packs. Another for the canoe. It looks like a two-mile portage one way. That's ten miles of walking."

It turns out to be a two-and-a-half-mile portage one way.

We disembark near an old Vietnamese man in stained clothes quietly fishing from the dock. We tie up and begin heaving out our packs. The dam cuts off any breeze, and the sun is high and hot.

We lift our two 50-pound packs and start walking, a half mile up an incline to the dam, up and over, and down another mile, where we dump the packs in grass near a parking lot. We can see the put-in a mile ahead, but decide to return for our other supplies and consolidate our goods here before attempting the last mile.

We walk back to Clueless. To save ourselves the third trip, we shoulder into the remaining packs and hoist the canoe over our heads and set off up the steep roadway toward the top of the dam. It's very hard going, and the heat is intense. Finding a little shade under some pines, we drop the canoe and our packs and sit down panting.

This is, of course, absolutely nothing compared to the Corps' many portages. After leaving the Clearwater River and entering the Snake, Lewis and Clark traveled 140-odd miles to the Columbia River, meeting at the confluence crowds of Indians. Their two Nez Perce guides, the old man Twisted Hair and the younger Tetoharsky, were willing to travel with them only as far as the great rapids six miles downstream. "On October 23," writes Stephen Ambrose, "the expedition came to the beginning of a spectacular but dangerous stretch of the river that extended fifty-five miles. It contained four major barriers (all inundated today by dam reservoirs), beginning with the Celilo, or Great Falls. In one short stretch of violent, roaring cataracts, the river dropped thirty-eight feet through several narrow channels between cliffs as high as three thousand feet." Clark reconnoitered the vicious rapids, the Short

Narrows, a quarter-mile long stretch where the massive river poured through a chute 45 yards wide. He writes: "I determined to pass through this place notwithstanding the horrid appearance of this agitated gut swelling, boiling & whirling in every direction, which from the top of the rock did not appear as bad as when I was in it."

Several times the Corps had to lug their heavy dugouts up and over the steep trails beside the falls and rapids, renting horses from local Indians to carry the heavier supplies. Sometimes they were able to send the emptied dugouts down the rapids tethered by braided elk-skin ropes. Several times they shot the rapids in their dugouts (while hundreds of Indians watched from above to witness the almost certain drownings), but they were expert dugout canoers by this time and somehow made the difficult passages with few mishaps. It is impressive that these men, several of them nonswimmers, survived thousands of miles of river travel, some of it spectacularly treacherous.

After they managed the Short Narrows, Twisted Hair and Tetoharsky told Lewis and Clark that they could no longer accompany them because the Chinook tribe below the rapids and falls were especially hostile. Their relatives above the rapids had even warned that the Chinooks would kill the Corps too. Lewis and Clark saw this as another opportunity to establish peace between tribes and talked their two interpreters and guides into staying for two more days. At the bottom of a set of rapids, they met with a Chinook chief, and Lewis and Clark reported that they were confident they had established peace between the Nez Perce and the Chinook. As Ambrose points out, this was wishful thinking, "neither side could understand a word the other side said, and the sign language of the Plains Indians that [Drewyer] used was imperfectly understood by the Chinooks."

At that point, Lewis and Clark had a parting smoke with their loyal Nez Perce guides and promised to see them again in the spring.

***

On we trudge. We see blackberry bushes alongside the road and drop the canoe to spend ten minutes picking and eating, drinking warm water from our canteens, and resting in the shade. Then we strap on our packs, heave the canoe onto our heads, and start packing up the road again. Panting, sweating, and telling each other it will be easier on the downslope beyond the dam.

A maroon pickup pulling a jet boat on a trailer pulls up beside us and stops. We tip Clueless to the side and let him slide to the ground.

A deeply tanned, red-faced man with a white, bald head leans out and asks, "You carrying that around the dam?"

"Yes."

"Throw it in back." He jabs a thumb toward the back of his pickup.

Smiles all around. What an incredible relief.

His name is Jim Downing. We do as instructed, sliding the canoe up beside a little blond, golden retriever in back, then throw in our packs, and climb in with dog and canoe. He drives us up over the dam, and down past our packs, then on down the road that extra mile to the put-in on the river. The kindness of strangers.

We give him hearty thanks, then leave our two packs and canoe to start the mile-long walk back to our other packs we'd left in the grass next to the parking lot. There's a visitor's center under the dam, so we walk in looking for cold drinks and food; we'd skipped breakfast and lunch. We find cold drinks in a vending machine, but the only food available is candy bars.

A woman in uniform hobbles up on crutches, and we ask her about the problems locking through. She tells us some Boy Scouts were permitted to lock through once in canoes, but they had made arrangements weeks before their arrival. She has long, black hair and sad eyes. You can't argue with a sad-eyed woman on crutches, and she is certainly more sympathetic than the security guard whose conversation was limited to, "You can't."

I know there are several more dams downstream, and I'm thinking we'll have to portage every one. Not something I'm looking forward to.

A long, clear, plastic tube three feet in diameter winds down from the dam and passes through the Visitor's Center. It flows with clear water, and all sorts of fish are fighting their way up the tube against the current: salmon, trout, catfish of various sizes, carp, lots of fish slapping their way up to algae haven.

Alex and I head the other way, on our way downriver, carrying our big backpacks.

We load Clueless, shove out into the swift current, and paddle down to the north side where we find a camping park. There we walk into a little shop and cafe where we fill our bellies and borrow a landline phone. Our cell has not had service since near Lewiston. I call Mark and tell him we need a ride out. I've lost my will to paddle a series of long lakes and portage around massive dams. We also ran across a sign below the dam that forbids the lighting of campfires the rest of the way to the Columbia, which means we would have no way of cooking. "You can't. You can't. You can't."

Mark says he'll send his son Michael the next day in his pickup to retrieve the Clueless Corps of Discovery.

FORT CLATSOP AND THIEVES

The real Corps of Discovery, after surviving the 55 miles of intermittent rapids and falls on the mighty Columbia River found
themselves again among deeply forested mountains. They fought
their way through strong headwinds, violent storms, high tides (as they
neared the coast), fogs, and seemingly constant rain. At length, paddling
down the north side of the four to five-mile-wide Columbia River on
November 7, they spotted what they thought to be the Pacific Ocean.
Clark scribbles in his notes: "Ocian in view! O! the joy." In reality the
Pacific was still 20 miles away.

Making their way along the north shore in their five dugouts proved
incredibly difficult. On November 12, Clark writes: "A Tremendious
wind from the S. W. about 3 oClock this morning with Lightineng

and hard claps of Thunder, and Hail which Continued until 6 oClock a.m.when it became light for a Short time, then the heavens became sudenly darkened by a black cloud from the S. W. and rained with great violence until 12 oClock, the waves tremendious brakeing with great fury against the rocks and trees on which we were encamped. our Situation is dangerous...all wet and colde our bedding is rotten and we are not in a Situation to supply their places in a wet bottom scercely large enough to contain us...Canoes at the mercy of the waves, altho Secured as well as possible, Sunk with emence parcels of Stone to wate them down to prevent their dashing to pecies against the rocks."

After finally reaching the Pacific coast, Clark walked nine miles north, scouting the shoreline. (They had hoped to encounter one of the trading ships that sometimes anchored near or in the mouth of the Columbia in order to obtain supplies for trading with the Indians on their return trip.) He found nothing but a savage coastline wracked by waves and wind. After returning to the others, they all voted, including Sacagawea and York (the first time a woman and a slave are recorded as voting in an election) to spend the winter south of the river in a region the Chinook Indians told them had many elk.

They crossed the miles-wide river in their shallow dugouts, boats not built to pass through sea waves, and forced their way up a tributary on the south side where they found a rise near a spring and set about building a rather snug, 50-foot-square log fort with two long huts on either side of the enclosure, where they spent a miserably wet winter within a forest of massive trees. The western hemlocks were thick and prodigiously high, with broken, dead limbs sticking out from all sides of the trunk, the live limbs hardly visible in the high, shadowed canopy above. Ferns matted the forest floor, and wet, green mosses climbed the damp trees. The river banks where they tied their heavy dugouts were slick, sticky mud. It was a cold, wet camp.

All winter the hunters searched far for the increasingly elusive elk while Lewis and Clark traded off much of their remaining supplies for food, and for an Indian canoe with a high prow, adapted for travel on the windy Columbia. They kept a close eye on their goods, noting that Chinooks, in their conical, woven-reed hats, kept pilfering anything left lying around.

By the time they were ready to leave the fort in late March, their trading goods were almost gone: "two handkercheifs would not contain all the small articles of merchandize which we possess," writes Lewis. "The balance of the stock consists of 6 blue robes one scarlet...one uniform artillerist's coat and hat, five robes made of our large flag, and a few old cloaths trimed with ribbon. On this stock we have wholy to depend for the purchase of horses and such portion of our subsistence from the Indians." They traded the artillerist's coat for another Indian canoe. They very much needed one more canoe but couldn't afford the asking price, so they stole one and departed for the Rocky Mountains.

This time they had to paddle up the current against the spring floods along the southern shore of the Columbia River. The Chinook Indians they met kept stealing everything they could lay hands on, even running off one day with Clark's pet dog Seaman. Clark told three men to track down the thieves and shoot them if they resisted. He loved that dog. When the trackers got within sight of the Indians, the Indians let Seaman go and ran for the trees. The Newfoundland happily ran back to his owners.

Once, Lewis became so incensed with the thieves that constantly hung around that he beat up an Indian who had just taken an iron socket. Lewis then threatened to shoot any thieves and had his men drive the Indians out of the camp.

The Corps had a terrible time purchasing fish, roots, and dogs to eat now that they were down to those few trading supplies. The Indians, too, were famished, having eaten most of their own winter supplies and were naturally unwilling to sell their remaining food. The salmon run they depended on was still said to be a month away. On April 3 they met some Indian families coming down the river in search of food. "These poor people," Lewis writes, "appeared to be almost starved. They picked up the bones and little pieces of refuse meat which had been thrown away by the party." The elk had moved to higher elevations, and the expedition's hunters only now and then brought in a duck or a deer.

Finally, as they paddled up the river, they began seeing a few horses in the occasional villages. Clark and Lewis began trading for these horses, hoping to transport their goods by land rather than pull their canoes up the impossible gorge of the Columbia. But prices for horses were very high. At one point Lewis traded their last two large cooking kettles for two horses, something he had consistently refused to do in the past. They were left with four small kettles, one for each cooking fire.

Sometimes they were invited to sleep in the huts of the Indians, but Clark writes that after lying down on a mat to sleep, he "was prevented by the mice and vermin with which this house abounded and which was very troublesome to me." Once they came upon a recently abandoned village that was carpeted with living fleas. When they walked into the empty huts, black clouds of fleas leaped upon them. The men had to immerse themselves in water to get rid of them.

They managed somehow to paddle and pull their canoes up several very difficult rapids, losing one of the better Indian canoes when, as the men strained to pull it around a rock, the five-strand rope of elk skin was jerked from their hands. They didn't recover it. The stolen canoe now floated back toward its owners.

At length they acquired ten horses and bartered some of their wooden canoes for wampum beads to trade with later. Their remaining dugouts they split and burned, unwilling to give them to Indians who persistently stole their axes, tomahawks, robes, spoons, anything. Lewis once appealed to a local chief who promised to intervene with the thieves. "I hope," writes Lewis, "that the friendly interposition of this chief may prevent our being compelled to use some violence with these people; our men seem well disposed to kill a few of them." But as they moved up the river, the stealing and angry conflicts continued.

THE NEZ PERCE AGAIN

April 18, 1806. Clark writes: "Early this morning I was awoke by an indian man of the Chopunnish Nation [the Nez Perce] who informed me that he lived in the neighborhood of our horses [and Twisted Hair's camp about 200 miles away]. this man delivered me a bag of powder and ball which he had picked up this morning at the place the goods were exposed yesterday." (The Corps had dug up one of the caches they had buried in the fall and had missed seeing the bag of powder and ball.)

This was a startling change: an Indian handing over goods he had found. The young Nez Perce furthermore offered to return with the party as a guide.

On April 21, Clark writes, "our guide continued with us, he appears to be an honest fellow. he tells us that the Indians above will treat us with much more hospitallity than those we are now with."

On April 23, they met another Nez Perce man and his family who were returning up the river and decided to join the Corps. This man had thirteen horses and agreed to lend some to carry supplies. The next morning they set off over the high, grassy plains, leaving the Snake River to cut across country toward the Lewiston area.

Clark began treating visiting Indians with the medicines he carried, which brought the travelers goodwill and some food. He set a man's broken arm with a splint, rubbed salve on wounds, and treated many sore eyes: "sore eyes seem to be a universal complaint among those people; I have no doubt but the fine sands of those plains and the river contribute much to the disorder."

The Corps crossed to the north side of the rushing Snake River and made their way past what is now Clarkston and Lewiston where they met Tetoharsky, the young chief who had canoed with them the previous fall. He once again agreed to accompany them on their way upriver to meet Twisted Hair, who was to have cared for their horses.

Food was still extremely scarce. They traded for scrawny, half-starved dogs and roots. Finally, on May 6, Clark treated a woman with an abscess in the small of her back. He cut open the abscess, smeared on a little fragrant skin ointment, and flour of sulphur. Her husband gave the Corps a horse, which they immediately killed, cooked, and ate—the first full meal they'd had in many days. By the next day, the woman seemed to be recovering from the abscess.

They crossed the Clearwater back to the south side where another Nez Perce gave them two lead canisters of powder that his dog had sniffed out from where they had been cached the year before: "as he had kept them safe and had honisty enough to return them to us, we gave him a fire Steel by way of compensation." Again, Lewis was struck by the honesty and good will of the Nez Perce.

CUT NOSE, TWISTED HAIR, AND BROKEN ARM

On May 8 the Corps met the principal chief of the area, a man they called Cut Nose, who had been away on a retributive raid against the Snake Indians to the south when Lewis and Clark passed through the previous fall. Clark gave him and his men the entrails of two deer as well as the four unborn fawns within them, and some horse meat and deer meat. The party then took their way up a trail into the high hills on the south side of the Clearwater to find Twisted Hair and their horses. They were accompanied by Cut Nose and Tetoharsky.

They traveled four miles into the grassy hills which were "steep and emencely high to a leavel rich country thinly timbered with pine."

There they met old Twisted Hair and some of his men, but Twisted Hair seemed on guard and soon an argument broke out between him and Cut Nose. Lewis and Clark couldn't understand the argument, but made signs that they all needed to proceed to water and encamp. They were still a day's ride from where the horses had wintered.

The Indians followed in separate groups and camped apart from one another. Lewis was communicating by way of a Shoshone boy, who would speak to Sacagawea, but the boy told Lewis that this was a conflict between chiefs and not his business. He refused to interpret, so Drewyer used his sign language. Apparently Cut Nose was jealous or angry with Twisted Hair, accusing the old man of having ridden Lewis and Clark's horses and of not making sure they were well watered during the winter months. Twisted Hair accused Cut Nose of taking the horses—which may well have been the case. Fortunately for Lewis and Clark, both chiefs agreed to return the horses.

Late the next evening, 21 of the 38 horses were returned along with about half the saddles and some powder and balls. "The greater part of the horses were in fine order, tho' five of them had been rode & worsted in such manner last fall by the Inds. That they had not recovered and are in very low order, and 3 with sore backs." Lewis paid Twisted Hair with an old beat-up musket he had bought from the coastal Indians for two elk skins and said he would give him another gun and ammunition when the rest of the horses were returned.

They were still camped on the high prairie when a cold, violent wind blew down from the mountains, followed by a plague of rain and hail. After dark, the rain turned to thick snow that continued all night. By morning eight inches had accumulated. The men of the Corps had traded away much of their winter clothing and buffalo robes over the course of their journey, so the cold penetrated. They pushed on several miles through the snow to the camp of Broken Arm, to whom they'd given an American flag the year before. They found the flag standing before his lodge, and he provided them with about two bushels of camas roots, four cakes of root bread, dried fish, and two young horses to butcher. Clark writes: "Those people has shewn much greater acts of hospitallity than we have witnessed from any nation or tribe since we have passed the rocky Mountains. in short be it spoken to their immortal honor it is the only act which diserves the appelation of hospitallity which we have witnessed in this quarter." The Nez Perce previously had provided food for the Corps, but usually at a price.

Clark also writes that the Nez Perce "not withstanding they live in the crouded manner before mentioned [they spent winters in reed-mat longhouses, sometimes 30 families to a longhouse] are much more clenly in their persons and habitations than any nation we have seen since we left Illiniois...They are expirt marksmen & good riders. they do not appear to be so much devoted to baubles as most of the nations we have met with, but seem anxious always to riceve articles of utility, such as knives, axes, Kittles, blankets & mockerson awls." Because the mountains ahead were still deep in snow and travel up the Lolo Trail would be delayed for at least a month, Broken Arm set up a leather tepee for them in the village.

The delay was bad news for the Corps, who were longing to get into buffalo country beyond the Rockies where food would be more plentiful. But they had no choice. They swam their horses to the north side of the cold Clearwater, carried their goods over on borrowed dugouts, then set up camp to await the melting of the snows. Patrick Gass guided the construction of a grass-thatched hut and began the process of burning and cutting a new dugout while the hunters wandered the steep hills, the gullies, and wooded streams. The day they crossed the river Collins managed to kill two bears, Sacagawea dug for fennel roots, which the men enjoyed, and one of the hunters stole a salmon from an eagle near camp. The fish gave them hope that the salmon would soon make their run. But the men were usually hungry and cold, having little to trade to the Indians for food. Lewis and Clark handed out a few awls and cut the buttons off their own coats to offer in trade, which brought in enough roots to keep them alive.

Three of the men recrossed the Clearwater to the south side in the newly made dugout, but it was "driven broadside with the full force of a very strong current against some Standing trees and instantly filled with water and sunk," losing not only their meager trading supplies, but three blankets and a coat which they could little afford to lose. Only three men now owned more than one blanket apiece. Clark wrote: "having exhosted all our merchindize we were obliged to have recourse to every Subterfuge in order to prepare in the most ample manner in our power to meet that wretched portion of our journey, the Rocky Mountains, where hunger and Cold in their most rigorous form assail the waried traveler, not any of us have yet forgotten our sufferings in those mountains in September last, I think it probable we never shall."

Meanwhile, Sacagawea's little son was cutting teeth and developed a fever. Clark, who loved the little boy, writes that he was "dangerously ill. his jaw and throat is much swelled...We apply a poltice of onions, after giving him some creem of tarter &c." Two days later the child was worse: "it's jaw and the back of it's neck are much more swolen... tho' his fever has abated considerably."

Also, William Bratton, who, because of a serious back injury, had been unable to walk was now unable to sit up without great pain. "We have tried every remedy which our engenuity could devise, or with which our stock of medicines furnished us, without effect. John Shields observed that he had seen men in a similar situation restored by violent sweats. Bratton requested that he might be sweated in the manner proposed by Shields to which we consented."

Shields dug a circular hole three feet in diameter and four feet deep, built a large fire within, let it burn down, then shoveled out the sticks and ashes. "A seat [was] placed in the center of the hole for the patient with a board at bottom for his feet to rest on; some hoops of willow poles were bent in an arch crossing each over the hole, on these several blankets were thrown forming a secure and thick" awning about three feet high. The blankets were secured on all sides, and Bratton was given a vessel of water which he sprinkled on the bottom and sides of the hole creating "as much steam or vapor as he could possibly bear." He also drank as much hot horse mint tea as he could take. After 20 minutes he was taken from the hole and twice plunged into cold water. He was then returned to the sweat lodge for 45 minutes, taken out, covered in blankets and allowed to cool gradually.

By the next day, Bratton was walking, nearly free of pain.

Shields's remedy prompted another experiment. At eleven that morning a dugout canoe arrived with three natives, one of them a man of middle age who had entirely lost the use of his arms and legs, though he was capable of eating and drinking and his muscle tone was still good. "He is a cheif of considerable note among them and they seem extremely anxious for his recovery," Clark observes.

They enlarged the hole used for Bratton, as the chief could not hold himself up in the hole, and the chief's father, "a very good looking old man, went into the hole with him and sustained him in a proper position." After sweating the man and his father, and then plunging the chief in cold water, and repeating the sweating, the chief complained of considerable pain. This seemed a good sign, since he had felt nothing in his body before. Lewis gave him 30 drops of laudanum (an alcoholic mixture of opium) "which soon composed him and he rested very well."

Lewis, after witnessing the little concern the Plains Indians displayed for their old people, was struck by these natives' attention to this man as well as the father's willingness to hold his son in the almost intolerable heat of the sweat lodge: "this is at least a strong mark of parental affection. they all appear extremely attentive to this sick...the Chopunnish [Nez Perce] appear to be very attentive and kind to their aged people and treat their women with more rispect than the nations of the Missouri."

Nine days later, the chief was gradually recovering the use of his limbs, little Pompi was nearly well, and William Bratton was walking around. Five days after this, after more treatments, Clark writes: "The Sick Chief is much mended, he can bear his weight on his legs and recovers strength." This was all good news, but the mountains to the east were still covered in snow.

JUSTIN

ark's son Michael arrives in his pickup below the Lower Granite Dam the next day and gives us and Clueless a ride into Clarkston. There, we call my wife Joy and she tells us Alex's older brother Justin is driving up from Kansas to surprise us. He's got his mountain bike and he wants to join us for a few days. Ever since Justin and I made a 1000-mile canoe trip, he's loved the outdoors. After that journey, he went to college, dropped out after two years, married, divorced, patched things up with his ex (to some extent), and they now have two daughters. We contact Justin on his cell phone and make arrangements to meet him the following day.

***

After picking up our car, Alex and I leave it at the motel and walk to a Mexican restaurant. Alex is feeling good. He walks along beatboxing: spitting out rhythmic stutters and clicks and growls while doing a snaky little dance, making swervy, crazy gestures with his arms and hands to freak out the passing drivers. We walk by restaurants of various descriptions. He says he wants to open one called Johnny Fitzgerald's Famous Chinese Cuisine, or Wang Su's Italian Bistro, or Juanita's Cheeseburgers. He makes a list of his favorite movies: *Training Day, Braveheart, The Last of the Mohicans, Master and Commander, Cinderella Man*—all macho adventures we've watched together. He spots a girl far up the street with factory-ripped jeans. "Wow," he says, "I think I like ripped jeans."

"You've got the eyes of an Indian scout," I say.

"Speaking of spotting girls," he says, "Justin used to be a first-class girl spotter. He could see a pretty girl in the next county. You'd look up and ask, 'Where is she? Where is she?' but she's nowhere to be seen. The reason you can't see her is she's still in the next area code."

We find the Mexican restaurant and eat, then walk four miles to a Baskin Robbins for dessert.

It's been a tough two weeks hiking the mountains, hitchhiking, and canoeing a part of the Lewis and Clark route. Now, we're both ready to return to the Lolo Trail and try to complete that difficult passage. This time we'll ride the mountain bikes we have strapped to our car, though Alex thinks riding horses is smarter.

***

Justin arrives. He's put on some solid weight since our canoe trip; he's now a strong young man, not the thin, sixteen-year-old I canoed with fourteen years ago—his strength and added weight will be both helpful and damaging in the next several days.

Five days ago Justin crashed while out riding his new bike, falling hands down on the asphalt, which took a big patch of skin off his right palm. He's got it wrapped up in antibiotic ointment and gauze bandages he bought from a Montana drugstore. The clerk said the ointment was used for horses. He bought several rolls of the gauze and some bright blue rolls of stretchy wrap so he can change dressings in the days ahead.

"Are you sure you can bike with that?" I ask him.

"I think so. The skin's starting to grow back."

I've looked at the hand. The skin is gone. A little whiteness is growing around the edges of a two-inch-square wound on the heel of his hand. It looks bad, but he's unwilling to forego the adventure.

We stop for a few hours in Orofino, the little town below the huge concrete dam where Alex and I met the Onion Man and the Knife Lady. We make a run to the lumber store to buy straps to tie our gear onto our bikes, then stop at the local Mexican restaurant where Alex and I watched the World Cup Soccer finals.

I see a grey-bearded man with long, curly hair and a deep tan riding a bicycle loaded down with equipment: three layers of bags strapped to the handlebars, saddle bags hanging to either side of the back wheel, a backpack, water bottles, smaller bags tied on top of that, and a walking stick sticking out the back like the tail of a stingray. He looks like a well-supplied, homeless traveler.

Because we're planning to load up our own bikes today and head out, I walk across the street and follow him into a Chinese restaurant to ask him for advice. He's seated on a bench just inside the door, perusing a menu. "So, how far have you been riding?" I begin.

The man stares at his menu.

I try again. No response. I turn to the woman behind the counter who tries to help me out. She asks him, "How far have you been riding?"

"I heard what he said." He looks up at me and glares. "I just get into town and am attending to my hunger, and someone walks up to me," he suddenly splays his fingers in front of his face and shouts, "and blows up in my face! I'm looking at a menu!"

I glance at the woman behind the counter, smile, and leave.

STOPPED ON THE LOLO

On June 10, Lewis and Clark finally moved out, each man riding a horse, with a second horse for supplies and several extra horses available for replacements or, if necessary, for food in the high mountains. The Nez Perce had eventually returned 32 of the 38 horses Lewis and Clark had left in their keeping. Somehow, perhaps through barter and medical services, they had obtained an additional 34 horses for a total of 66.

First, they stopped on the Weippe Prairie (where the Corps had first met the Nez Perce the previous September) intending to lay in a stock of dried meat for the journey up the Lolo Trail, but the hunters killed little. The days were warm and the mosquitoes on the wetland prairie, "our old companions," had become "very troublesome." Across the gently undulating prairie, the camas was in bloom again. "At a Short distance," writes Clark, "it resembles a lake of fine clear water, so complete is this deseption that on first Sight I could have sworn it was water." They had packed bags of camas root cakes they had acquired from the Indians. Apparently their stomachs had grown accustomed to the rich roots.

They were impatient to move on. The snows on the Lolo Trail had already delayed them five weeks. So, on June 15, in spite of rain falling all morning, they saddled up and set out into the Rocky Mountains once again, this time without a guide. It was "with great dificulty that the loaded horses Could assend the hills and Mountains the[y] frequently sliped down both assending and decending those steep hills" on the wet snow. In places the horses were climbing snow drifts eight and ten feet deep. The snow had crystallized and was hard enough to carry their weight, which relieved them of climbing around and over the many rocks and treefalls they had encountered on their way down the year before, but the Corps often lost sight of the blazed trees that marked the trail. When they found a place to camp, grass for the horses was buried beneath deep snow. "Here," writes Clark, "was Winter with all it's rigors; the air was cold my hands and feet were benumbed."

On the third day out, they recognized that their horses would not be able to make the four- or five-day journey to needed grass and that the chances of their losing the way were real: "If we proceeded and Should git bewildered in those Mountains the certainty was that we Should lose all our horses and consequently our baggage ensstrements perhaps our papers and thus eventually [risk] the loss of our discoveries which we had already made if we should be so fortunate as to escape with life."

The captains sent Drewyer and Shannon to find Indian guides, offering them rifles and horses if they'd take them over the Lolo Trail. It was clear to the captains that they still needed the Nez Perce.

On their way back to the Weippe, Joseph Potts badly sliced his leg with a large knife. Perhaps he fell or his horse rubbed against a tree trunk and the knife in its scabbard shoved into his leg. Whatever the case, they had to halt and bind up the wound. Then Colter's horse fell while crossing the rushing Hungery Creek. I can see the creek in spring spate, the grey waters churning down the mountain, pouring through fallen trees, roaring around rocks, and through leafing willow brush and leaning fir trees still footed in snow. Colter's horse stumbles and its legs go sideways in the strong current. Colter clamps his legs to the horse as it slams into the freezing water. Rolling beneath his horse, he somehow keeps a grip on his rifle. They both surface, riding a chute between boulders, both gasping for air, then rolling again. The rocks and current scrape him off his horse, but he does not let go his rifle. I can hear the men shouting above the roar of the waters as he comes up again, the horse flailing to find its feet in suddenly shallower water. It is quickly over, man and horse scrambling into brush and up the bank to stand there side by side snorting and coughing and shaking. He still gripped his rifle.

Just another day in the mountains. Lewis barely mentions the event.

On June 23, Drewyer and Shannon returned with three Nez Perce who had agreed to act as guides for the payment of two rifles. One was a brother of Cut Nose. All three, writes Clark, were "young men of good Charrector and much respected by their nation."

BUBBA

Alex, Justin, and I drive down to the Orofino laundromat, a small, white, flat-topped building. After ten days hiking and canoeing in the mountains, Alex and I need to wash the clothes in our backpacks. Outside next to a dented black pickup stands a short, pudgy man in jeans and a sleeveless T-shirt that falls four inches short of his belt, exposing a hairy belly that's tattooed in three-inch, Old English script proclaiming HILLBILLY. A brown goatee sprays from his chin and he's wearing wire-rim glasses and a black baseball cap that reads, FBI. As we carry in our laundry, I glance out the window and notice the little man taking a pinch of powder from a Tupperware container and sniffing it up a nostril.

The laundromat is hot. Half the washers aren't working, and the floor needs sweeping.

Hillbilly walks in while we're sorting clothes. Justin is dropping shorts, jeans, and socks into two machines as we fall into conversation with the man. He calls himself Bubba. He's from South Carolina, but he grew up in a Los Angeles ghetto. "Lots of gangs. I was small and white and had a big mouth, got into lots of fights. My father tells me, 'You'll either be a professional victim all your life, or you'll stand up and fight.'

"I fought. Got in with some really ruthless people. Ruthless, man. Finally, my aunt, my niece, and me left to join my grandparents here in Orofino. I'm glad I got out of there."

He transfers his own clothes from the washers to the dryers, slots quarters, then steps outside to smoke. I follow him out and sit down on a five-gallon plastic bucket next to the door. It's partially filled with sand for cigarette butts. Alex comes out and squats down on the sidewalk beside me. Another clear-sky day, the heat moving into the nineties.

Bubba leans back against his hoodless pickup in the strong sunlight, sucks on his cigarette, then goes on: "My first job up here was a fire fighter. They dropped me, a city kid, out in the middle of this forest with one other guy. Wow! Did I feel all alone! Mountains as far as you could see and me and him stuck up there all alone." He pushes his wire-rim glasses up his nose and takes another pull at the cigarette.

"There was this fire that had burned maybe two acres in two days. Not doing much. The pencil-pusher back in the main office who ran things said, 'Go up there and put it out, then cold train it.'"

"What's that?" Alex asks. We're both sitting in a sliver of shade cast by the flat-top building.

"Just stick around till you're sure the fire's out. Anyway, they dropped this crew of us down near the little fire and dropped off all our supplies in a helicopter sling: food, water, gasoline for the chain saws, everything a ways up the mountain.

"Then the wind picked up and the fire blew up in our faces. That ridge they dropped us and our supplies on was above the fire, which got that pencil-pusher in a lot of trouble later. The fire started running straight up the mountain, right at us. I got my saw and two containers of water out, broke the water open and poured it over myself, then ran uphill. The fire was leaping from tree top to tree top; it was blowing that hard. The trees were just blowing up. Damn, was I scared. City kid. That two-acre fire was burning through a thousand acres in no time, running right up the mountain at us. Then the wind took the fire sideways, and we lived." He takes another pull at his cigarette and looks at his boots.

"So we climbed up to the helicopter landing zone, but one guy wasn't there. None of the guys wanted to go back down and find him; the fire was too close, flames and smoke just pouring up out of there. I thought, man, he might be knocked out by the smoke or burned down there. I've got to go. So I start walking on down the mountain toward the fire and here he comes. I call out, 'Where you been, man?' 'Oh, no problem,' he says, 'I just went back for my weed.'

"Man, was I pissed! That idiot going back for his stash could have killed me!

"Later, I told the guys we ought to beat the shit out of him. But they said no, his dad's a big honcho around here. So we didn't."

He drops his cigarette butt and grinds it out with the scuffed toe of his boot. He reaches into his pickup cab and pulls out a two-liter of Mountain Dew and takes a long guzzle.

"Later, I went to work logging in the steep mountains. I was a hooker, down on the ground. We had these inch-and-a-half steel cables, the high wires strung down the mountain. Then these cables hanging from the high wires with chokers hanging down. We'd hook a choker to the log and signal with our talkie-tooters."

"A tooter what?"

"It's a walkie-talkie with a button. Uses a series of toots you can hear across the mountain, so everybody knows what's going to happen.

"Anyway, we'd hit the button so many times to let everybody know we had the log, then we'd run like hell along the side of the mountain to get away. Then come back and hook another and run like hell. If the cable up above was high enough, the log went up smooth, but after attaching the choker, the log would drag along a few feet, maybe catch a stump. Sometimes they snapped a cable and it shot through the air like a rifle shot. Once I saw two supporting cables go; one pulled a stump out, but the other one just snapped. The whole high cable leaned over and fell with all the logs it was hoisting.

"Run like hell or die was our motto."

I stand up from the bucket I'm sitting on. "You had to be in great shape to work like that."

"I ate all the time. Twenty-to-forty-thousand calories a day. Almost no body fat. Every time I hooked up a log, I'd reach in my pocket or in my backpack and pull out a powerbar or a candy bar. Ate all the time. Had to."

I step over beside Alex to get out of the sun and lean against the plate glass.

"When we logged with helicopters, the rotating blades would build up static electricity. When you touched the cable, you'd get shocked. For two days, when I was new, the guys didn't tell me what was going on. They'd just break up laughing every time it happened. I'd pull the choker down and when it touched the log or swung by a limb, bam! It got me. Then I noticed that they'd take a stick and drop it on the cable or choker to ground it. I finally caught on, but it would really zap you. Course, I laughed at the next new guy who came along."

He takes another swig of his Mountain Dew and tells us about a perfect log they found, one that had a long, thick trunk without branches that they could cut for veneer. He tells us how they lifted it out with a helicopter and that you'd get a big bonus for finding a log like that. He lights another cigarette and pulls at his rough goatee.

"Then, when I finally graduated to operating the high cable, it's the machine at the top of the mountain that drags the logs up, I noticed these four guys would disappear into the brush for an hour at a time. They'd hook up logs, then poof! they was gone. Nowhere to be seen.

I'd wait and wait and after twenty minutes or half an hour, here they'd come, straggling out of the forest. I finally got pissed and shut the machine down, walked down there, and found all four smoking meth. Fired all four of those suckers on the spot."

He flicks the cigarette ash with his finger and puts it to his lips.

"Maybe I was too hard on 'em, but man, someone could get killed on that mountain. I mean I've done my share of drugs—growing up in LA and all: weed, meth, cocaine, crack, alcohol, the whole shitroll. But you can't get strung out up there on the mountain, you're going to kill somebody."

Justin's inside the over-heated laundromat folding clothes he's taken from the driers, so Alex and I step in to help. Bubba follows us through the door and checks on his machines. I thank Bubba for his stories. We bag our clothes and walk out. Bubba follows us into the sunlight. We open the trunk of the car and drop the bag in.

Bubba walks over to his beat-up truck and leans against the door. "Man, my wife was raised hard and poor, so when I started making all that money logging, all she wanted to do was party on the weekends."

We walk to the doors of our car. I ask him how much he made logging.

"Three-hundred dollars a day."

"That's good money."

"Yeah. So all she wanted to do is party. But when I got home, all I wanted to do was sleep and eat. She'd spend $1000 on a single weekend... and then I'd have to ask her for lunch money the next Monday. It's a hard life for a family man. I was flying back and forth to Los Angeles where we had a house, so the weekends is all we had."

He pulls his pack of cigarettes from his jeans pocket, taps another one out, pulls out a plastic lighter, and flicks the flame. "She took the house, the kids, everything."

He takes a long drag on the cigarette and slowly expels the smoke. "Now I'm broke and don't even own a washing machine." He runs a hand up a stubbled cheek, adjusts his glasses, and looks away toward the mountains beyond the town. "But it's beautiful up here...better than LA." He smiles. I can see he's missing some teeth.

I walk around our car in the heavy sunlight and open the door. I see him reach inside his cab and click on his truck CD player as I step into our car. We can hear the lyrics from the song: "I hurt myself today, to see if I still feel."

He's leaning against the front fender of his ratty little truck that has no hood, looking away toward the mountains. "I focus on the pain, the only thing that's real."

I start the engine of our car.

"The needle tears a hole, the old familiar sting./ Try to kill it all away, but I remember everything."

Alex leans out our car window and calls out, "I know that song! Johnny Cash!"

We see him smile and nod his head. He looks away to the mountains. "What have I become? My sweetest friend./ Everyone I know, goes away in the end./ And you could have it all, my empire of dirt..." We back out, turn, and drive back across the Clearwater, taking a left onto Highway 12.

HIGH UP THE LOLO

The next morning the Corps of Discovery and their Nez Perce guides set out up the Lolo once again, climbing back to Hungery Creek and their stashed supplies. That night the Indians set several fir trees on fire, believing this would bring fair weather for their journey. These fir trees "have a great number of dry lims," writes Lewis, "near their bodies which when set on fire creates a very suddon and immence blaze from bottom to top of those tall trees. they are a beatifull object in this situation at night." The men were huddled in their few robes of worn elkskin, tattered wool, or ragged buffalo, their hands held out to their campfires as a small rain fell. They watched the huge trees roaring into the dark sky, flinging sparks hissing high into the rain, the wavering glare reflecting from the wet flanks of the hobbled horses whose heads had all come up in alarm at the sight. One of the new Indian guides was sick and shivering. Lewis handed him a buffalo robe, the man having no cover but his moccasins and a wet deerskin shirt.

Early the next day the men collected their horses beneath a grey sky and intermittent rain and set out again, stopping at noon for Sacagawea to gather "a parcel of roots which the Shoshones Eat. it is a Small knob root a good deel in flavour and Consistency like the Jerusalem artichoke." A little before dark the rain returned and fell quietly through the trees on the shadowy column of men and horses moving ever higher into the mountains beneath a leaden sky. They stopped near dusk to unload the wet packs, set up the wet tents, and strike fire into damp wood.

The following day, their guides led them "over and along the steep sides of tremendious mountains entirely covered with snow." Late in the evening they arrived at a steep, south-facing side of a mountain near a spring where at last there was plenty of grass for the horses. Clark complained of "a violent pain in my head which has tormented me ever Since, most violently." Again it rained before dark as the men broke off dry limbs from the tree trunks for the fires, and cut spruce limbs for their beds.

On June 27 they stopped at the request of the guides on a high, nearly treeless ridge where previous Indians had built a conical pile of rocks about six feet high. There they smoked together, the place being sacred to the Nez Perce. "From this place we had an extensive view of these stupendous mountains principally covered with snow like that on which we stood; we were entirely surrounded by those mountains from which to one unacquainted with them it would have seemed impossible ever to have escaped, in short without the assistance of our guides, I doubt much whether we who had once passed [this way] could find our way to Travellers rest in their present Situation...those indians are most admireable pilots." They found they could sit their horses and slide straight down banks of snow rather than taking a route that wound down the mountains as they had the previous fall.

The hunters, who always preceded the travelers, were again

unsuccessful, so Lewis issued a pint of bear's oil to be cooked with a mess of camas roots. Lewis mentions that Potts's leg, which had been much swollen and inflamed from the knife cut, was much better. Lewis applied a poultice of pounded wild ginger, which gave Potts some relief from the pain.

On June 29, they crossed the continental divide and at last "bid adieu to the snow," making their way down to a stream which was about 30 yards wide "and runs with great velocity." Near the river they found a deer the hunters had left, which pleased them all, having now been reduced to eating roots without oil or salt.

Early that evening they arrived at the hot springs they had passed the previous September. The hunters brought in another deer, so they ate well. Both whites and Indians took baths in the hot springs, the Indians then jumping into the cold creek and returning to bathe again in the hot springs. Clark wrote that the water was so hot, he could barely stand it for ten minutes, and that other adjacent springs were even hotter.

They were now following a rushing creek to the place they called Traveler's Rest, where they intended to stop for a few days, before dividing the party. Lewis and several men would follow the Bitterroot River north to where it flows into Clark's Fork, then follow it up the mountains. This, according to the Indians, was a shorter path to the Missouri River. Lewis also wanted to explore the Marias River, a northern tributary of the Missouri, to find out how far north its sources were. If it flowed from Canada, this would push the Louisiana Purchase north into then British Territory.

Clark and the rest of the Corps would meanwhile ascend the Bitterroot Valley and cross the Bitterroot Mountains using a more easterly pass than the difficult one they had taken the year before. They would then find their way to Camp Fortunate, where they had cached supplies and hidden their dugout canoes. The plan was for Clark to then send one team down the Jefferson River to the Missouri and meet up with Lewis while Clark traveled with a second team to explore the Yellowstone River, meeting the others at last where the Yellowstone pours into the Missouri. It was an ambitious plan.

On the way to Traveler's Rest, they climbed a steep hill where Lewis's horse slipped. Lewis went off backwards, hit the ground hard, and slid and rolled nearly 40 feet down the hill before he could stop himself. The horse too went tumbling down the slope, almost rolling on top of him, but it managed to scramble to its feet and both horse and man were once again unhurt.

That evening they finally arrived at Traveler's Rest, "leaveing those tremendious mountanes behind us—in passing of which we have experiensed Cold and hunger of which I shall ever remember," writes Clark.

On July 1, they rested their horses, sent out hunters, and divided baggage for the trips ahead. Their hunters came in with six "large fat Bucks" and six does. "This," says Clark, "is like returning to the land of liveing a plenty of meat and that very good." They set up poles and began drying strips of venison.

Their guides now wanted to leave in order to find their Salish friends, but Lewis prevailed upon them to accompany him for two more days so they could show him the proper route over the mountains. He gave their leader a small medal and the leader then insisted on exchanging names with Lewis, a ritual of friendship. Lewis's newly given name would be White Bearskin Folded. That evening, they held foot races with the Indians and watched the young Nez Perce race their horses. "These are a race," wrote Lewis, "of hardy strong athletic active men."

LEWIS EAST

O n the third of July, Lewis set off up Clark's Fork with nine Corps men and the three Nez Perce guides toward the high pass that would eventually take them down to the falls of the Missouri River. After seven miles, the Indians advised crossing the river which at that point was 150 yards wide and running strong. The Indians made deerskin boats for their supplies and swam their horses over, while Lewis's nine chopped trees to make three small rafts, transporting their supplies in several trips. Lewis accompanied the last two men, who could not swim. The raft rushed downstream for a mile and a half, a wild and dangerous ride, before their desperate poling and paddling brought them near the far shore. Lewis was torn off the raft by a willow branch and had to swim for it just as the raft began to sink. The two men hung desperately to the sinking raft and somehow kicked it to solid ground.

At camp that night, the Nez Perce pointed out the way ahead, telling Lewis by signs that if he followed what is now the Blackfoot River he would find a beaten path over the mountains. The Nez Perce were afraid of encountering the Blackfeet, and intended to leave the next morning to search for their Salish friends.

The following morning Lewis gave the Indians deer meat to take back with them, as well as a shirt, a handkerchief, and a little ammunition for their newly acquired guns. The Indians warned him that the Blackfeet would "cut [them] off" and expressed sincere regret at leaving their new friends. Lewis called for a last smoke with "these friendly people," then saddled the horses, and at noon bid them a final adieu. It was the last they would see of the Nez Perce, the tribe that had sustained and guided them both fall and spring.

CLARK SOUTH

C lark and his contingent, including Sacagawea and little Pompi, filed south up the Bitterroot Valley, a lovely valley from ten to fifteen miles wide and surrounded by snowy mountains, the center partially timbered with cottonwood, birch, willows, and pines. Because the Salish Indians regularly burned off the low brush in the valley, there were wide meadows of grass and wildflowers. The column moved through these meadows of clover and "Sweet cented plants, flowers & grass," wading across ten rushing streams flowing from the mountains, several with strong currents.

The next day they pressed on up the valley, fording more streams, the last so deep and powerful that it swept several of the horses down some distance and flowed over the backs and packs of some of the smaller pack animals, soaking some of their goods. They found tracks of two men on the far side of a stream. The Salish and Shoshone seemed to be keeping out of sight. Had the Shoshone guide Old Toby and his son made it back to their village over the snowy Lolo Trail last fall or had they been lost in the mountains? The Corps would never find out.

It was July Fourth, so Clark celebrated the holiday in true American fashion with a big picnic at noon: fat venison and cous roots mush. That night they camped on the north shore of the West Fork of the Bitterroot River and the next morning crossed the river with some difficulty and soon found the East Fork and the trail they had descended the previous fall. There was fresh sign of two horses and a fire that had been left burning to the side of the pathway, but no Indians. Why the Salish or Shoshones would not show themselves was a mystery. It's possible that the campfire was not Salish, but that of a small raiding party of Blackfeet, who often invaded the valley in the spring and would not want to be found by their enemies.

After stopping to dry out their goods, Clark's crew packed up and climbed the mountain into the high valley called Ross's Hole. There they camped, going through the now familiar routines of hobbling the horses, building campfires, skinning deer, roasting venison, boiling roots. When they rolled up in their blankets, the night was so cold Clark couldn't sleep. The moon was waning and the high mountain stars kept him company through another long, restless night.

Sleepless nights, even violent headaches (which Clark had suffered for days on the Lolo Trail) never stopped these men. At Traveler's Rest, Lewis mentions in his journal that two of his men were suffering intensely from symptoms of syphilis they had picked up among the Chinook during the winter months—or among the Mandans the previous winter—but the parties rode on.

On the sixth of July, a light frost lay across the meadows as Clark's party ascended the Bitterroot Mountains, intending to take a western pass, now called Chief Joseph Pass, rather than return over the torturous passage they'd taken the year before. High in the mountains, they found where the trail branched, and took the eastern path, eventually finding the head of a creek now called Trail Creek.

Clark notes old buffalo roads made by mountain buffalo years before, the Indians having cut down and eliminated herds east of the Rockies and within the mountains. They moved down the creek, fording it often, passing hundreds of ground squirrels that whistled at the passing column and scampered to their holes. Reaching a more level plain where the Indian trail went off in several directions, Sacagawea said she knew the place well (It would be near this place that the Nez Perce would one day suffer a sudden and unexpected attack by U.S. soldiers and citizens who were the successors of Lewis and Clark).

After wading the small river, they began moving south and east up the valley of dry grass and sagebrush. Heavy clouds were building over the snowy mountains and they spotted a terrific storm pouring down out of the mountains. Black clouds were dragging dark sheets of rain across the valley. A sharp, cold wind picked up, flinging dust, sand, and sticks. Clark called a halt and grouped his column together and turned their horses' tails to the wind. The storm struck with force, the cold rain slashing horizontally, drenching them in seconds. The column bowed their heads and stood together, taking the onslaught for an hour and a half.

After the cold winds passed away down the valley, the thoroughly soaked and bedraggled column made camp in a small dry timber the storm had missed. Here Clark saw where Shoshone women had dug camas roots, but once again, no Indians were in sight.

They unsaddled their horses, built their fires, ate, and slept.

Next morning, before dawn, they found that their grazing horses had wandered out of sight. Clark sent men in every direction to find them. By six, the men had returned with all but nine. As the missing nine were their best horses, they speculated that they had been stolen by Indians. Nevertheless, Clark left five men to find the horses as the main party packed up and rode on, coming upon a hot spring where Clark experimented by boiling two pieces of meat.

On July 8, Clark's main party arrived at Camp Fortunate. The men of Clark's party who were tobacco chewers were so impatient to get the tobacco they had buried in the caches they "Scercely gave themselves time to take their Saddles off their horses before they were off to the deposit." Clark found "every article Safe, except a little damp. I gave to each man who used tobacco about two feet off a part of a role took one third of the balance myself and put up 2/3 in a box to Send down with the most of the articles which had been left at this place, by the Canoes to Capt. Lewis."

The next day was windy and cold. They hauled the sunken dugouts out of the ponds where they had left them, then washed them and let them dry, repairing one dugout that had split. The five men who had gone in search of the lost horses caught up that day, having overtaken the strays running up their backtrail into the mountains.

The party waited through the morning and afternoon. The cold dry winds were effectively drying the dugouts, so Clark planned to leave the next day.

On July 10, the men awoke to yet another hard frost. They shoved their dugouts into the water, loaded them up, packed a few goods on horses, and set off downriver, the route much easier paddling downstream than pulling upstream the year before: on the first day, they passed six of their encampments of the previous year. Clark rode one of the horses, paralleling the river with the companions he intended to take overland to the Yellowstone River.

As before, beaver dams blocked streams and river, creating pools and lakes and bogs. Countless beavers lay along the banks, sleeping in sunlight, and then, as the horses approached, slapping warnings and slipping into pools. Young geese and ducks were everywhere, sandhill cranes flapped away in pairs, and from the dry hillsides antelope watched. On July 11, they passed the brown, rocky bulk of Beaverhead Mountain as a high wind howled down off the snowy mountains behind them. "The violence of this wind retarded our progress very much," wrote Clark, "and the river being emencly Crooked we had it imediately in our face nearly every bend"—a real problem for the men in the dugouts. "At 6 P M I passed Philanthropy river which I proceved was very low. the wind Shifted about to the N. E. and [blew] very hard tho' much wormer than the forepart of the day." At 7:00 p.m., they encamped at Wisdom River. (They had named the two forks of the Jefferson River Philanthropy and Wisdom to honor the virtues of their president. Philanthropy is now called the Beaverhead River, and Wisdom is, unfortunately, The Big Hole.) After eating, the men sat around their four campfires whittling paddles made from the boards of a pirogue they had left there the year before, and listening to the concussive sounds of beavers continually slapping the water with their tales in the marshes and bogs all around them. Once again, Clark could scarcely sleep.

The next morning he climbed into one of the canoes and the men set out on a strong current. Another hard northwest wind arose "and rendered it very difficuelt to keep the canoes from running against the Shore." By early afternoon, the wind was still strong, and a sudden gust drove Clark's canoe under a log that projected from the bank. The man in the stern was caught between log and canoe. The crew freed the man and after much work freed the canoe, but then the wind drove the canoe under a projecting bank, and the current tipped it. They clambered out into shallow water and began unloading supplies. The men in the following dugouts beached their canoes and forced their way through thick brush and briars to help, but by the time they arrived, Clark's crew had reloaded, shoved their canoe back into the stream, and were off again on the quick current.

On July 13, near the Three Forks of the Missouri, Clark's canoes caught up with the party that had been traveling by horseback led by Sergeant Pryor. The horsemen had killed six deer and a grizzly. They were finally in the land of plenty. From there, according to plan, Clark sent the canoes downriver on the Missouri under Sergeant Ordway to meet Lewis's party to the north. Clark with ten men, and Sacagawea, moved east on horseback over what is now Bozeman Pass to explore the Yellowstone River. Sacagawea was familiar with this land and its rivers, and Clark says of her, "The indian woman who has been of great Service to me as a pilot through this Country recommends a gap in the mountain more South which I shall cross."

It was risky: two parties setting out in different directions and hoping to coordinate their travels with a distant third party to meet finally at the confluence of the Yellowstone and Missouri Rivers.

BLACKFEET

After leaving their Nez Perce guides in the Bitterroot Valley and crossing the continental divide at a pass now called Lewis and Clark's Pass, Lewis and his party made their way down to the high plains where they shot two elk and a brown bear. They were back in bear country. Patrick Gass and John Thompson, who had been sent ahead on horseback to set up camp, were chased by a big grizzly. The men were afraid to fire upon the pursuing bear lest their shots spook their Indian horses, which were unaccustomed to gunshots, but they managed to keep ahead of the charging bear, and it eventually slowed to a walk and turned away.

That evening they saw vast herds of buffalo down in the Missouri River Valley. Lewis says there must have been 10,000 within a circle of two miles. Huge packs of wolves followed the buffalo. It was mating season for the buffalo and "the bulls keep a tremendious roaring. We could hear them for many miles and there are such numbers of them that there is one continual roar"—which spooked their horses.

The next day they shot eleven buffalo and set about cutting the meat and making two canoes of willow limbs and skins. They used these to transport meat and goods across to the south side of the Missouri, which here was about 100 yards wide and crowded with islands. Reaching the other side, they dug up a cache from the year before, but high waters had ruined much of what they had buried, including all the plant specimens Lewis had collected—a real disappointment.

Lewis left three men at the river to recover the white pirogue that had been hidden there while he took three men to explore the Marias River. Here, near the Great Falls of the Missouri, a man was again attacked by a grizzly. McNeal's horse came within ten feet of the bear in heavy brush without seeing or scenting the bear. Suddenly the horse jumped away, throwing McNeal at the bear's feet. The grizzly stood up on its hind legs to give battle, and McNeal leaped to his feet and slammed the butt of his rifle on the bear's head. The gun snapped off at the breach, which stunned and cut the bear, knocking it to the ground. While it pawed its head with its rear feet, McNeal ran for a nearby willow and scrambled up before the bear could recover. It got to its feet and walked over to the tree, where it waited for him for hours, finally leaving late in the evening. After some time, McNeal slid carefully down from the tree, tracked his horse for two miles through the late twilight, caught up with it, and returned to camp with his broken musket.

Lewis remarks, "there seems to be a sertain fatality attatched to the neighbourhood of these falls, for there is always a chapter of accedents prepared for us during our residence at them." And the mosquitoes were again a scourge. They "continue to infest us in such manner that we can scarcely exist: for my own part," writes Lewis, "I am confined by them to my bier at least 3/4ths of the time." The dog Seaman "even howls with the torture he experiences from them, they are almost insupportable, they are so numerous that we frequently get them in our throats as we breath[e]."

More trouble lay ahead. After Lewis left Gass and two men on the river with the white pirogue, he rode away with Drewyer and the Fields brothers, excellent hunters, to explore the Marias River. For days they rode alongside the river over hills of buffalo grass seeing distant mountains to the west. Finally, they turned back after determining that the river bent westward into the Rockies and did not, as Lewis had hoped, continue north into Canada.

On their return, the four men at last encountered the dreaded Blackfeet. This was the tribe the Shoshones, the Salish, and the Nez Perce had warned them of. They were allied to the British of Canada from whom they purchased rifles and ammunition, which gave them a distinct advantage over their southern enemies. Lewis spotted about 30 horses on a river bluff and thought there might be as many Blackfeet. He knew that running would indicate he was their enemy, so he approached a group of eight who were peering down into the river bottom, apparently watching Drewyer who was down there hunting.

When Lewis and the Fields brothers got within a quarter mile of the Indians, one of the Blackfeet leaped on his horse and charged to within a hundred paces, reined up hard, then turned and galloped back to his friends, who mounted up and began walking their horses toward Lewis and the brothers. Lewis was convinced that "if they thought themselves sufficiently strong, they would attempt to rob us in which case be their numbers what they would I should resist to the last extremity prefereing death to that of being deprived of my papers instruments and gun."

Fortunately there were only eight, though several more horses were saddled nearby. When Drewyer eventually climbed the bluffs and joined them, they were able to communicate with sign language and the two groups agreed to camp together.

Lewis kept the first watch around the campfire, shaking Rueben Fields awake near midnight to take the next watch. About daylight, the Indians woke up and crowded around the fire. Joseph Fields, who was on watch, had laid his gun down behind him and the leader of the little band of Indians slipped behind him and snatched it up. At the same instant, two others seized Drewyer's and Lewis's guns. Fields, seeing this, turned to pick up his rifle and saw the leader sprinting away with both his and his brother's guns. He shouted and his brother Rueben leaped up, understood the situation, drew his knife, and chased the Indian. Running him down after 50 or 60 yards, he stabbed him "to the heart with his knife the fellow ran about 15 steps and fell dead."

Meanwhile, Drewyer awakened as an Indian grabbed his gun. He instantly jumped up and wrestled it away, crying out, "Damn you! Let go my gun!"

Lewis rolled out of his blanket asking, "What's the matter? What's the matter?" He turned to reach for his rifle only to see an Indian running away with it. Lewis drew his pistol and sprinted after the Indian, shouting for him to lay the gun down. The Indian stopped, laid the rifle in the grass, turned slowly, and walked away. The Fields brothers, running up with their rifles, wanted to shoot the man, but Lewis said no.

Several of the Blackfeet, seeing that they had lost the guns, ran for the horses, driving not only their own horses before them, but the Corps' horses. Lewis shouted to fire on the Indians, then turned to follow a young warrior who was running to join a companion already driving off some of the horses. "At the distance of three hundred paces they entered one of those steep nitches in the bluff with the horses before them." Lewis was nearly out of breath and could pursue no further. He called to them as he had done several times before that he would shoot them if they did not give him his horses. Of course they didn't understand a word. He raised his pistol and one of them jumped behind a rock and shouted to the other, who, armed with a rifle, turned toward Lewis, thirty steps away. Lewis fired, shooting him through the belly. The Indian fell to his knees, rolled onto his right elbow and fired at Lewis, the shot singing past Lewis's head ("I felt the wind of his bullet very distinctly," writes Lewis). Without his shot pouch, Lewis ran back to camp. By this time, Drewyer had captured several of the Indian horses, and was saddling them and throwing packs on others. After the Fields brothers returned with four more horses, they loaded on some of the buffalo meat the Indians had left. Lewis took time to gather four shields, and the bows, arrows, and quivers the Indians had left behind. He threw them all on the fire.

The party then set off at a gallop.

They rode all day, resting their horses for two hours at evening, carefully watching their back trail, and then set out by moonlight and traveled more slowly. Heavy thunderclouds were building around them as they moved on through occasional moonlight. Through the long night, they passed immense herds of buffalo, the bulls fighting and bellowing, some of them catching wind of the party and pounding away in the dark, till around two in the morning, the men turned their horses out to graze and lay down to rest in the plain "very much fatiegued as may be readily conceived."

They awoke at daybreak so sore from the ride they could scarcely stand. They hobbled about, saddling their Indian ponies, then stiffly mounted and rode on, finally reaching the Missouri River just as the white pirogue with Gass and his men came paddling down the river from their camp at Great Falls—perfect timing.

They loaded the canoes, left the horses behind, and set off down the river, intending to encounter Clark and his men at the mouth of the Yellowstone.

Ten days later they came to the mouth of the Yellowstone River. Clark and his party had earlier left a note on a pole, not wanting to wait because game was scarce and mosquitoes were thick. Lewis found a remnant of the note and hurried on down the river. Within days, they caught up with Clark and his whole party. The Corps of Discovery was reunited, though Lewis had been wounded. The day before, Cruzatte had accidentally shot Lewis through his left thigh while they were hunting for elk in thick brush on an island. Clark's party reported some trouble, too: several days before, they had lost all 50 of their horses to raiding Crow Indians.

The united Corps made their way on down the Missouri, dropped off Charbonneau, Sacagawea and Pompi at their Mandan village, paid Charbonneau for his services, and then descended the Missouri, finally returning to civilization near the end of September.

They were celebrated everywhere, and their maps and journals encouraged rapid westward expansion, initially for the fur trade, as was intended, and then, inevitably, for settlement.

NEZ PERCE
FLIGHT TOWARD FRE

BEAR PAW
BATTLEFIELD

BIG HOLE
BATTLEFIELD

CANYON CREEK
BATTLEFIELD

CAMAS MEADOW
BATTLEFIELD

THE LOLO AGAIN

Lewis and Clark's was not the only epic journey that passed up the Lolo Trail and through the Bitterroot Valley. The very tribe that by the Corps' own accounts helped them most, that had fed them, sheltered them, guided them, and cared for their horses, would, over the next decades be pressed into ever smaller sections of their ancient homeland where they would be harried by settlers, invaded and harassed by gold miners, and hemmed in by the U. S. military. When war finally broke out, the U.S. army would chase over 700 members of several Nez Perce bands up the Lolo Trail, through the Bitterroot Valley, over Chief Joseph Pass, and along the valley that led to Camp Fortunate—retracing Clark's return trip.

***

Alex, Justin, and I drive up Highway 12 where Alex and I had hitch-hiked. We pass our failed entry point to Wendover Ridge, and drive on to the Lochsa Lodge where the mayor, Kevin Poole, had dropped us off. After consuming our hefty ration of hamburgers, salads, blackberry cobblers, and ice cream, it's three in the afternoon when we leave our car and start pushing our fully loaded bicycles up the gravel road that leads to the Lolo Trail. The road cuts back north into the mountains about a mile above the Lochsa Lodge, four miles east of where Alex and I started in the last time. This time I know where to find the Lolo.

We've strapped our gear down on the racks attached to the back wheels of the three bicycles. My bear pistol is wedged beneath bungee cords on top of our sleeping bags and tent. The sun is high and hot, even at this elevation, and there's little shade along the white gravel road. A few hundred yards up the road along the only flat stretch we'll encounter over the entire afternoon, we climb on our bikes and start pedaling. We pass a road crew laying down new gravel, but within a few hundred yards, the road veers up the mountain and we dismount. Then it's up, up, pushing our loaded bikes. The sweat is pouring down my forehead and into my eyes. I can't see. Shirtless Alex hands me his bandana. I wipe my eyes and hand it back, but he tells me to keep it. I wipe my eyes again and tie the blue bandana around my head.

Alex and I agree it's not nearly as difficult to push loaded bicycles up the mountain as it is to carry 60-pound backpacks, but it's still serious work and as the air thins we find ourselves stopping to rest in shady spots every fifteen or twenty minutes. Justin is in good shape and by nature a stubborn soul. He can outdistance me a long way if he wants to, but he keeps a steady pace and waits in shady spots when I fall behind.

After a couple of hours, we're still climbing, still hoping for our first joyous downhill. One forested ridge leads to another, higher one, which climbs into another. We keep pushing on and up for five or six hours more and gain only eight sweaty miles according to the map.

Finally, the road bends over another of its interminable turns and eases downhill. At last! We step onto our bikes and begin rolling: down around bends, bouncing over ruts and rocks, twisting left and right, the three of us elated, the wind cooling our sweaty faces. Braking down the steeper slopes, we ride for one downhill mile to Papoose Saddle where signs inform us that we've reached the Lolo Motorway, Forest Service Trail 500, which is very good news to us. The bad news is that Trail 500 immediately starts climbing. It's too steep a grade for us to pedal with our bike racks loaded, so we have no choice but to start pushing once again. Step by step. Up and up. Alex mentions that he could use a pack horse.

About seven in the evening, a dark blue SUV rolls up the road behind us. The slim young man behind the wheel used to work for the Forest Service: "fire fighter, timber sales, pretty much everything." He's now a landscape architect in Coeur d'Alene. He says he comes up every summer to camp and hike.

He wishes us well and drives on up the single sandy lane. We keep pushing. The road is still ascending the ridge lines. The trees along the mountain have been swept by a forest fire that caught this steep slope and parts of the next one. All the slopes are steep, and the gravel-sand road just keeps on winding and climbing. The sunlight is intense.

By sunset, we're still shoving our loaded bikes, feeling "much fortigued," as Lewis would have it. Deep, dark shadows have risen out of the valleys and submerged all but the highest peaks, which take on the appearance of green islands scattered across a wine-dark sea. It must be around nine or ten in the evening; my watch has quit working and our cell phones are useless up here, so we can judge time of day only by the sun—and the summer sun drops late in these northern climes. We're hungry and exhausted, but there isn't a single level place to plant a tent, and we haven't seen water for miles. The slopes plunge down at what looks like a 45-degree angle. A carpenter would call this a 6-12 or 7-12 pitch, almost impossible to walk up without sliding back down. On and on. We could stake our tents on the road itself, but I had a friend who once slept in his tent right beside a road, and a drunk in a pickup ran him over.

Halting for another rest, I look back. The last, long, jagged ridge on the horizon far to the south stands above the tree line, catching the fading red light of the setting sun. It looks like the serrated edge of a long, blood-streaked stone knife. Along this very trail we're climbing, the Nez Perce fled for their lives. Through seven decades of friction with whites, the Nez Perce never fought the Americans, even when surrounding tribes did. In 1855, various bands of the Nez Perce agreed to a treaty with the United States which allowed them to keep almost 8,000,000 acres of their homeland. But in 1877, the U.S. government reduced their reservation to 700,000 acres, less than a tenth of what they had agreed to in the earlier treaty.

General Oliver O. Howard, a Civil War veteran, was sent to force the outlying bands of Nez Perce into this terrifically reduced reservation. This story has often been told and I will not retell the entire story here, but the irony remains: the very people who saved the Lewis and Clark expedition, the same tribe that fed them, pastured their horses over the winter, and guided them back over the Lolo Trail were driven out of a homeland they had defended for perhaps 10,000 years. They would become illegal emigrants as the real illegal immigrants (according to treaties signed by both parties) chased them into Canada or imprisoned them in Kansas and Oklahoma.

With fewer than 200 fighting men, over 550 women and children, and a herd of well over 2000 horses and pack mules, the bands of the Nez Perce who had refused to sign the latest treaty (often referred to as the non-treaties) fought several times with U. S. citizens and soldiers in what is now Idaho, then fled across the Clearwater River to the Weippe Prairie (the place Clark had first met the Nez Perce). 750 Indians prepared to make their way over the difficult Lolo Trail.

WATCHERS

Justin, Alex, and I push on up the long and winding Lolo Trail. Always up. The light in the west is almost gone and the mountains fall away into a somber darkness. We're exhausted, hungry, and thirsty, having reserved just enough water for our evening meal.

Justin points out a little ridge below the road. He says we can slide down and set up our tents on the rocky, humpy ground beneath some pines, but I take a look at it and tell him we need to push on. On we push, the bicycle pedals catching our shins and ankles and leaving scrapes and blood and scabs. A turquoise glow in the far west outlines the distant mountains and the road climbs ever upward, the ridgeline where the Nez Perce herded their horses never far above us on our right. The high heat of afternoon is long gone; we stop to pull on shirts and jackets and resume shoving our loaded bicycles up the winding, sandy road, three hobbling shadows struggling over a rocky roadway.

Coming around a bend, we see that at last, at long last, we have reached the top of the high ridge. In deep shadows to our right, we can make out a pale circle of stones where someone once built a fire. We push into the clearing and lean our bikes against pine trunks, unstrap our bundles, and begin setting up our two tents while Alex goes for wood. We're clearly the first campers to camp here this year, so there are plenty of fallen branches and snow-broken trees for firewood. The two tents blossom as Alex drags in branches and one heavy tree trunk.

I collect some dried grass and pine needles, snap off little sticks and build my usual stick tepee over the kindling. I reach in my pocket for the plastic lighter and soon have the fire going. I shake out the tote bag that holds our pans, and pour most of our remaining water into one pan. By the time the water boils, we've gathered around the fire. I pour the boiling water into the freeze-dried containers, and we sit back, drink a little bottled water, and eat. It's a big fire circle and we've stacked on the limbs. The yellow flames lap up the dried wood and leap for the sky, sending sparks careening into the still night air, constellations of sparks floating into the stars.

Sore but happy, we three lie back against a big log near the fire and gaze into the sky: "all the firefolk sitting in the air." There is no moon, so the stars are intense and many, the same star patterns that Lewis and Clark watched 200 years ago, the same circling companions of the Nez Perce in 1877. Not long ago in the course of cosmic affairs, but a long time in human affairs.

The black landscape has lifted us high into the ancient sky, sky that gives the illusion that change can be arrested, for these mountains remain, and this ancient, braided trail still wanders the same ridges, that Lewis and Clark walked just last September when the snow was falling, and returned the same afternoon. On the Weippe Prairie, the Nez Perce camped just weeks ago.

Gathered on the high, rolling prairie of the Weippe in makeshift shelters (they had lost many of their tepees and tepee poles in a two-day battle with General Howard's men), the headmen of the various bands—Looking Glass, White Bird, Toohoolhoolzote, Thunder Rolling Up the Mountain (or Chief Joseph) and his brother the war chief Ollokot—debated whether to flee over the Lolo Trail or stay and continue to fight for their homeland. Chief Joseph made an impassioned speech, arguing that if they were not fighting for their homeland, what were they fighting for? How could they leave the graves of their fathers? But most of the assembled men sided with Looking Glass who thought they could find refuge with the Crow tribe whom he had helped in a recent conflict with the Sioux. Joseph and his brother Ollokot didn't like it, but decided not to abandon the tribe.

An old medicine man named Wind With Him rode into the Nez Perce camp on the Weippe. He was looking for his son, Speaking Thunder. He told his son, "I want you home with me. Death awaits you on the trail you are taking. It is dark with blood! I do not want to know you are killed. All going will die or see bondage." A rather accurate prediction as it turned out.

But his son refused to leave the exiles. Tears came into the old man's eyes. "I am willing," he said, "that you go. It is all right for you to go help fight. But soldiers are too many." His son did fight through the whole 1200-mile retreat, but was taken prisoner in the last battle near the Bear Paw Mountains in northern Montana and died an exile in Indian Territory in Oklahoma, never seeing his father again.

The next morning the bands set out up the difficult Lolo: 750 men, women, and children, driving the loose horses and mules before them up the twisting trails through thick forests and brushy meadows, along rushing streams, on up onto the rocky ridgelines. They camped that first night near Mussel Creek where they waded into the cold waters to collect mussels, for they knew how to live off the land.

When I was a boy, trying to live off the land in Kansas, I once picked up a mussel from a muddy creek, roasted it that evening in the coals of my campfire, rolled the blackened shell out of the ashes with a stick, let it cool a little, then pried open the shell with my hunting knife, and ate, or rather, chewed. It tasted like creek mud and chewing took a long time. That mussel, with a small, roasted dove and a leafy wad of boiled dock (a weed so fibrous that no amount of chewing would allow me to swallow) was my evening meal. By morning I was famished. My skinny, teenage body carried little body fat, so I left my backpack on the side of the hill and walked back down the valley across fields of milo and potatoes to my friend Mark's house, where I caught a ride home.

It turned out to be a most peculiar day. I suspect my hunger and ignorance saved my life. That afternoon several tornados ripped through that valley, one of them stripping Mark's house to its wooden floor, scattering lumber and shingles across the fields, carefully setting down a coffee table in a pasture a quarter mile away; the table still held a vase with a single long-stem rose. A passing love gift from the raging winds.

From their picture window, Mark's family, with my older brother who was visiting them that day, had been watching two twisting monsters as they writhed and ripped their way down the little valley. All ran for the basement but the boys. Then, as the slashing winds leaned hard against the house, one of the roaring, spinning monsters turned toward them, and the boys scampered down the basement stairs just as the tornado, with a mighty roar, swept the first floor clear of roof and walls. All below survived unhurt.

I was by that time already home, where one of the marauding tornados tracked me down. Peering out a ground-level window with my parents and little sister, I saw the trees of the adjacent orchard shoved down flat against the ground as the air went grey with whirling debris. Briefly, the air cleared, and the apple trees stood back up, trembling. Then the chaos returned, whipping the trees flat in the opposite direction, tearing some of them up by the roots, then demolishing the roof of the Baptist church next door.

The next day, when I returned to my abandoned campsite to retrieve my backpack and sleeping bag, I found that a tornado had ripped through the creekside forest just feet from my camping spot, tearing havoc through the trees, rending the trunks and branches, ripping the forest into a mangled confusion of splintered trunks and shattered limbs. If I had stayed there that afternoon and been cooking the snapping turtle I found I had caught on a baited bank line, I would have run for lower ground, directly into howling destruction.

Justin spots a falling star and then Alex sees one. I keep looking up from the fire too late to catch their quick bright lives. In time we're all gazing into the flames as the fire heats up a bed of red coals. It's cold on the high mountain, but our thirsts keep returning, and we share the last of our water. We lie there talking of times gone by, laughing at memories, wondering whether we will be able to push on if the roads keep rising as they have through this long afternoon and evening. We've traveled twelve or thirteen miles, almost all of it on foot. We have enough food for five or six days more; 80 or 90 miles of ridge and rock and forest lie ahead.

Justin points out a satellite passing slowly among the stars. Soon we all see it, a distant light moving through the black limbs of nearby pines, a lone wanderer of the skies, still attracted to earth, looking down upon this swirling black marble of sea and continent and cloud. I would not trade this rich world for a flight into deep space. Old Edward Abbey had it right: "I'd sooner exchange ideas with the birds on earth than learn to carry on intergalactic communications with some obscure race of humanoids on a satellite planet from the world of Betelgeuse. First things first."

After a few minutes, Justin says, "There's something out there."

"Where?"

He points. "Out there. See it?"

We do see: a pale, ghostlike deer in the faint light, perhaps a buck, standing beneath the dark trees like some ancient watcher of the pri-meval forest. The figure drops its head and moves, then looks up, step-ping through the farthest glow of the fire just this side of the trees, then fades into the black forest wall.

But to what shall we awake? That thoughtful traveler, Hilaire Belloc, found himself one night in an old inn he had long loved in his beloved corner of England. He sat before a fire beneath a low, black ceiling hung with candles and conversed with a stranger who had just come in from the night. Belloc argued that "Color is for the eyes and music is for the ears," and therefore our thirst for something that will not perish, our deep desire for a permanent good, is evidence that there is an imperishable life. The stranger from the night surprisingly agreed with him and said, "I have sometimes seen it clearly, that when the disappointed quest was over, all this journeying would turn out to be but the beginning of a much greater adventure, and that I should set out towards another place where every sense should be fulfilled, and where the fear of mutation should be at rest."

And Belloc said to him, "You think, then, that some immortal part in us is concerned not only with our knowledge, but with our every feeling, and that our final satisfaction will include a sensual pleasure: fragrance, and landscape, and a visible home that shall be dearer even than these dear hills?"

The man stared into the fire, shrugged, and said, "Something of the sort." His shoulders were broad and "conveyed in their attitude that effect of mingled strength and weariness which is common to all who have travelled far and with great purpose, perpetually seeking some worthy thing which they could never find."

And here we lie, our heads on a log on a clear August night beneath a black ceiling hung with stars. The cold deepens. A stick snaps and throws sparks erratically into the Milky Way. The fire settles to burn quietly, as if meditating its own demise. The red light reveals the quiet faces of my sons, the smoke swerving sometimes this way, sometimes that, the sharp scent catching us, blinding us and turning us away.

Justin has always wanted his own way, and like all of us, his own pleasure, which makes us all sometimes disagreeable companions. He married, had two lovely daughters, then had an affair that shattered his marriage and his relationships with all of us. Miraculously, his wife forgave and took him back, but a stubborn vein of hard, glittering iron pyrite runs through his generous heart and it often makes him a solitary prospector. The young often believe that rebellion is an expression of freedom, that rules restrict and laws imprison, but that old Kentucky poet Wendell Berry is right when he looks up at the sky and sings, "The cloud is free only/ to go with the wind./ The rain is free/ only in falling./ The water is free only/ in its gathering together,/ in its downward courses,/ in its rising into air./ In law is rest/ if you love the law,/ if you enter, singing, into it/ as water in its descent." Berry also says of the marriage commitment: "Forsaking all others, we/ are true to all." It follows that forsaking the beloved, we are true to none, least of all, to self.

But I was once a rebel too. Each child turns from home and wanders away. Only in ready forgiveness and persistent love is union possible. And I am happy Justin has come with us, joined with us, and made us a family again.

Suddenly, Justin is quoting an old poem we memorized when he was a boy. Each word falling quietly into place: "On a starred night Prince Lucifer uprose./ Tired of his dark dominion swung the fiend/ Above the rolling ball in cloud part screen'd,/ Where sinners hugged their spectre of repose./ Poor prey to his hot fit of pride were those./ And now upon his western wing he leaned,/ Now his huge bulk o'er Afric's sands careened,/ Now the black planet shadowed Arctic snows./ Soaring through wider zones that pricked his scars/ With memory of the old revolt from Awe,/ He reached a middle height, and at the stars,/ Which are the brain of heaven, he looked, and sank/ Around the ancient track marched, rank on rank,/ The army of unalterable law."

I am watching Justin's face in the light. "I can't believe you still remember every word of that poem," I say. "It's been what? twenty years since you recited that with your sisters on their way to that little country school house?"

Justin smiles and watches the fire. Neither of us can remember the poet's name, and I have forgotten most of the words, but each word has returned to him these long years later. "A word has power," says N. Scott Momaday, "in and of itself. It comes from nothing into sound and meaning." Riding words we find a mountain campsite among the Nez Perce; upon words sacred and profane we make our own journeys over the edge of the sky.

***

Near Mussel Creek, the Nez Perce were building their evening fires and roasting mussels when a scout named Wetyettamaweyun (I Give No Orders) rode into camp shouting, "Soldiers coming! I am wounded!" He had been shot through his upper arm.

One of the headmen gave the order to move camp a half mile off the trail. As they packed their supplies on the horses, a number of warriors rode away to watch the back trail. Night came on and no soldiers appeared. Sometime around midnight, a leader told half the men to return to camp. The seventeen who stayed waited through the long night.

The next morning, they followed an experienced leader named Rainbow back toward the Weippe Prairie, trying to locate their pursuers. They eventually approached a small creek. There they heard a voice through the trees, then a second one speaking the Nez Perce language, saying, "There are fresh tracks. Tracks made this morning."

Rainbow and the others dismounted, tied their horses, and waited in the thickets near the stream. The approaching Indians were a handful of General Howard's Nez Perce scouts, members of the *treaty* Nez Perce who had chosen to stay on the new reservation. As the scouts rode up the trail, the seventeen hidden in the trees opened fire, knocking from his horse a young Nez Perce scout named John Levi and wounding two others. All but John Levi wheeled their horses about and galloped away. When Rainbow's men dismounted and lifted the young man from where he lay wounded, they saw he was still alive. They recognized him, but no one said anything. One of the warriors cocked his rifle and shot him through the heart.

TREEFALLS

I crawl from my sleeping bag, unzip the tent door and peer out into a bright mountain morning. A buck with a full, velvet-covered rack of horns stands just twenty yards away beneath a pine tree. He's watching me. Then, seemingly unconcerned, he drops his head and noses around near my bicycle, then walks past the ashes of our fire, stopping to sniff. He glances at me over his shoulder, then walks away along the timbered ridge. Apparently we passed his inspection.

We're stiff and sore from the long climb of the previous day, but we're all thirsty and pack up quickly, without eating breakfast, and take to the trail, searching for water. The forest-service road winds between scattered pines along this high, rocky ridge. The morning scent of pine is in the air, and as far as we can see, dark green mountains fall and rise toward granite-peaked horizons. We can pedal the more level sections of the roadway, but we often have to dismount and trudge up steeper slopes.

We live for the downward dashes. Coming to a summit, we mount the bikes and go rattling and bouncing down, swerving around fallen rocks, our packs jumping and shaking behind us. Always too soon the road turns up and we swing reluctantly off our bikes and walk again.

We start finding big patches of snow near the roadway, some of the melt water seeping across the trail. Within a half hour, we find a little rivulet bouncing down from a high ravine through lush green grass and bushes. We stop to drink our fill, then pump full our canteens, water bottles, and camelbacks. So cold, so delicious.

The sun rises above the mountains and the heat returns. We dismount and begin pushing up another long slope. A white pickup with a hardbitten little man with a stubble beard roars up the road behind us. A blonde woman with heavy, black eyeliner watches us from the passenger seat. We stand aside and nod as he guns the engine past us. In time the road levels out. We mount up again and pedal along the boulder-strewn ridge. Suddenly the road turns and drops away along the mountain side and we're flying and crying out like mountain jays, bouncing and turning, the wind in our faces, the road dropping swiftly. Speed and rest combined: it's the American ideal. But too soon the road twists back up the long mountain and we're reduced to life as two-legged animals, shoving our loaded bikes up through strong sunlight.

About midmorning we come upon Keith, the landscape architect's campsite. He is camped beside a huge snowbank that covers the road. "I thought I'd see you guys sometime this morning," he says. "I didn't want to bottom out plowing through the snow, so I just stopped here for the night. Some other guy came by this morning and plowed right on through, but I'm going to take a hike." He slings on his backpack. Just then, the white pickup we'd seen go by us an hour before comes plowing back through the snowbank, the truck veering off the road to where the snow is only two feet deep, the motor roaring, the truck sliding and fishtailing, finally four-wheeling it to a stop on dry roadway.

The tough little man with the stubble beard climbs out, a long-barreled pistol strapped to his belt. He rubs a hand over his chin and steps through the wet snow. The woman with bleached blond hair and the heavy eyeliner climbs out the other side of the truck.

He has a high, raspy voice: "We couldn't get through down there," he says. "Big tree fallen across the road." He looks at our bicycles. "You guys shouldn't have no trouble. You can get around it or under it." The two of them are out for a high-mountain drive, and this seems to be their limit. "The Forest Service," he says, "ain't made it up this far to cut out the treefalls yet, so we're head'n on back."

We bid them all goodbye and push our way around and through the snowbank, then mount up, and stand on our pedals, cruising down the winding road, vibrating over the rock-pitted surface.

We brake before a big ponderosa pine fallen across the road. It's two feet in diameter, angling down from the upper slope, leaving just sliding room for us to lay our bikes down and push them under. Justin, with his strength, takes his bicycle to the lower edge of the road and lifts and pushes it through and over the branches and trunk.

Then it's down and down, swerving, leaning, braking, vast trees-capes of fir and spruce and pine greeting us at every turn, some slopes scattered with standing dead trees, others burned, others thick with living firs. Often the great trees rise high on both sides, deeply shad-owing the path for hundreds of yards, a complicated tunnel of green light. The melting snows seep and pool across the road, our tires skitter through puddles and wet sand. Then our passage turns around a heavy mountain shoulder, opening again to vast vistas of receding mountains held by the high mountain sun: "the solace of fierce landscapes."

We swerve down the mountain and watch each other leaning left then right, ripping through patches of slushy snow, pumping up surfaces of cracked limestone, each anxious that the others not slip or slide or tumble down one of those precipitous slopes. We ride our brakes until the slope levels, then rises, stand on our pedals and pump hard while clicking down through the gears as the slope increases, till we can't pump any longer.

Panting, we swing off our bikes and start pushing again.

Once, after a long decline to a low saddle between ridges, we stop to drink and check our supplies. Justin's can of sunscreen has rattled out from under the bungees. He's always had sensitive skin and needs the stuff. He leans his bike against the roadside bank and walks back up the road searching. Alex and I sit down in the shade to rest.

Forty-five minutes later, Justin returns with a smile, having located the sunscreen. We eat granola bars, drink more water, and start the long push up the next mountain.

It goes on like this through the long morning and heated afternoon: much more time spent pushing up than time riding down. Treefalls occasionally block our way, but Justin is strong enough to lift our bikes over the larger trunks or we push the bikes around or over smaller branches. It's grueling work. Once, catching up to Justin, who has been waiting in the shade of some pines, I lay my bike down and lean over, panting. I look up and ask my sons, "How'd I talk you guys into this?"

They both laugh, and Alex says, "I think you sold us with the trail mix and granola bar offer."

Later, afternoon clouds rise over the mountains, and a cool breeze catches us on the western slopes. We climb and push our way up a steep grade and begin finding fallen trees at almost every turn. A storm has knocked havoc into this section of mountain forest. The treefalls are a great deal of work: Justin will climb over the fallen trunk and one of us will push his loaded bike into and through the stiff branches as Justin, with his solid strength, lifts and pulls. We do the same for the next two bicycles. Then it's on up and around another turn where there's another treefall or two. The clouds darken and rain comes, falling softly across the mountains, fading the far slopes, darkening the sandy road. We push on through the showers, losing ourselves in thought. For me, the rain is full of ghosts: mounted Indians strung out for miles along these ridgeline trails, moving through blue-green forests that fold and fade into the rainy mountains. Old men and young women hunch over their mustang ponies, their wet heads bowed against a gusting rain, the dogs pacing between the horses across pine needles and through wet bear grass, boulders and brush. Children of six and eight and nine, already expert riders, are wrapped in wet blankets or buffalo robes, rocking to the movements of their horses as they ride the high mountains they have never seen before, with the recent screams of their mothers and sisters and the blast of incoming artillery from the two-day Clearwater Battle still cutting their dreams. Horses snuffle and blow and slip as they make the hard ascent, and children lean forward with the clink of pots and pans and bracelets muffled in the hush of the falling rain. Older boys and young men ride out ahead, moving hundreds of loose horses steadily up along the ridges and down the braided trails, the shadowed shapes of roans and buckskins, reds, and blacks, and appaloosas threading through the dripping pines and spruces and firs, jumping over fallen timber, maneuvering through jumbled granite and treefalls. Behind them they hear the cry of a baby who will not sleep in its mother's arms, and it all becomes an image of Meriwether Lewis and William Clark, Patrick Gass and Rueben Fields, Drewyer and Charbonneau, York and the big dog Seaman, young Sacagawea and her baby following their Nez Perce guides on this same trail seven decades before.

For us, the sudden rain passes, and with the sun, the heat returns. A mountain grouse paces across the road just ahead and walks sedately up the steep gravel of the slope above, as if we're no real bother at all. While we watch, a bright green hummingbird swoops close in a sudden whir, hangs before a cluster of choke-cherry flowers, and flashes away, "a resonance of emerald."

On we go. Sometimes we push the bikes up off the road and force our way through bear grass and bushes to get around large fallen trees. Having pushed and pulled over maybe thirteen or fourteen trees in the space of two hours, we finally find a downslope and off we go again. After two miles of leaning around corners and sliding through snow-banks, we stop to check our gear and discover my pistol has jumped its bungee cord and disappeared. It's a depressing thought to lose an expensive .357 magnum we've brought along for bear protection, so

my two sons volunteer to walk back up the road and scout around for
the pistol, giving their old man a needed rest. It's more lost time, but I
don't mind sitting in the shade, breathing in the day.

Two hours later they come walking down the road and I see them
smile. Having investigated every treefall we pushed through, Justin
thought to lift up a spruce limb just below the road and found the silver
pistol: good news, but the delay has cost us hours. If we keep this pace,
we won't have enough food to get us to the Weippe Prairie.

Now we make sure our canteens and packs and tents are cinched
tight with flat straps; the bungees are too flexible to hold on the shaking
downslopes. I strap the pistol to my belt.

***

Late that evening we camp again, where others before us have built
stone-circle fires. But again there's no water on this high ridge, so Justin
suggests we melt the snow from a nearby snowbank as Lewis and Clark
did. It takes time. You scoop up pans of snow, and set them to melt
over the fire. As the snow in the pan melts down, you scoop up more
gritty snow and push it into the pan, wait for it to melt, scoop up more
till the pan is full. Finally, to avoid disease, you bring the water to a
boil for at least a minute, then pour the boiling water into canteens and
bury them in the snow to cool down. The water tastes of smoke—and
iodine pills, which we begin using because it takes too long for the water
to boil and cool.

The fire burns hot and the stars burn cold in the black sky. We sit
on rocks or stand near the fire holding out our sore hands to the heat,
tossing on limbs as the fire subsides. Justin sits on a stump and unwinds
the long, stretchy bandage from his wounded hand, then peels away the
stained gauze. There's a white border of skin growing around the wound
that covers the heel of his hand, but it will take weeks to heal properly.
He smears on the antibiotic salve and lays on clean gauze, then wraps
the stretchy blue bandage several times around his hand. It's looking
better than the night before. The first day he'd wrapped the gauze with

duct tape, thinking it would better shield his hand from the constant rub of the bicycle handle, but when he ripped off the duct tape that night, the gauze beneath was soaked and his hand was wet and puckered as if he'd been swimming for hours.

We're all exhausted and soon retreat to our tents, but Alex and I haven't been keeping up our readings of the hobbits' journey, so inside our tent, after we slide into our sleeping bags, I read of their wonderful stay in the valley of Rivendell where the sunlight is golden and the air is woven with the sounds of running and falling waters, and the evening scented with trees and flowers. Frodo is recovering from a terrible wound, but his friends are with him and old Gandalf the wizard has returned. They sit and speak of many things, but especially of the Dark Lord "whose power," says Gandalf, "is again stretching out over the world."

The Nez Perce were, like the hobbits and their "fellowship of the ring," fleeing directly toward the lands held by the power that opposed them. But the Indians held no magic ring with which to destroy its growing power, and the tribe's danger increased with every mile they traveled, for the great power of the East had been growing for three-hundred years and its messages were sent on magical wires, its armies carried at speed on fire-breathing beasts along tracks of steel, and its determination to conquer was relentless.

The next morning we dig our water bottles and canteens from the dirty snowbank and drink cold, smoky, medicated water. As the boys break camp and pack the bikes, I cook up some oatmeal and brew some coffee. We've been eating too much of our freeze-dried evening meals, and have enough left for only three days. It looks like we'll be living on oatmeal and beef jerky for a day or two—better food than Lewis and Clarks' dried soup.

The day turns hot and the up-mountain pushing is the usual sweaty ordeal. The great, blue-green mountains, a vast ocean of stone and forest, roll away on every side, rippling into pale summits that lap the distant horizons. Sometime around noon we come to a clearing along a high ridgeline where fir trees scatter dark pools of shade across the trail. Far down a steep, open slope of broken granite sprinkled with yellow wild-flowers, we see a still, blue lake. We're hot, so Justin and Alex decide to go swimming. I'm not up for the long, precipitous hike down, nor the longer climb back up, so I sit back and rest in the sunlight as they find their meticulous way down, slowly diminishing to tiny figures clambering over rockfalls far below.

Bees hum in the afternoon sunlight, moving between flowers that cluster among the rocks, competing with swerving flies for the nectar of purple lupine, bluebells, and yellow stonecrop. A half hour later I see the boys' naked bodies, so small they're just flakes in the sun, disappear into the forest near the lake. Soon I hear faint cries as they plunge into the icy water.

An hour later they've climbed their sweaty, dusty way back up and we ride on, weaving, winding, climbing. We seem to have passed the uncut treefalls; here the Forest Service has sawed through any fallen trunks and pushed the pieces to the side (a service the Nez Perce were missing), but General Howard, before setting off in pursuit of the retreating Nez Perce, thought to call in 50 axe men to cut a trail for his cannons and Gatling guns.

PURSUIT AND ESCAPE

After John Levi and the Nez Perce scouts working for General Howard were ambushed, the surviving scouts rode back to Captain Miles's cavalry on the Weippe Prairie and reported. Miles, rather than risk another ambush by pursuing the escaping Indians through thick timber and up the mountainous trail, returned to Howard's main force down on the Clearwater and waited on the general to make up his mind about what he intended to do.

Howard collected supplies and waited on reinforcements, some being sent by rail from as far away as Georgia. Meanwhile, General Philip Sheridan, headquartered in Chicago, telegraphed a message to Colonel John Gibbon, then east of the Rockies on Sun River in Montana, to gather troops to defend Montana settlers in the Bitterroot

Valley. Gibbon, says historian Josephy, was "a vigorous and efficient leader of volunteers in the 'Iron Brigade' in the Civil War and a veteran of the recently concluded campaign against the Sioux." He gathered men from Fort Benton and Fort Baker and set off across the high mountain passes to Missoula in the upper Bitterroot Valley.

After some confusion, Howard gathered his forces on the Weippe Prairie and began the pursuit early on the morning of July 30, five days after the Nez Perce reached the crest of the Lolo Trail and were already descending toward the Bitterroot Valley. Howard had 700 men and 350 pack mules. "In a steady rain," writes West, "men, horses, and mules trudged through a sop of mud. The trail steepened and tapered to a path through thick underbrush, tangled vines, and a forest of white pine and spruce." They found cold, dead horses left by the Indians, and initially had a very hard time pulling the cannons and Gatling guns through the thick stands of trees till the 50 axe men, recruited from Lewiston and the Camas Prairie, caught up and began chopping trail. The forest resounded with the chop of axes, and the cracking, hushing fall of trees.

At night they slept where they could, sometimes stopping for the night on steep ridgelines. Howard's military correspondent, Thomas Sutherland, writes: "According as the tents were pitched, or beds made in them, we slept almost erect or standing on our heads."

***

On a high, open ridge, we three come upon two large rock piles. This was one of the holy places of the Nez Perce. A sign calls it the Indian Post Office, a name that diminishes its significance. This is likely the place where Lewis and Clark stopped to smoke at the insistence of their Nez Perce guides. It was a place of prayer. Lewis and Clark seemed little inclined to pray, but stopped because their guides desired it. When religion is lost, the world loses a deep dimension, a profound way of seeing. "Now," says essayist Annie Dillard, "we are no longer primitive; now the whole world seems not-holy. We have drained the light from the boughs in the sacred grove and snuffed it in the high places..."

Novelist Graham Greene puts it this way: "with the loss of the religious sense went the sense of the importance of the human act." *With* the religious sense, "we are aware of another world against which the actions of characters are thrown into relief...acts of supernatural importance." The Nez Perce took this view for granted, as did Pierre Jean De Smet and much of nineteenth-century America.

That afternoon Alex and I find a streamlet and stop to drink and fill our water bottles. The live water pours down from above us, cold and clear through rich grasses, sedges, and young fir trees. Justin has fallen behind us to keep an eye out for dropped supplies. By the time we've filled our containers, using the little water purifier pump, he still hasn't caught up. I walk up the road and find him a half mile up the mountain, working on his bicycle. His bike rack has lost two screws, the rack's bars are bent and his tent and pack are sitting on the rubber tire of the back wheel. We try to pry and lift the rack off the tire. We take our bike tool and extract screws that hold his water bottle in order to replace the lost screws. Alex comes walking up the road just as we get the whole contraption jury-rigged off the back tire.

On we go, down to the clear little waterfall, giving Justin time to drink and fill his water bottles, then we begin pushing up the long, winding trail to the top of the next mountain, stopping often in little patches of shade to rest. Then down we go, letting Justin lead, for fear that his bike rack will break again. Which it does. I hear his bike (ahead of us) angrily buzzing down the mountain like a giant bumble bee, his packs rubbing the knobbly tires of his mountain bike. Justin's weight keeps the tires turning down the trail, but every time he hits ruts or flat-rock surfaces, the packs shake down on the tire and it buzzes louder. When Alex and I find him at the saddle of the mountain, his back tire is stuck fast.

We go to work again on the rack but find a connecting bar on one side has snapped. There's nothing to do but divide his gear between Alex and me, and pry the rack free of the tire. We get this done, but it's clear we can't keep going up the Lolo Trail this way. Fortunately, a gravel road intersects the Lolo just here, a gravel road that, according to my map, winds down the mountains back to Highway 12.

Off we go, swooping down the switchback road like birds of prey, with no need to pump or push our way up another slope. Once we come upon a boulder the size of a small car that broke from the mountainside and tumbled onto the roadway. On we go. We're moving too fast for safety on gravel, but the thrill seems worth the risk. After nine or ten miles, the road finds the two-lane asphalt of Highway 12. I brake hard and turn in a tight circle, waiting for Justin to arrive, and then, after no mishaps at speed, I unceremoniously tip slowly over and slam down on my side into the gravel. It's a hard hit to ribs I'd cracked three weeks before, but what can you do? You get up, endure Alex's grin, and wait for Justin. When he arrives, he tells us his bike's back tire slid on loose rock and he wrecked. Leaping over his handlebars, he hit some part of the falling bike and bashed a big knot in his shin, somehow landing on his feet. It's a good thing he has not fallen on his skinned and bandaged right hand.

We glance up the two-lane highway and down, then roll out onto the tarmac, turning toward Kooskia, 60 miles down the mountains. Even though there's a slight downhill grade, with the loads Alex and I are carrying on our fat-tired mountain bikes, it's still work to pedal.

Late that afternoon we find a campsite beyond a bridge on our left that takes us over the Lochsa River. The raspberries and huckleberries are ripe, so we spend a half hour building up our sugar levels, our fingers sticky sweet. We're also sweaty and filthy from three days in the mountains, so we find a narrow footpath down to the river, strip naked, and wash in the rushing, icy waters. We sit in the numbing current and watch the setting sun throw pink across the vanilla clouds and dye the river red.

***

The fleeing Nez Perce bypassed three-dozen soldiers and a number of Bitterroot settlers who tried to block their escape on Lolo Creek. Then, knowing they had outdistanced Howard, the tribe took their time moving south up the Bitterroot Valley, taking about the same route

Clark and his Corps had traveled 71 years before.

All might have gone well for the Nez Perce refugees had it not been for the telegraph. Howard had been in communication not only with General Sheridan in Chicago, but also with General William Tecumseh Sherman, who was then Commanding General of the United States Armies. Howard had even been in direct communication with Washington D. C. The tap, tap, tapping of the Morse code kept outflanking the retreating bands.

THREE DEVILS AND THE ANTLER ARTIST

After cold baths in the Lochsa River, a quiet night's sleep in our tents, followed by an hour's work on Justin's broken bike rack (helped along by a fix-it man named Hayes from southern Idaho), we three take to the highway, pedaling steadily for several hours through the morning sun. About noon, we stop to eat at Three Devils rapids, where Alex and I had capsized. It's a beautiful place of deep forests and white-sand beaches. Having eaten lunch, I wander down to the river, where Alex and Justin are swimming. I notice that Alex is staring up current. He's waist deep in the cold water and his gaze is fixed on a point beyond the trees that screen my view. I think he's watching Justin swim, so I walk back a hundred yards to get my camera. When I return, I'm immediately worried. Alex is fixed in the same place, still staring up the river. Something's wrong. I slosh into the water and look. There, halfway across the river, just this side of the crashing waves of the rapids, I see Justin, stroking through the turbulence. He seems fixed in place. The waves are rising and falling all around him and his arms are rising and falling as he pulls himself through the current, but he's not going anywhere. He's caught in that dreadful backwash. He still seems to be swimming strongly, so I stand there, shin deep, and watch, hoping he can pull himself out. His arms keep stroking, but he has no flotation device. The blue-bandaged hand regularly rises above his head and slaps into the current, pulling and rising and pulling and rising and pulling. But his head remains in place. I begin to feel desperate, thinking he needs help, wondering if two of us, caught in the river's power, will help or hinder rescue. On he goes, without going, stroking, stroking. I wade in knee deep and start working my way toward him. Then suddenly, as if some river demon who had him by the ankle has suddenly let go, we see him stroke heavily into calmer waters and then to shore.

I wade along shore to meet him. He's leaning over, hands on his knees, panting. "Dad," he says, looking up. "You were right. That current had me and wouldn't let go!"

***

Hours later, we pedal into little Kooskia and find a café. By the time we've eaten and had a beer, the sun has already moved behind the forested mountain over the South Fork of the Clearwater. I've arranged for my car to be here and we are loading our bikes on the bicycle rack when a red-and-silver Ford pickup with an antler couch fastened to the truck bed rolls by, does a U-turn, and parks on the adjacent street.

"That's got to be the brother of those two guys with the Liberty Bell we met down by the river," I tell Alex. "Remember? They mentioned they had another brother who helped them make antler furniture?"

A tall, thin young man with a long blond ponytail steps out of the

THREE DEVILS AND THE ANTLER ARTIST

truck. I walk over and introduce myself, telling him I met his brothers on the river a couple of weeks ago.

"Right on. Right on," he says, "That's cool."

"Where do you get the elk horns to make the furniture?"

He loves his craft and wants to talk. "We buy from pickers who know more or less where the elk herds discard their antlers every year. It's pretty good money. They can make $300 a day, just scavenging the right draws or canyons where the elk shed their horns. Mushroom pickers can make a good living too. When we all lived in Alaska, we picked morels and made $50 a bucket. My brothers could bring in maybe $300 a day."

"You lived in Alaska?"

He pulls out a pack of cigarettes and lips one from the pack, snaps a lighter, and lights up, then takes a long draw. His eyes are a pale grey, his face thin and drawn. He looks up the street and says, "There's three boys and four girls in our family. Our dad was a handyman and we lived like gypsies when we were kids. Spent some time in Alaska."

"What are your prices for elkhorn furniture?"

"Well, you know the rich mentality: if you charge too little they don't think it's worth anything. So we start by figuring the cost of the elk horn: $10 a pound. That couch in the pickup has 200 pounds of horn, so already we've got $2000 in it. Then it takes me a month to build it, working late. I don't just punch out at five o'clock. I'm more into the art of it."

There's a dark-haired girl leaning against a storefront, smoking a cigarette and watching us. He glances over at her and looks back at us. "Call me up, and I'll send you an antler lamp; do it for the cost and shipping."

"Really?"

"I'm not much of a business man. But this is my passion." He walks to his truck and motions us over. "You see how on this antler I cut off the spline? And attached it to the armrest, because it's got that perfect curve. And that center one comes from Arizona: they've got different genes. See how it curves? They're all different elk families, gene distributions: California, Arizona, New Mexico, Colorado, Idaho."

I look over at the young woman smoking. She glances away.

He drops his cigarette on the street and stubs it out with the toe of his boot. His grey eyes drift over the mountains and glance up at a clear evening sky going gold behind the mountain. "It's going to thunder and lightning tonight," he says. He nods goodbye and walks over to join the dark-haired girl.

As we drive into the night with our bikes strapped to the rack behind the trunk, the thunder finds us, and the rain. We're on our way west, then north to Coeur d'Alene to find De Smet's missions.

***

The Nez Perce moved slowly up the Bitterroot Valley, stopping near Stevensville and trading with the storekeepers for flour and bullets. "Store owners Henry Buck and his brother," says West, "found that the Indians had plenty of gold coin and promised to pay for everything." They seemed anything but wild Indians on the warpath.

The band's leaders met with their longtime ally, Charlo, the Salish chief. He had been living in peace near the Jesuit mission founded by De Smet and wanted no part in the war.

DE SMET AND THE BITTERROOT

The Salish Flathead led by Chief Charlo was the last tribe to live freely in the Bitterroot Valley. The story of their loss is a complicated one.

De Smet, after making his first successful contact with the Salish at the Green River Rendezvous in 1840 and traveling with them into their homeland on the buffalo plains near the Beaverhead Mountains, returned to St. Louis to bring supplies and recruits to build a mission among his new friends. He arrived in St. Louis on New Year's Eve. Reporting to his bishop, De Smet was devastated to learn that the bishop had less than half the money required to begin a mission in the Rockies, a mission that would require wagon loads of supplies: "We had need of provisions, fire-arms, implements of every kind, wagons, guides, a good hunter, an experienced captain—in a word, whatever becomes necessary when one has to traverse a desert of 800 leagues [2400 miles], and expects nothing but formidable obstacles to surmount, and thieving, and sometimes murderous enemies to combat—and swamps, ravines and rivers to cross, and mountains to climb, whose craggy and precipitous sides suddenly arrest our progress, compelling us to drag our beasts of burden up their steep ascents. These things are not done without toil and money." De Smet was at first depressed, thinking that he would break his firm promise to return to The Grand Face and his waiting Salish friends.

He began writing letters to established Catholic communities in Philadelphia, Kentucky, and Cincinnati, and took a riverboat south to New Orleans to raise funds. By the end of April, just four months later, he had raised the necessary funds. Two priests, Nicholas Point, a man with remarkable artistic and architectural skills, and Gregory Mengarini, (a fine sculptor and painter, musician, medical doctor, and carpenter) were appointed to join De Smet along with three lay brothers and artisans: a blacksmith, a carpenter, and a tinsmith.

They took a steamboat from St. Louis to Westport (near present-day Kansas City), then joined a party of travelers, some heading west for adventure, others to explore the possibility of settling in California. They stopped briefly near Topeka (Kansas Territory), where they visited the Kansa Indians, who had recently attacked a Pawnee village while most of the Pawnee warriors were away. The Kansa had killed about 90 women and children and enslaved the others, a devastating destruction of a village, but a scene that had been repeated across the continent over the centuries.

As the travelers and De Smet moved west and north up the Oregon Trail, they met a band of Pawnee on their way to avenge the destruction of their village. Days later, the warriors returned, passing De Smet's party with a single fresh scalp. And I wonder about that single soul: perhaps a woman gathering roots or filling a water pot or a boy out hunting squirrels and rabbits with his little bow. Suddenly he hears the war ponies pounding across a meadow and he runs...

This time, De Smet's trip west was unusually difficult because he and his companions were hauling farm implements and building materials on several wagons. Somewhere along that long journey they met a delegation of Salish who, as The Grand Face had promised, had departed to meet De Smet after the flowers appeared in the mountains. This band of men had traveled 800 miles to meet the priests. Among them was an aged man whom De Smet had baptized the previous year. He was so decrepit he needed a stick to lean on even when seated, yet he had insisted on joining the young warriors on the dangerous journey to meet the priests, "urging his steed forward, whip in hand, he led his youthful followers at the rate of fifty miles a day." The old man brought with him his grandson of six or seven who, "having served at the altar the preceding year, would not be refused permission to accompany his grandfather." Young Ignatius, the son of Old Ignace La Mousse (who had been killed at Ash Hollow), came too, as did his brother, Francis Xavier, and Gabriel Prudhomme, a mixed-blood who served as interpreter.

"Now that we were together," writes De Smet, "both parties were full of vigor and hope." They reached the Green River Rendezvous near the end of July, but the Flathead Salish who had been waiting for them had run out of provisions and left, some of them convinced that the black robe had broken his promise to return.

On they went, forcing their way through a difficult landscape: "Six times Father Mengarini tumbled from his horse, "and Father Point quite as many." Once while riding at full gallop," writes De Smet, "my horse fell and I flew over his head, and not one of us in these various occurrences received the least scratch"—which must be something of a grateful exaggeration.

Eventually they made their way over South Pass and on to Fort Hall, a Hudson's Bay fur trading post on the Snake River in arid sagebrush country, where the American emigrants they had been traveling with left them, the adventurers to return to the east, the others to head across the vast deserts to California—some to die at the hands of a raiding party of Indians. De Smet, Mengarini, Point, the three artisans, and the little band of Salish moved north and east up Henry's Fork, crossing what De Smet thought to be "the most barren of all the mountain deserts... We had to resort to fishing [Little Ignace jerked a line and hook expertly back and forth, snagging a number of fish] for the support of life, and our beasts of burden were compelled to fast and pine; for scarcely a mouthful of grass could be found during the eight days which it took us to traverse this wilderness." They then recrossed the continental divide, and as before, moved over the plains to Beaverhead Rock. There, De Smet's wagon party finally met the main Salish encampment. The trip from Westport on the Missouri River had taken four months.

The Grand Face and his people greeted the party with joy: "The mothers offered us their little children, and so moving was the scene that we could scarcely refrain from tears. This evening was certainly one of the happiest of our lives."

From there, the Salish and De Smet's party took their way back up Deer Lodge Creek into the Bitterroot Valley and began building their first mission in the Rocky Mountains, several miles above the mouth of the Bitterroot River (in present-day Stevensville) at a traditional winter camping ground of the Salish. They constructed a stockade against the raids of the Blackfeet and within the stockade they built a church they called St. Mary's. The Salish pitched their many tepees around the church and along the east banks of the Bitterroot River.

Nearly the whole tribe had converted, and regularly attended daily prayers and Sunday liturgies. De Smet and his fellow priests catechized, baptized, and began to teach the nomadic Indians how to plow and plant and raise cattle, to read, write, decipher arithmetic, and sing hymns. The missionaries hoped to settle the Indians into a more sedentary lifestyle that would prepare them for the white invasion they knew they could not stop. To change an entire culture of nomadic hunter-gatherers and warriors was a radical undertaking. Even the Jesuit general in Rome wrote that De Smet's hopes to repeat the seventeenth-century successes of Jesuits in South America seemed hopeless. As historian Lucylle Evans notes, "The land was different, Jesuit resources far less, the Indians too nomadic, and the whites too free to settle there."

The Indians knew of the power and technology of the white man. They tended to associate power with religion and thought that if they accepted the white man's faith, they would receive the power inherent in the whites' religious system, but they were not ready to change their whole way of life. De Smet and his associates worked hard to establish a settled mission that could serve as a bulwark against the coming invasion. They knew they had little time, but no one guessed how very little. Once, walking across a stream in the Bitterroot Valley, De Smet stooped to pick up something bright in the flowing water. A gold nugget. He stood there for a few seconds examining it, then slipped it into his pocket and told no one for over twenty years. He knew that if word got out, a rush of miners would surely follow. Nevertheless, the gold rush of 1849, just eight years after the establishment of St. Mary's, would flood the West with prospectors and settlers. Alex, Justin, and I drove by great piles of gravel that had been shoveled from streams 150 years before and still stand as monuments to enterprise and greed. It was gold along Elk Creek and near Orofino in Idaho that hastened the breaking of treaties and the beginning of the Nez Perce War in 1877.

De Smet's first mission prospered. Over 4200 adults and many children were baptized that fall of 1841, but De Smet, as became typical of his life, was quickly sent on another journey. He would always long to settle down in this mission in the beautiful Bitterroot Valley, but again and again he was required to travel, by muleback, horseback, on foot, snowshoe, dogsled, steamboat, train, and sailing ship. Each year he wrote down the year's mileage. By the end of his life he calculated he had traveled 260,929 miles, the equivalent of ten-and-a-half times around the earth.

In October of 1841, he agreed to journey to Fort Colville (over 300 miles of rough mountain travel northwest to near the Canadian border) to purchase seeds and other supplies for the new mission and to contact allied tribes who had asked for missionaries. Accompanied by ten young Salish warriors, he headed north down the Bitterroot Valley. He describes his Salish guides as warriors who "had already been often pierced with balls and arrows in different skirmishes;" they were a tough, boisterous group, and he enjoyed their company. A man noteworthy for his sense of humor, he mentions their "rare hilarity," a group of young men off on a long and dangerous journey, excited and full of laughter.

Soon after setting out, "snow fell in large flakes, notwithstanding which we continued our march. We crossed in the course of the day, a fine stream [Lolo Creek]—the same one which the famous travelers, Lewis and Clark, ascended in 1805." Like Lewis and Clark, De Smet observed qualities of soil, distinctive features of animals, birds (he calls the bald eagle the nun's eagle "on account of the color of its head, which is white, whilst the other parts of the body are black," and landscape: "The mountains which terminate [the Bitterroot Valley] on both sides appear inaccessible; they are piles of jagged rocks, the base of which presents nothing but fragments...while the Norwegian pine grows on those that are covered with earth, giving them a very somber appearance."

While setting up tents near Clark's Fork River, De Smet spotted what he took to be a Blackfeet warrior "in the act of hiding himself," but De Smet did not speak of it to his young companions, "fearing that I might not be able to prevent a bloody struggle between them. I, however, took the precaution of having a good watch kept over our horses." This willingness to protect the arch-enemies of the Salish would prove damaging to the Jesuit mission in years to come. De Smet and his fellow Jesuits, like Lewis and Clark before them, were committed to establishing a confederation of northwestern tribes who would be at peace with each other. In this they seem as idealistic, and perhaps naïve, as Lewis and Clark.

A WILD AND DIFFICULT RIDE

A s De Smet had hoped, the party received warm welcomes from both the Pend Oreilles and the Kalispel tribes, who had already learned Catholic prayers and practices from a young man they had sent to St. Mary's that fall. The men of the village hid their rifles beneath their blankets and suddenly pulled them out and fired a welcoming salvo, which sent De Smet's mule Lizette bouncing and bucking, and set the tribe to laughing.

Leaving the Kalispels, the party worked its way down a difficult valley and had to climb a slope so steep Lizette couldn't carry De Smet's 200 pounds. He slipped off, grabbed the mule's tail and hung on, stumbling behind, "crying at one moment aloud, and at other times making use of the whip to excite her courage, until the good beast conducted me safely to the very top of the mountain." From there he stopped to catch his breath and view the "magnificent prospect, the windings of the river. On one side hung over our heads rocks piled on rocks in the most precipitous manner, and on the other stood lofty peaks crowned with snow and pine trees: mountains of every shape and feature reared their towering forms before us. It really was a fine view and one which was well worth the effort we had made."

They rode on, passing through a deeply shadowed forest so thick, they could "scarcely see beyond the distance of twenty yards" for three days. Their horses "suffered a great deal in it from want of grass...It was a real labyrinth; from morning till night we did nothing but wind about to avoid thousands of trees fallen from either fire, storms or age." The trees of the forest were massive. He measured one cedar with a circumference of 42 feet, and another, fallen one at 200 feet in length (the height of a twenty-story building.)

At last they came out of the dark forest above a lake that appeared to be 30 miles long and several miles wide, "called Pend d'Oreille, studded with small islands covered in woods," and populated by deer, elk, and wild horses. Once, when De Smet fell behind the party, he found himself on a narrow rock shelf with a 1000-foot precipice on one side and a rock wall rising on the other. He suddenly pulled up at a crevice that fell hundreds of feet. "The slightest false step," he writes, "would have plunged the mule and her rider into the abyss beneath." The mule hesitated. "I recommended myself to God, and as a last expedient sank my spurs into the sides of my poor beast; she made one bold leap and safely landed me on another parapet much larger than that I had left."

They descended the mountain and passed into another wet, dense forest. Ever the evangelist, De Smet walked off the trail through shadows to a small hut. With the help of his interpreter, he converted and baptized an ancient woman living there. "I had scarcely regained the path, when I met her husband, almost bent to the earth with age and infirmity; he could hardly drag himself along. He had been setting a trap in the forest for the bucks. The Flatheads [Salish] who had preceded me had told him of my arrival. As soon, therefore, as he perceived me, he began to cry out, with a trembling voice, 'Oh, how delighted I am to see our father before I die. The Great Spirit is good—oh, how happy my heart is.'" He visited with the old man and his wife, and before leaving, baptized the old man too.

Later he came across a little hut of bulrushes where five old men lived. "Three of them were blind, and the other two had but one eye each; they were almost naked, and offered a real personification of human misery." They, too, had heard of his coming and asked to be baptized. During his journey of 42 days, he writes that he baptized 190 persons and preached to 2000 Indians, including the Coeur d'Alenes where he received an even more positive welcome than he had among the Salish.

***

The following year, 1842, because Fort Colville had insufficient supplies for St. Mary's, De Smet traveled west again, this time reaching the Columbia River. His boat capsized, drowning several of his companions in the very rapids that had almost taken the Lewis and Clark dugouts, but the rest of the party finally paddled down to Fort Vancouver near the Pacific and purchased supplies. De Smet then set out to return to St. Mary's once again. He was again welcomed by the Coeur d'Alenes. On returning to St. Mary's in the Bitterroot Valley, he appointed the priest Nicolas Point to build a second mission among the Coeur d'Alenes.

This mission's church building still stands on a hill near the banks of the Coeur d'Alene River. Called The Old Mission, its church is the oldest standing structure in Idaho.

THE OLD MISSION AND THE BROTHEL

After driving back to Lewiston with our bikes strapped to the back of the car, we three head north for the Old Mission. It's a clear summer day. Dust devils, like tall, lazy tornados of dirt, twist slowly into a hot summer sky, visible for miles. We turn east and drive through Spokane, on past beautiful Lake Coeur d'Alene, and finally to the Old Mission on its rise of ground above the river. Caught in sunlight, it looks like a wooden version of an old Southwest mission building, an arched flat façade held up by six rounded pillars. The National Park Service now has custody of the building and has built a visitor's center nearby.

Father Nicolas Point settled among the Coeur d'Alenes for two years, then, in 1848, Father Ravalli, a physician, architect, and sculptor, was sent from St. Mary's to replace the original bark church with a more permanent building on higher ground near the Coeur d'Alene River. For tools he had a broad axe, an augur, a saw, some ropes and pulleys, and a pen knife. For workmen he had two lay brothers and the Indians.

They set about felling trees, carrying rocks for the foundation, cutting saplings to weave between pillars, and mixing adobe mud to fill in the lattice of saplings woven with grass. The building was (and is) ninety feet long, forty feet wide, and a full thirty feet high, an extraordinary building for the virgin wilderness of northern Idaho. The sawing was done in a dug sawpit, says historian Edmund Cody, "with an improvised whipsaw," cutting and squaring "uprights about eighteen inches square and rafters about ten inches square." Planing and shaping the beams was done with the broad axe, and the uprights were drilled and fastened to the rafters with wooden pegs. "Huge timbers were cut for the floor and carefully placed to procure a smooth surface."

Walking inside we see a handsome, grey-haired man sitting on the east side of the church talking earnestly to his two granddaughters, who seem less than interested. We introduce ourselves and ask him about the place. He points out the statues carved by Ravalli, one an elegant and beautiful carving of St. John the Evangelist. He tells us the candle holders were fashioned out of used tin cans. One of the lay brothers carved seventeen panels for the ceiling, each of a different design. We look up and see the ceiling panels colored a faded blue. The man explains that the Indians were not used to praying in an enclosed space, so the priests rubbed the ceiling with huckleberries to stain it sky blue. We walk around the sanctuary to look at the fourteen pictures of the Passion of Christ framed and hung from wooden pegs, at a large picture of the Sacred Heart, and paintings above the side altars depicting Heaven and Hell—paintings like nothing the Indians had ever seen. Walking behind the sanctuary into the back rooms, we can see Indian handprints in the old adobe.

Conflicts arose among the converted tribes in the following years. Father Point joined 200 lodges of the Salish Flatheads on a buffalo hunt in lands that had once been Salish, but then were occupied by their well-armed enemies the Blackfeet. For three weeks it snowed. "Many of the Indians," writes De Smet, "suffered from snow-blindness, and during a terrific storm the Father [Point] nearly succumbed. Had not some of the hunters quickly lighted a fire when they saw him turn a ghastly pallor, he would have died of cold."

Later, hunting the open plains and rugged mountains, sixty Salish warriors surrounded seventeen Blackfeet. "In this plight the captives appealed to the black-robe for mercy; and he insisted that the [Salish] spare them. They did, but most reluctantly, and became highly incensed against the Father for this meddling in the matter," says Evans.

After the snow storms, the tribe kept searching for buffalo, but with no luck. At night, their starving dogs would eat the leather ropes that tethered the horses. Point asked the Indians to pray for food. He wrote in his diary that the following day, "toward midday we reached the sumit of a high mountain. What a transformation! The sun was shining and the cold less penetrating. We saw an immense plain before us, good pasturage, and herds of buffalo. The expedition halted, the hunters assembled and set off for the chase." Before sunset, 155 buffaloes fell.

The Blackfeet were a constant threat, and the Salish could not understand the missionaries' desire to give to them the same powerful religion that they, the Salish, had received. Once, after a battle with the Crows in which the Salish had, out of necessity, joined their enemies the Blackfeet to defeat this common enemy, these Blackfeet expressed a sudden willingness to convert to the new religion. They noted that the Salish had offered Christian prayers before bravely fighting the Crows, and attributed their success to this new religion. De Smet, who was present on this occasion, agreed to instruct the Blackfeet. He also made the mistake of giving them a gift of tobacco he had originally promised to the Salish, which of course upset the Salish. He also sent Father Point to build up a mission among the Blackfeet.

De Smet's overtures to the Blackfeet caused intense anger among the Salish. And members of the far-flung Blackfeet, despite the conversion of some, continued to raid the Bitterroot Valley. One of the brothers living at St. Mary's wrote: "The Blackfeet were a great trouble to us, so much so that at 3 miles from the Mission we were not sure of our lives. Brother Joseph and I spent many a weary night in sharp lookout on the top of our bastions with our guns. Fr. De Smet bade me never to undress at night, and to make a wooden cannon to keep the Blackfeet away. Ahead of the bastion I made a corral for the horses of the Indians, 2 of whom were constantly watching there in their lodge." Lone Salish returning to camp in the evenings or leaving for a hunt were often ambushed and killed.

Nevertheless, the mission prospered. De Smet brought a man to St. Mary's from Fort Vancouver who built a flour mill to grind the wheat that the mission grew. This mill replaced one that Ravalli had constructed. The ingenious Ravalli contrived, in addition to the flour mill, a saw mill, made out of a steel wagon tire flattened and hammered into a blade that he toothed by chiseling and much filing. Four more wagon wheels were welded together for a crank to work the water-powered saw. Adept with medications, Ravalli brought medicines from St. Louis and collected herbs from the Indians, creating a little pharmacy attached to his log cabin. He treated the Salish with a smallpox vaccination he devised from cowpox. None of the Salish came down with smallpox when an outbreak broke out among the Nez Perce who were staying there and had refused the vaccinations. Smallpox had been the scourge of Indian populations across the continent. Waves of the plague swept Indian encampments from coast to coast. Salish historians estimate that 20,000 Salish lived in the Bitterroot and Clark's Fork valleys before the arrival of Lewis and Clark, but repeated pandemics had already reduced the tribes to no more than 2000 by the time the Corps arrived.

By 1846, St. Mary's mission was producing 7000 bushels of wheat and almost 5000 bushels of potatoes annually. They had 40 head of cattle, as well as poultry and other animals. They were even extracting sugar from potatoes. In material ways, the mission seemed to be succeeding. "The spiritual and moral condition of the mission," writes Evans, "was as satisfactory as its material prosperity. With the abolition of polygamy the population had sensibly increased. The abandonment of children, divorce, and the shedding of blood were now unknown among the [Salish]. Young girls were permitted to marry for choice; and the sick were cared for, and no longer allowed to die in misery. Education of the children was regarded as a religious duty, and gave promise to the missionaries of a Christian generation."

Outside the mission, success was not so evident. In the spring of 1846, after De Smet had left again to raise funds and gather recruits, another buffalo hunt led to a battle with the Blackfeet. The Salish killed 24 of the enemy and lost four of their own. Father Mengarini, who accompanied the Salish, told the Salish to stop the fight. His presumption angered the young men. New leaders arose and opposed the priests.

When several of the older leaders who had been faithful Catholics died, opposition to the priests and constant harassment by the Blackfeet led to the closing of St. Mary's just nine years after its founding. It was a devastating setback for De Smet's hopes.

However, sixteen years later, at the request of the Salish, the priests did return and reestablish the mission. Meanwhile, other missions had been planted among the Kalispels and Pend Oreille to the north and the Coeur d'Alene to the west. Then, in 1855, Isaac I. Stevens, "an impatient, politically ambitious military man," according to Alvin Josephy, arrived in the Bitterroot Valley to negotiate a treaty with the tribes. He insisted that the Salish tribes move to a reservation at the north end of the Bitterroot Valley. Victor, a Flathead Salish chief, refused to give up his native land. He asked the president of the United States to come and see that the Flathead section of the valley was much more suitable for the reservation. Stevens backed down enough to allow a federal survey to choose the best land for a reservation and decide the issue later. Victor had, at least temporarily, won his point and kept his people near St. Mary's.

In 1872, James A. Garfield, not yet president, arrived with a commission and persuaded two of the Flathead chiefs to move their families to the northern reservation so that white settlers could have the valley, but Chief Charlo, Victor's son and successor, like his father, refused to sign the document or move, though someone on the commission fraudulently signed his name for him. When, five years later, the Nez Perce refugees arrived in the Bitterroot Valley, fleeing General Howard's column, Charlo was still living there in peace with his white neighbors, having convinced a visiting federal commission that he had never signed the Garfield treaty.

***

Outside the Old Mission church, Alex climbs on Justin's shoulders and begins picking ripe yellow cherries from a nearby tree, dropping them into an empty plastic water bottle. Eating cherries, we tour the old priests' home and the graveyard nearby, then head for the parking lot.

There, the grey-haired man, James Connell, his wife, and two grand-daughters drive up and tell us of a restaurant a few miles away called The Snake Pit. They say it's a building with an interesting history and that we should take a look.

Following his directions, we drive along the winding river and approach a two-story wooden building of considerable age, with elk horns mounted above the second story balcony. Inside is an old stone fireplace, stuffed animals, antiques of the old West, including elk-horn chairs. We sit down in a booth next to a shelf of old canned food. I read the label of a bulging can:

Road Kill Stew with Veggies.

Packed in Mississippi River water. Not over three days on the road: long enough to bring out the flavors. Not long enough for botulism.

Contents: rabbit, skunk, possum, cat, coon, squirrel, tire, frog, and carrots.

Calories: 29

Sodium: 1200 grams; Calcium: 8 teeth

Another can reads: "Dehydrated Water: Empty contents of can into one gallon of water, stir until dissolved. Chill and serve."

The owner, Joe Peak, comes to our table and introduces himself. He tells us about the history of the building: "Every two-story building in this part of the country was a brothel. So this place used to be a brothel for all the miners who worked these mountains. There was a bar and food on the first floor, the second floor was for other activities."

After hearing about our visit to the Old Mission, he tells us that for years his son was a tour guide at the mission. He's now a chaplain in Afghanistan. Joe goes back to the kitchen and returns with a printed email from his son. The son writes that he has celebrated 500 masses and traveled thousands of miles over the country in airplanes, helicopters, and armored vehicles: "This year I had the privilege and opportunity to bring God's presence in the Sacraments to thousands of troops in Afghanistan." Joe, and his wife, who later comes to our table, are very proud of their son. But they want to introduce us to another friend, Jean Vosberg, a retired school teacher and principal who loves her hometown and hates the EPA. She walks up, pulls up a chair, and joins us.

Jean Vosberg is a short, stocky woman who wears glasses over her sharp old eyes. Her hair is white and her jaw is strong. She takes a look at the three of us and says, "I'm not nice, and I'll beat up the sonofabitch who tells me I am. I'll be 80 years old in March, and you can drink green beer on my birthday."

Alex, Justin, and I say hi.

"When you get done eating, I want to show you my town."

We order our food as she tells us the history of Kellog, Idaho, that lies just up the road. It's a mining town. "The military," she says, "needed a road from Fort Benton on the east side of the Rockies all the way to Fort Walla Walla on the Columbia River to deal with the Indians and connect the coasts. So they started blasting the road through the mountains. It took years and a boat load of money.

"Anyway, one day this man was walking along that road they'd built and went off to explore along the river for 35 miles. He found gold.

This was back in the 1880s."

She looks at Alex and Justin. "Have you ever seen the movie *Paint Your Wagon*?"

They look at each other and shake their heads no.

"Well, that's your homework, kids. That's the best intro to our area. Anyway that guy who found the gold naturally let the word slip and within a year there were 3000 people up here digging in the gravel and panning in the creeks.

"Then one day a couple miners are caught in this tent with a jackass that won't leave the tent. They tell this guy Kellog they'll give him a grubstake to start mining if he gets rid of the stubborn jackass that won't leave their tent. So Kellog pulls the jackass out of the tent and takes it over the hill, but the jackass breaks loose and he chases it. When he finds it, it's pawing at the ground and staring at him. Kellog walks up to the animal and notices something gleaming in the dirt. It's galena, silver ore. So that's what got the town of Kellog built. It was discovered by a jackass and is still inhabited by jackasses."

As we finish our food, Joe Peak walks up with free dishes of huckleberry ice cream.

Jean hands around the dishes and says, "Here, eat your ice cream; it's good for you."

"You know," she says, "they've dug 500 miles of tunnels in our hills. People come here and say no one's working, but they're all back there in the tunnels. Then the EPA showed up. You know, don't you, that those initials stand for Enemy of the People of America. They made us shut down all the silver smelters in town, lost us 2000 good jobs. Now we have to ship all our silver ore to Japan to process where they smoke up the world on their end. I don't like the EPA."

After our huckleberry ice cream, we walk out the front door, down the wooden stairs and into the gravel parking lot. Jean tells us she was a school teacher who taught four generations of students. "I even taught Mary Peak, Joe's wife." She glances back at the building. "You know they both have cancer now. I'm worried about them."

We're about to climb in our own car when Jean says, "No you don't! You're coming with me." Justin and Alex aren't so sure, but they shrug and we all pile into her compact car. Off she goes, kicking up gravel from the parking lot and speeding up the winding river road, then flooring it onto the interstate, swerving off onto an exit ramp and cruising into the town of Kellog. She points out a distinct species of fir trees that rises up the mountain in terraces beyond the town, and tells us that the Bunker Hill Mine hired an arborist to plant the trees: "People said the smelter smoke was killing off the forest trees, so this arborist named Ed used grow lights in the mines to start the trees growing and then moved them out and planted them. He planted five million trees."

She swerves her little car around a slower vehicle and yells out the window, "Get your ass out of the way, you stupid man!"

She tells us that after teaching school she became a principal. "Women could be school teachers and principals; men couldn't."

Still in town, she speeds us along a forested road. "We had a mother bear lived in that white house up the hill." She points up a forested rise. "That bear went downstairs in the basement to have herself a baby bear. He was part of the neighborhood, used to visit everybody. Friendly little cuss."

Flying through a stop sign, someone roadside jumps quickly back onto a sidewalk and yells after her, "Hey, that's a stop sign!"

"Oh geez! Missed the sign! I'm notorious around here, I've got to watch it."

She points out various landmarks. "There's the Dodge dealership. That guy's the biggest car dealer around. He's a pain in the ass, really and truly. He took over the high school and we had to build another high school up on Jackass Gulch Road, but after we built it up there, the people figured they had to change the road's name. So they call it Jacob's Gulch Road now. Stupid people."

She takes a bridge over the river and turns back onto an entry ramp to the interstate, pushes the pedal to the floor and roars back onto the four-lane highway. "Modern people think they can change Mother

Nature, but she doesn't like that. This engineer came to town once when I was a girl and said he was going to build a road through the mountains."

The river parallels the interstate and I see a moose feeding in the shallows. Jean steps on it and we fly around an eighteen-wheeler.

"When we grew up we didn't know we were supposed to hate people. People came from every country in the world to work the mines. We all got along just fine. I grew up back there in Little Italy."

Her car drifts into the passing lane and slowly back into the other lane. Cars brake and swerve to avoid us. "Someone got concerned that the miners weren't getting enough sun, must have been the EPA. I don't like the EPA. So they built this solarium and the miners would go in there and get a day's equivalence of sun. Even us school children were bused to the solarium to get our ration of sun. Our day was Tuesdays.

"Anyway, this engineer shows up when I'm a little girl and says he's going to build a road through the mountains. I say, 'You are?' He says, 'Yes, I am. I'm an engineer.'

"See that hacked-off mountain over there? I was a girl when that mountain came down. A sad day."

She jerks the steering wheel right and we swerve off the highway onto an exit ramp. Justin and Alex are hanging onto their arm rests as she turns up the river toward The Snake Pit. Soon we're pulling into the graveled parking lot of the tall, gabled building. "You know the madams here at the brothel used to donate school uniforms for the poor kids." She hits the brakes. "Yeah, that's right. They were some pretty good-hearted souls."

We thank her for the tour, and she announces, "If I die, I'm dead. If anybody needs spare parts, be my guest. And please place my ashes at the bar of The Snake Pit. Or better yet, put them in five aluminum cans and put those cans on my grave. The EPA considers beer cans so hazardous they won't remediate the land if it has cans on it, so that'll preserve my grave!"

She smiles and looks at us. "Remember your homework, boys. Watch *Paint Your Wagon*."

BITTERROOT

After meeting Chief Charlo of the Flathead Salish in the Bitterroot Valley and spending $1200 on bags of flour, ammunition, and cattle, the Nez Perce moved slowly up the valley day after day, convinced that the settlers were friendly and that they had, as Looking Glass had predicted, left the war behind them. The tribe harmed no one. Yet all was not well. White Thunder, who was 21 at the time, says there was a feeling in the camp that "none of us could understand." Shore Crossing rode through the camp one morning calling loudly, "My brothers, my sisters, I am telling you! In a dream last night I saw myself killed. I will be killed soon! I do not care. I am willing to die. But first, I will kill some soldiers. I shall not turn back from the death. We are all going to die!" And Lone Bird, also a brave fighter, rode about calling, "My shaking heart tells me trouble and death will overtake us if we make no hurry through this land! I cannot smother, I cannot hide that which I see. I must speak what is revealed to me. Let us be gone to the buffalo country!"

But Chief Looking Glass scoffed at their fears. He told them that the settlers here had no quarrel with them. He refused to hurry. Along the way, they met the Nez Perce leader Lean Elk (whom the whites called Poker Joe) and his small band returning from the buffalo plains. Lean Elk was an experienced buffalo hunter who knew the trails through the Rockies and was a natural leader. He and his followers decided they had little choice but to join the exiles.

They made their leisurely progress across the east fork of the Bitterroot River and up into Ross's Hole (where Lewis and Clark had met the Salish on that cold, rainy day so many years before). Then the bands followed Lean Elk (Poker Joe) over the high mountains and down to an old camping place along a river well known to the Nez Perce buffalo hunters. It was the Big Hole River that Sacagawea had recognized when passing through with Clark's men. The tribe forded the river and set up camp in open grass and sagebrush just beyond the willows and thickets that bordered the meandering stream. The horse herd was left to scatter along the mountain slope on the other side of the river to graze. The Nez Perce once again wrapped themselves in robes and blankets and slept in the open beneath a dark sky (they had lost their tepee poles at the Battle of the Clearwater weeks before).

The next day Looking Glass announced that they would stay there a few days to fatten the horses and give the women a chance to cut and dry new lodge poles. Ten or twelve of the young men, including White Thunder, wanted to scout the back trail as they had done along the Lolo Trail. They asked an old man, Burning Coals, if they could borrow his fast horses, hoping to retrace the difficult mountains back to Ross's Hole to see if they were being followed, but Burning Coals refused and Looking Glass told the young men, "No more fighting! War is quit." Five Wounds, a respected warrior, argued with Looking Glass, telling him to let the scouts go back, but Five Wounds finally threw up his hands and said, "All right, Looking Glass. You are one of the chiefs! I have no wife, no children to be placed in front of the danger that I feel coming to us. Whatever the gains, whatever the loss, it is yours."

That day they rested beside the river. Children and dogs played in the shallows; boys hunted the little ground squirrels that darted from the sage brush, the women began chopping down lodgepole pines, hacking off the branches, and peeling the bark. They set up tepees for the first time in weeks and built their cooking fires inside.

Meanwhile, Colonel Gibbon, that "vigorous and efficient leader" had moved his infantry out of Missoula on wagons and had, for the last few days, been moving up the Bitterroot Valley at twice the speed of the fleeing bands. He picked up 38 mounted citizen-volunteers as he went. If the scouts White Thunder had wanted to join had been allowed to reconnoiter, and if they had spotted Gibbon's men, the Nez Perce could have trapped and destroyed Gibbon's small command in the mountains (or so White Thunder later believed). Instead of sending out scouts, the Nez Perce held a parade that evening. The warriors rode their horses around the camp, shouting and singing songs, "all making a good time," recalls White Thunder, "everybody with good feeling. Going to the buffalo country! No more fighting after Lolo Pass" [the skirmish with a few dozen soldiers and citizens who had tried to block their passage out of the mountains and into the Bitterroot Valley. The Nez Perce had simply bypassed the log barricades and soldiers by taking a side path around a mountain, holding the soldiers in place with a few snipers]. "War was quit. All Montana citizens our friends," said Looking Glass. It seems Chief Joseph, whom American newspapers across the country were claiming to be the Nez Perce leader and strategist who had fought off Howard's attack at the Clearwater, had little to do with these decisions. White Thunder was a relative of Chief Joseph and often spent time in his tepee during this retreat.

Chief White Bird's ten-year-old son was playing the stick and bone game with some boys down by the creek: "Having lots of fun, we were noisy. Finally dark came, and we had fire for light and warmth." The boys saw two men appear beyond the fire wrapped in grey blankets, their hats pulled down over their eyes. "We saw they were white men. Foolishly we said nothing to the older people about it. We ran away, and then came back to our playing. The strangers were gone. We resumed our game, having great sport."

After a while, the boys grew tired, and walked back to their parents' tepees. That night the old warrior Wottolen dreamed of soldiers.

BIG HOLE

Justin picks up his car in Lewiston and we drive both cars again into the mountains, over the continental divide, and down into the Bitterroot Valley. The light is gone by the time we turn up the long valley. It's after midnight when we climb the highway that leads past Ross's Hole and over Chief Joseph Pass, spooking deer and elk as we wind over, then down the mountains.

It's two a.m., a cold, black night, when we park at the closed gate that blocks the road to the Big Hole Battlefield National Park and Museum. I turn the key off and pull on a jacket while Alex takes his red blanket, steps out of the car, and wraps it around his shoulders. Justin gets out of his car; he's wearing a hooded sweatshirt. We ease the car doors shut, not wanting to wake the rangers sleeping in nearby buildings.

Then, under starlight, we walk toward the battle.

Cold. Quiet. The mountain slope on our left stands half black with trees against a range of stars. The nearer slope of open meadow is faintly visible in the palest light of a quarter moon, a faint light neither soldiers nor Indians had that moonless, starry night in 1877.

Walking by the park buildings, we cut left through sagebrush and grass, click on small flashlights, then choose our way down a slope toward the river that is maybe a quarter mile away. Stepping between stiff clumps of sagebrush, we sweep our flashlights across the dry grasses and dead flowers of late summer. The black mountain where the horses grazed rises slowly into the stars as we walk down the slope. We're heading northeast, approaching the tepees.

By 2:00 a.m., Gibbon's men have already crept down to the base of that grassy slope we can barely make out in the thin moonlight. They remain for the present on the other side of the shallow river from the Indian camp, taking up positions in a long line directly across from the tepees clustered nearby and others farther down the creek, leather lodges pale beneath the starlight. To our left is a black wall of willow thickets along the river. The three of us slide down into what must be a dry irrigation ditch and scramble up the other side. We walk a few feet and slide into another dusty irrigation ditch, then, grabbing handfuls of bunch grass, pull ourselves onto the low prairie that slopes gradually to the river. The tepees are close.

Twenty-one year old White Thunder is sleeping in Minthon's tepee. Minthon is a younger friend whose lodge lies near this southern edge of the scattered camp. Chief Joseph's tepee, where White Thunder usually stays, is at the far end of the encampment; White Thunder's rifle and ammunition are in Joseph's tepee.

The young man wakes in the night and hears a horse wade across the creek—the splash and clop of hooves on rocks—then the movement of horse and rider through the brush and thickets along the river, north and away. The night is still. He falls back asleep.

Colonel Gibbon has laid his plans. Just before midnight, he

distributed ninety rounds of ammunition for each of his 149 regular soldiers and 38 volunteers. He faces around 200 sleeping warriors, and 500
women and children, though reports have put the numbers far higher.
He has left his cannon and a mule carrying 2000 rounds of ammunition
behind, afraid the mules and cannon will make too much noise moving
through the trees and brush. By one in the morning, he has his troops
lined out along the river—across from Justin, Alex, and me.

Now, about two, the soldiers can see the dim glow of the smoldering
campfires within the tepees. Sometimes they hear a woman talking or
the fretful crying of a baby.

My sons and I move on down toward the river; we can barely make
out the black trees just ahead. We stop and wait. The sleeping Indians
are near, their dogs curled up inside the tepees, their fires going to
ash, some 2000 horses on the far slope grazing slowly across the steep
meadow. The three of us can see little but the bright stars that salt the
black night. Alex still has his blanket wrapped around his shoulders.
Justin has put his hood up. Behind us we can see the silhouette of the
low building that commemorates August 9, 1877. No one builds memorials to the boys who played the bone game, to the women who spent
the day cutting down lodgepole pines, laughing, gossiping, boiling the
dried buffalo Lean Elk's people brought from buffalo country, cooking
bread or a little camas root cake over the coals, maybe boiling a pot of
dried bitterroot. We don't write stories of the boy who waded across
the river that afternoon to check on the grazing horses and called his
favorite pony to him, letting it nuzzle his hand for a nibble of sweet
camas cake, or for the boy who waited a half hour behind a clump of
greasewood till the little ground squirrel poked its head from its burrow,
then watched as it dashed through the grass and stopped, sitting up
on its tiny hind legs as the boy drew his arrow to his cheek and let fly.
These were the good hours, the fine, sunlit hours of ordinary life that
we take for granted. No, we build memorials for blood.

About four in the morning, a ten-year-old boy wakes to hear the low
voice of his father, Red Elk, outside their tepee. He is saying something

to Chief Chuslum Moxmox (Yellow Bull) about maybe seeing soldiers across the river. Just then a shot barks from the darkness to the northeast, somewhere along the river, maybe a quarter mile away. Two or three more shots. Then rifle fire breaks out all along the river, flames spurting from unseen barrels. The boy jumps up and ducks out of the tepee into the cold, dark morning. Someone is shouting, "We're attacked! We're attacked!" The boy can see spurts of fire crackling from the repeating rifles all along the river willows. Then a man's voice across the river shouts something in the American tongue, and there are shouts and shots and the sounds of many men breaking through brush, sloshing and stumbling across the black river.

Women scream as they grab their children in the dark, the sound of bullets clicking through leather tepees and humming past their heads. Some of the children duck under their buffalo robes and lie very still, listening, their little hearts pounding in their ears. A dog yelps.

With the first shots, twenty-one-year-old White Thunder opens his eyes and listens. Maybe he is dreaming. Then come the staccato bursts of rifle fire all along the river to the north, the shouts of men. He and little Minthon roll out of their blankets, and White Thunder grabs his moccasins and magic war club in the dark of the tepee, slipping its thong over his wrist. He has no rifle. He steps out of the tepee with Minthon beside him and peers into a darkness cut by stars and rifle fire. Far to the east behind him, a vague grey light begins to silhouette the prairie horizon. It still seems like a dream.

Most of the shooting is coming from farther north toward the main camp. The women have run from Minthon's tepee and have thrown themselves down in sagebrush. One of them calls out, "Why not all you men get ready and fight? Don't run away!"

Young Minthon hands White Thunder his rifle, telling him there's only one bullet. Soldiers are yelling as they scramble through thickets, stopping to fire low into the pale grey tepees. White Thunder takes a few steps toward the fighting and sees a man running toward him from the tepees on his right. Coming close, the man says, "Rainbow is killed!"

White Thunder thinks this is a mistake. Rainbow, who led the seventeen scouts on the Lolo Trail. Rainbow, whose advice the young men respect. He sees Five Wounds wrapped in a black blanket a few feet away, stepping nervously back and forth. Five Wounds turns and says, "Any you brothers have two guns? Let me have one." Five Wounds had been wounded in the hand at the battle on the Clearwater; his hand is still wrapped. A man runs over and hands him a rifle, saying, "Take this gun. It has five shells in the magazine and one in the barrel." Five Wounds says, "They're enough," and drops the blanket and takes off running toward the river. It's the last time White Thunder will see him alive.

White Thunder, already a veteran of several battles, takes Minthon's gun and dodges through the sagebrush and grass toward the spurting rifles and the shouts and the screams. The gunpowder drifts like morning fog through the camp. He can see shadows running among the tepees. Two warriors join him as they run toward the firing. They see a man staggering near them. It is Jeekunkun (Dog). Blood is running from his head. White Thunder cries, "Trade me your gun! You have plenty of cartridges and I have none. Trade, and then get away from danger!"

Jeekunkun says, "No! I must have the gun. I don't want to die without fighting!"

Another Indian, shot in the right arm and carrying his rifle in his left, hurries toward them. He too refuses to trade guns. He has been shot a second time through the stomach. Rifles are firing everywhere. The high-pitched squeals of terrified boys and girls, the shouts and curses of women and men, the harsh barks of frightened dogs all cut the smoky dawn. Running around the tepees, White Thunder sees a soldier staggering, falling as if drunk. White Thunder swings his war club and slams it into the soldier's skull and sees the man's teeth fall part way from his mouth. He reaches down and pulls a set of wooden false teeth from the soldier's mouth; he has never seen anything like that before. He drops Minthon's rifle, grabs the soldier's rifle and takes his cartridge belt, then moves forward, approaching a small thicket of willows. Black Trail comes out of the thicket, stooping as he runs; he calls to White Thunder, "My nephew, I got shot. I am wounded, shot through the shoulder."

White Thunder, now well armed, sees soldiers running between the lodges and firing their guns. Some of the tepees are already being kindled by soldiers who have grabbed burning sticks from the fires. Old, dry buffalo and elk hides are beginning to flame up.

He is hot with anger: "Women, children, and old men who cannot fight are in those tepees!" A voice calls out from a hundred steps away, "My brothers! Our tepees are on fire! Get ready your arms! Fight! You are here for that purpose!" A number of warriors respond with war cries.

Near the river, he sees Five Fogs, of the Palouse tribe, with his bow and arrows, crouching in front of his tepee. It is growing a little lighter in the east and the soldiers are no more than ten or fifteen yards from Five Fogs. He shoots an arrow as several rifles fire; he skips sideways and lets go another arrow. Three times the soldiers fire and miss, but the fourth round of shots knocks Five Fogs down and kills him.

White Thunder runs to within 20 steps of the river and finds a vantage point away from the Indians in camp. He aims at a soldier and pulls the trigger, knocking the man down; he levers in another bullet, aims and hits another soldier, levers in another, aims, and fires quickly. He charges in and grabs their guns and cartridge belts, one after another, draping the belts across his shoulders.

Above the camp and across the river, Chief Joseph and No Heart after the first barrage have waded quickly across the river and over the rocks in bare feet to rescue the vital horse herd. Without their horses, the tribe will be at the mercy of their enemies. The two men have run up the slope toward the frightened horses. They catch horses, then start driving the herd up among the trees, away from the fighting. Someone in camp yells that Salish allies of the settlers are driving off the horse herd, and a warrior jumps on the horse staked near his tepee, and splashes through the willows and up the hill to save the horses. He catches up to No Heart and shoots him down, thinking he's a Salish stealing the horses.

Down below, Shore Crossing, who just days before prophesied his own death, drops behind a small log and aims his rifle at the willows through which the soldiers are charging, their muzzle flashes banging through the brush. His pregnant wife is right behind him, and he orders her to flee. She starts to run, but is hit by a bullet and crawls back behind him. Shore Crossing puts his sights on a soldier breaking from the river willows and shoots, and the man folds over and hits the ground. Several soldiers simultaneously break through the river brush and fire. Shore Crossing is hit. His wounded wife grabs his gun and shoots down a charging soldier just as several soldiers fire and kill her.

Children screech and run bent over for any cover at all. Eelahweemah (About Asleep) is twelve years old. His father Likinma (Last in a Row) points to a shallow gully and tells his sons and the women emerging from his tepee to go hide there, then turns and begins firing at the charging soldiers. About Asleep, his little brother, and five women crouch in the shallow gully, but soldiers begin firing at the shadows huddled there. The boy sees his father shoot down one soldier, but suddenly his mother moans and collapses. The smoke of gunpowder fills the still air, the drifting clouds rising slowly into the grey light of earliest dawn. The twelve-year-old boy glances back and sees that all five of the women are shot dead or badly wounded. He tells his brother, "We must get out of this place!" The two boys jump up and run as bullets whisper past them. They sprint to the river and jump and slide down the bank, where they see an Indian lying dead. They flatten themselves in the sand and dirt beside the body.

Between tepees, a woman lies dead. The baby lying on her chest is swinging its broken arm and crying. The little, bloody hand, hanging by a string of flesh and skin, slaps back and forth. An old man sits smoking beside his tepee, a dark shape against the tanned hide of the lodge. His name is Wahnistas Aswetesk. He is very old. A soldier shoots a bullet through him and he jerks, then goes on sucking his pipe, the smoke flowing from his lips. Other soldiers fire as they run past. Bullet after bullet cuts through him. Still he smokes. Sitting on his buffalo robe, he glances around at the running soldiers. He somehow survives his many wounds and lives the long retreat to northern Montana.

White Thunder turns and splashes across the river toward the slope of the mountain. Some of the soldiers and civilian volunteers are already retreating across the river, and several are shot down by the pursuing Nez Perce. Reaching an open space between willows, White Thunder sees a soldier moving through a grey patch of willows, stepping cautiously, stooping, peering through the dark brush, his gun ready. White Thunder moves quickly behind him, hoping to touch him while he lives, performing the feat that earns one of the highest honors a warrior can achieve, but when he's within four steps of the soldier the man whirls about and brings up his rifle. White Thunder fires, and the bullet hits the young man in the chest.

White Thunder moves on and sees a soldier standing at the water's edge, but his head is cocked to one side and he is staring right at White Thunder. The young warrior whips up his rifle, but the man doesn't move. "Then I understood. That soldier was dead! He was the only dead man I ever saw standing."

He runs upstream, back the way he'd come. Several soldiers lie wounded or dead along the river. A sixty-year-old Indian named Allezyahkon is dead under the riverbank, one leg in the water. Wookawkaw (Woodpecker) is dead a few feet farther along the bank, his dark blood seeping into the current. The soldiers have broken out of the river brush and are running away from the village, up to a little stand of trees on a level bench on the mountain side. There they begin scooping out little rifle pits with their trowel bayonets and knives, clawing up the soil with their fingers.

White Thunder weaves his way along the river to see what has become of his people. He finds a soldier lying with a knife in his left hand and his rifle dropped next to his right hand. He leans down quickly to pick up the rifle and the knife flashes by his face slicing his nose. He leaps aside, swings his war club, and breaks the soldier's head. He picks up the rifle and cartridge belt and moves on, his nose bleeding.

He finds a badly wounded soldier, takes this man's cartridge belt and finds attached to the belt a small bag holding hardtack and a little bacon, then wades again across the river to the village.

The eastern sky is brightening. Shots are still cracking from up the slope where the soldiers and citizen volunteers are besieged. About eighty Indians are dead or dying, most of them women and children. "The air," says White Thunder, "was heavy with sorrow. I would not want to hear, I would not want to see, again."

At the north end of the village he comes across a small tepee pitched by itself. Inside is a woman, the wife of Sun Tied, who has just given birth, and her aged midwife, Granite Crystal. Both have been shot. The newborn baby lies in its mother's arms, its head smashed in. Thick smoke from the burning tepees screens the rising sun.

Across the camp there are howls of rage and grief. Colonel Gibbon would later write: "Few of us will soon forget the wail of mingled grief, rage, and horror which came from the camp four or five hundred yards from us when the Indians returned to it and recognized their slaughtered warriors, women, and children."

White Thunder finds a horse, mounts it, and joins several other men, including his uncle, Yellow Wolf, to scout the back trail while Chief Ollokot (Chief Joseph's brother and war chief of their band of the Nez Perce) and several more warriors continue sniping at the soldiers huddled in the little stand of trees. By this time Joseph and others have herded the horses back across the river and into the camp. They begin tearing down the remaining tepees, tying supplies onto the horses, and making travois to carry the wounded. They bury their dead along the riverbank, pushing the overhanging dirt onto the bodies, or hide them in shallow graves among the trees and rocks. There is little time for ceremony. They hurry their work. No one knows how close Howard and his 700 are. In time the camp starts moving south and west away from the fighting. Almost the entire Nez Perce horse herd has been saved, so they are once again capable of moving rapidly.

White Thunder, Yellow Wolf, and four others ride up the open, grassy slope behind the besieged soldiers and spot the four-wheeled cannon being drawn down the mountain by six mules. It's a long way off up a steep slope, and while the six scouts ride toward it in the early light, they see a puff of smoke and hear the boom of the cannon. The scouts scatter and the cannon ball thumps down somewhere in the meadow without exploding. They ride on. Again the cannon booms, but the Indians are still some distance away and the shot does no harm. As they urge their horses up the slope, White Thunder sees an Indian moving through the trees behind the cannon. He recognizes the young man. It's Red Scout, who stops, aims his rifle and fires, killing one soldier. Another shot rings out from the trees behind Red Scout and one of the mules goes down kicking, entangling a soldier in the harnesses. Caught in the open, the other four or five soldiers run for the trees. The one caught in the leather traces, a fifty-six-year-old private, cuts himself loose and fires back at the two Indians who have approached him from the rear. He then manages to scramble away through the brush before the arrival of the mounted scouts.

Espowyes (Light in the Mountain), riding ahead of the scouts, cuts up toward a pack horse being led by a retreating soldier. The soldier sees the approaching Indians, leaves the horse, and runs for cover. Light in the Mountain leans from his saddle to pick up the horse's lead rope then gallops back toward White Thunder and the five scouts. When they ride up to Light in the Mountains and the pack horse, they cut the ropes of the wooden boxes, and pick up rocks to break the boxes open. Inside they find 2000 rifle cartridges. By then about 30 Indians have gathered, and they all dive in to clutch handfuls of cartridges, to fill their cartridge belts and bags.

Some of the Nez Perce meet in a clearing farther up the mountain to watch the back trail while others keep up the siege around the grove of pine trees and brush below. Word comes to the Indians up the mountain that Red Moccasin Tops, who started the war with Shore Crossing, has been killed near the soldiers in their makeshift barricades behind the trees. His father, Yellow Bull, says to the gathered warriors,

"We do not want to leave him there. We do not want to leave him for crazy white people who might cut him in pieces to make fun of a brave warrior. Who will bring his body away, bring him to this place?"

A western wind has picked up with the coming of day. Seven or eight men, including White Thunder, start down the slope, trying to stay out of range of the soldiers in the pine grove. Weweetsa, who was wounded earlier in his right side, rides behind the others and is suddenly hit by a long shot from the barricades. A few minutes later, Quiloishkish's elbow is shattered by a shot. The Indians pull back, taking their wounded with them.

Six or seven warriors try again to retrieve the body of Red Moccasin Tops by crawling down a shallow draw. Tipyahlanah (Eagle) jumps up, sprints to the body, and finds that Red Moccasin Tops is still breathing, though he's been shot in the throat. Eagle lifts him and carries him back up the draw a few steps, but a bullet strikes Eagle. He staggers a few paces and falls. Red Moccasin Tops stops breathing there, and Eagle crawls away through the grass.

The warriors decide to try one more time. Bighorn Bow, a big, strong man, crawls down to the body and pulls it back while the other Indians keep firing on the shallow trenches in the pine trees.

At one point, the Indians to the west and a little above the soldiers light the grass and brush on fire to burn the soldiers out. It is early August and the dry grasses roar into flame, pushed by the wind toward the little stand of trees that protects the soldiers. But the strong wind that should have swept the flames into the trees and trenches suddenly switches direction and the soldiers are saved. Lieutenant Woodruff, lying among the trees with his comrades, later wrote to his wife Louise, "I began to fear that I should never see you again. Our Heavenly Father was on our side and the wind changed and blew away from us...I never knew how much I loved you until I thought [we should never] see each other again."

As the day wears on, the soldiers in the trenches stop firing and the Indians think the soldiers are low on ammunition. But the Indians do not charge. They know that soldiers can replace their dead, whereas a single lost warrior cannot be replaced. The warriors remain to keep the soldiers pinned down while the women, the aged, and the children ride away down the valley.

If the soldiers or citizen volunteers lift a hand or hat above the shallow trenches, a shot rings out. Four soldiers have been killed in the same trench by an Indian firing from behind a fallen tree. Other Indian marksmen have climbed pine trees and fire down into the trenches, but by nightfall their firing dies away and both sides wait.

Night comes on. The stars reappear over another battlefield. There is no moon.

Crawling close to the soldier barricades and trenches that night, an Indian who knows English hears them talking and cursing: "Charley! Charley! Hold on there! Goddamn you, wait!" One man is weeping, others moan. The mountain cold settles down. Wounds stiffen. The only soldier with any medical experience has been shot through both legs, a hand, and a heel. Colonel Gibbon himself has taken a bullet through his leg. The two horses that survived the retreat across the river have both been shot and killed. Soldiers carve meat from one of the dead horses for those who can eat it raw. But their main problem is thirst. They have run out of water.

After full darkness, Colonel Gibbon asks for volunteers to crawl down to the river with canteens. Three volunteers, with a few riflemen to cover them, move from the black trees and slide down the steep slope toward the river, moving slowly on their bellies or sliding feet-first on their backs with the empty canteens tinking and clanking as they try to move noiselessly through the clump grass. They slide painstakingly down through hummocks and around stands of brush in the dark. Tense, concentrating on every shadow, grateful there is no moon, expecting any second to hear a shot and see the spurt of flame. Then, after the slow descent through fearful silence, they push through thick grass and willows to suck water from the shallows and allay a daylong thirst. They carefully push each canteen beneath the surface as eyes dart along the flowing water to the black willows, which stand against a sky pitted by a thousand stars; the few riflemen behind them lie on their stomachs and watch their back trail. Then they make the hard climb up that steepness with the full canteens bumping along the ground and dragging through the grass, every sound a signal to their enemies, not knowing that by this time almost all the Indians have left the scene, most of them riding away to join the retreating families, and only a few, like White Thunder, staying to watch for Howard's reinforcements.

Hours after midnight a voice from high up the mountain calls out: a harrowing, haunting voice crying out of the darkness. White Thunder whispers that it is a white man's voice, but none of his friends knows if it is a soldier or citizen volunteer, or why he calls. Everyone waits. No one responds.

The night grows colder. A few of the wounded fitfully sleep. Hours drag. The stars turn. Imperceptibly, a paleness begins to blur a distant ridge and another day slowly returns for the living.

***

Justin, Alex, and I stand up in starlight. We're stiff and cold. There's a faint glow on the eastern horizon. Alex wraps his blanket more snugly around his shoulders, and we turn and pick our way back through thistles and brush. Twisted branches of dead sagebrush catch our jeans. We sweep the ground with our little flashlights and climb up through dead needle grass, stepping on occasional red leaves of a plant that lies like blood stains on the ground. Cassiopeia hangs upside down among the stars. We slide back into the first irrigation ditch and crawl up the other bank, then down into the next dry ditch and up, and walk up through darkness.

***

About dawn, a soldier hurried his horse down the mountain above through the gathering light and into the trees and barricades where the soldiers watched. No one fired. The few Indians on watch heard the soldiers cheer loudly. They supposed the man had brought ammunition or news of reinforcements. Several Nez Perce untied their horses and took the trail up the mountain to scout the back trail once again for approaching soldiers. They saw nothing, missing Colonel Gibbons' pack train, which remained hidden in a wooded draw only 200 yards beyond the point where the scouts turned back.

After the scouts returned, Ollokot and the others who were with him decided to leave, seeing no more danger to their people from the besieged soldiers and having spotted no reinforcements. The Indians each fired two parting shots into the trees, jumped on their horses, and rode down the slope and across the river, through the ashes of the abandoned camp, and south to catch up to the retreating bands.

The day after the last Nez Perce men rode away, Howard's advance guard with seventeen Indian scouts hurried down the slope to relieve Gibbon's survivors. By that time they had been resupplied by their hidden pack train and seemed to be in good spirits.

The night before, wolves and grizzlies had torn buried Nez Perce bodies out of the ground across the river, scattering the bones, and that afternoon Howard's Bannock scouts dug up others, mutilating and scalping them. Through the night their bonfires roared and the drums beat as they leaped to the rhythms of the scalp dance.

***

How did the Nez Perce feel about the battle? They had successfully fought off the attack, yet they had lost 80 men, women, and children, by far their greatest losses so far. What were their chances now? They had to assume Howard's army was still on their trail, and the Indians now felt no settler could be trusted. And where were they going? Into buffalo country, but would their Crow friends receive them? The Salish, and Chief Tendoy of the Shoshones, though longtime allies, had already refused help.

They fled south over sagebrush prairie, crossed the continental divide at Bannack Pass (30 miles south of Lemhi Pass), moved down a rushing little stream past strange outcroppings of rock, then south again along the Lemhi Valley, skirting the western slopes of the mountains. Howard pressed his pursuit. A Nez Perce war party rode back and attacked his camp at night, driving off 150 of his pack mules. When Howard sent cavalry in pursuit, the Nez Perce ambushed them among dry lava ridges, aspen trees, and sagebrush. They eluded a contingent of Howard's troops sent to trap them near Henry's Lake in Pierre's Hole (where De Smet had first met the encamped Salish 37 years before), then the tribe rode up the Madison River into Yellowstone (designated as a national park just five years before). For two weeks, they passed through that strange land of bubbling cauldrons and steam-breathing mountains, capturing and releasing some prisoners, skirmishing with other travelers; then, as Howard's force caught up, they fled down a steep canyon into the Absaroka Mountains, out-maneuvering another cavalry contingent sent to trap them. On and on they fled, finding no friends among the Crow Indians, capturing supplies at Cow Island far north on the Missouri River, but finally getting run down by U.S. cavalry under Colonel Nelson A. Miles as they camped just 40 miles from refuge in Canada.

During a seven-day battle, 200 Nez Perce slipped away at night and crossed the snowy plains into Canada, but the rest, with Chief Joseph, were captured and sent into captivity in Oklahoma. And so, the tribe most respected by Lewis and Clark for their honesty, nobility, and hospitality were run down, exiled, and dispossessed.

HEADING HOME

After leaving the Big Hole Battlefield in the hours before dawn, we drive ten miles to the little collection of houses and businesses called Wisdom, Montana. We're exhausted and need a place to catch a few hours' sleep. They have one motel, but all its windows are dark, so Justin opens his car door and walks to the office. He knocks. We wait. He knocks harder. We wait. After a third try, he returns to the car. Apparently Wisdom will not have us.

Justin needs to return home, so we say our farewells, hug each other, and he drives away. Alex and I turn north and east, intending to travel through the Crow and Sioux lands that De Smet crossed many times over the years. We take turns driving through what's left of the night, north around the Pioneer Mountains and east, then north to Butte,

Montana, then east over a rocky pass on Interstate 90 to Bozeman until we eventually find a white stucco motel in Livingston.

We sleep late. Before noon we leave the motel and follow the directions of a sign to the Free Chicken Jamboree in Sacagawea Park on the banks of the Yellowstone River. Fried chicken, baked beans, potato salad, lemonade—and a free bluegrass-gospel concert put on by seven or eight musicians from a local church. The guitars strum, the banjos pickety twang, the electric guitar bumps through the bass notes, the drums thump patter thump, and the men and women step to the microphones and sing of Jesus, of standing on the Rock that does not move. A white-haired guitar player leans into a microphone and says, "I've known some people that need to move."

We need to move. Driving out of town we see a shirtless man with a beard to his waist and a strong, muscled physique. Alex says, "That's a bum who's ripped!" That he is. A weight-lifting vagrant? He looks like that mountain man who suddenly appeared on the sand beach at Three Devils with his wolf dog and vanished just as suddenly as I swam for shore.

Then it's east again on I-90, following the Yellowstone River, heading through time and tragedy across the Great Plains where De Smet again and again tried to arrange peace between the U. S. government and the native tribes. It is a land of prairie hills, distant mountains, and wide skies, a landscape that shows its age: eroded, rocky hills with stands of pine and juniper, faded bunch grass as far as the eye cares to see. Hills that border the river push their bony shoulders up, and a line of broken limestone along a ridgeline looks like bleached vertebrae. Later, a wide, flat slope angles down like a lean torso from a bald, pine-bearded hill to a belt of cottonwoods where the windows of two ranch houses connected by a fence reflect the sun, as if a wasted old man fell asleep and let his glasses slip to his waist. Flat river valleys. Eight antelope feeding in a field of green alfalfa. White gravel beaches of the winding Yellowstone River. Two black cows standing to their knees in the rushing blue water. White, high-prowed drift boats floating down the current, fishermen standing and casting. A grove of tall cottonwoods shades a passing cemetery of old gravestones.

The high Absaroka Range (through which the Nez Perce escaped) fades layer upon layer to the south.

Alex and I are silent as we drive the long highway. Our journey, like every journey, is closing down. Hour by hour, the white-blue skies fall down distant horizons that keep rolling away. I think of Chief Charlo of the Salish who refused help to the Nez Perce refugees, in order to maintain his friendship with his white neighbors. He, like Chief Tendoy of the Shoshone, was allowed to remain in his Bitterroot homeland—for a time. Unlike Tendoy, the government did not wait for the old man to die before they forced his removal. In an agonized speech denouncing white demands, he was recorded as saying: "[The whiteman's] course is destruction; he spoils what the Spirit who gave us this country made beautiful and clean...We were happy when he first came; since then we often saw him, always heard him and of him. We first thought he came from the light; but he comes like the dusk of the evening now, not like the dawn of the morning. He comes like a day that has passed, and night enters our future with him." Thus, another tribe that had welcomed Lewis and Clark in the mountains and had traded them horses, and had maintained peace with the whites for 85 years, was, in 1890, forced from their ancient homeland.

We pass through the city of Billings and curve south toward Sheridan, the highway rising onto high prairie cut by steep, folded, prairie hills. In a deep valley to our right, three pale antelope run for the shadows. A long-eared jackrabbit scuttles across the blacktop. The sun sinks into the Big Horn Mountains and a great darkness rises in the east: thick, opaque, with one distant thunderhead flashing intermittently, the tall anvil burning amber-red and gold in the last of the sunlight.

On we go, driving into night, and I feel as if I'm accelerating out of the past and into the rushing future where all of us go: warriors and explorers, chiefs and priests, ranchers and mayors, bee fighters and boatmen, craftsmen and loggers, dog trainers and school principals, all moving into the dark. The car seems not to move at all toward the ever-receding horizon, crossing and not crossing the edges of time, a small craft drifting without movement into the vacant, interstellar spaces. "The only wisdom we can hope to acquire/ Is the wisdom of humility: humility is endless," wrote T. S. Eliot, "I said to my soul, be still, and let the dark come upon you/ Which shall be the darkness of God." And the darkness that opens the endless skies of Montana to its crystalline stars seems very real, present, and powerful.

DE SMET AND THE SIOUX

One of De Smet's early encounters with the Sioux occurred in 1840 on that first long journey back to St. Louis from the Rocky Mountains. After spending a few days at the fur trader's post, Fort Union, at the confluence of the Yellowstone and Missouri rivers (the place De Smet bid goodbye to his Salish bodyguards), he and his guide, the former grenadier in Napoleon's army, traveled on horseback down the north bank of the Missouri to the Mandan villages where Lewis and Clark had wintered in 1804-05. They, like the Corps of Discovery, were welcomed and entertained by the Mandans and Minnetarees and Aricaras, though recently these tribes had been devastated by another smallpox epidemic. Crossing through a forest along the river, De Smet and his guide saw bones and rotting bodies wrapped in buffalo robes and tied, as was the Plains Indian custom, to the branches of the largest trees. The next day they found but ten families of the Mandans, "once such a powerful nation." De Smet, the grenadier, and a French-Canadian guide then headed south into the vast, treeless hills of Sioux country along the west bank of the Missouri River.

About noon one day they stopped in a secluded ravine of lush grass watered by a clear spring. They were congratulating themselves on the security of their position when they were suddenly surrounded by a war party of Sioux who had been tracking them for some time. De Smet stood up at once and walked up to offer his hand to the apparent leader. The leader refused his hand and asked, through De Smet's Canadian interpreter, "Why hide in this ravine?"

De Smet said, simply enough, that they were hungry and the spring was inviting.

The war leader, says De Smet, "looked at me with wonder [and said to the Canadian] 'I have never seen such a man in my life. Who is he?'

"My long black robe and the missionary cross that I bore upon my breast especially excited his curiosity.

"'It is the man,' responded the Canadian, 'who talks to the Great Spirit. It is a chief black-robe of the Frenchmen.'

"His fierce look changed at once," writes De Smet. "He ordered his warriors to put away their weapons and they all shook hands with me. I made them a present of a big twist of tobacco and everybody sat down in a circle and smoked the pipe of peace and friendship."

Ever after, De Smet sought to establish a mission with the Sioux, though the troubled years ahead prevented it. Still, they kept in contact. Sioux headmen often sent messages asking him to return. No doubt they were impressed with, among other things, his obvious courage. On that same journey down the Missouri river, he stopped at a Sioux camp where several warriors, blackened from head to foot as a sign of having killed, leaving only their lips free of the black stain, returned with a scalp of the Potawatomies, the very tribe De Smet had been serving in previous years. After observing the ensuing scalp dance, De Smet asked for a council, where he stood up and rebuked the gathered warriors for breaking an earlier promise negotiated with the Jesuits of Council Bluffs not to kill the Potawatomies. He argued that such killings would bring inevitable retribution from the injured families. Standing alone to rebuke hostile warriors right after the intense emotions raised by a scalp dance is no light matter. The warriors listened to his argument and surprisingly refused to argue the point.

After establishing the Rocky Mountain missions in the following years, De Smet returned to St. Louis in 1846 for more supplies and recruits. Unexpectedly, given his rapport with so many tribes, he was never allowed to return full-time to the missions he loved, though he did make repeated visits. Apparently, he was too valuable a recruiter and fundraiser to spend his time on distant missions. He was given a job as a financial officer for the Jesuits in St. Louis, a job he detested: "I hold the general purse," he writes, "and have to supply all needs; and this purse is never full; the greater part of the time it is flat; while I receive demands from all sides." He longed for heaven "where all ciphering, quibbling and account-making are at an end." He did not, however, force his desires upon his superiors; he was a Jesuit sworn to obedience.

In addition to these "ciphering, quibbling, and account-making duties," he was often sent to more distant places. By 1847, ten Jesuit missions were scattered across the Northwest, and De Smet became their emissary, traveling across the continent, over the Atlantic, and throughout Europe to raise money and inspire recruits, then back, around Cape Horn and up the coasts of the Pacific to the Columbia River and into the interior to visit the missions—again and again. Crisscrossing the Northwest and the Great Plains he kept encountering more tribes who invariably seemed interested in him and at least politely willing to listen to his message.

De Smet accompanied a delegation of Rocky Mountain chiefs to the territorial government in Washington Territory and, later, another delegation of Indians to Washington D.C. to negotiate treaties. More and more, military officers recognized that the various tribes trusted him.

They eventually persuaded De Smet's superiors to let him be an envoy, helping negotiate peace. When he travelled with government officials on such business, he refused payment, feeling it would compromise his position as a neutral arbitrator with both sides' interests at heart: "I shall not accept any remuneration for my personal services. I prefer to be altogether independent in money matters and my only object is to be of use to the whites and still more to the poor Indians. They are for the most part the victims of misdeeds of the whites...the incessant provocations and injustice on the part of the whites. When the savages raise the hatchet or go on the warpath, it is because they are pushed to the limit of endurance, and then the blows they deal are hard, cruel and terrible."

Near Fort Laramie, in 1851, De Smet was called upon to help negotiate a treaty with a number of tribes. He estimated there were 10,000 Indians gathered along the banks of the Platte, representing many bands of the Sioux, Cheyennes, Arapahos, "with several deputations from the Crows, Snakes or Shoshones, Aricaras, Assiniboins and Minnetarrees," that is, tribes who were often inveterate enemies. After agreements were concluded, De Smet was hopeful. All signs led the commissioners to see what De Smet called "the commencement of a new era for the Indians, an era of peace. In future, peaceable citizens may cross the desert unmolested, and the Indian will have little to dread from the bad white man, for justice will be rendered to him." This comment was naively hopeful. Like Lewis and Clark, De Smet and these commissioners were allowing earnest hopes to cloud their reason. The promises may have been sincere, but corrupt Indian agents, merchants, whiskey sellers, settlers, gold miners, delayed or insufficient government payments, and angry men on all sides would constantly subvert those promises.

On a later trip, De Smet writes: "They [the Mandan, Aricara, and Minnetarees near Fort Berthold] complained bitterly of the Government agents and the soldiers. They first deceive them and rob them in the distribution of their annuities, and the others demoralize them by their scandalous conduct. All last winter they were the playthings and slaves of a hard and tyrannical captain, who seemed to make it his business to torment the poor wretches. When the old women with their starving babies came up to the fort to pick up the filthy refuse thrown out of the soldiers' kitchen, they were pitilessly driven off with scalding water, thrown upon their emaciated bodies, covered only with rags in the severest cold weather...Their crop having failed, they were reduced to famine and all assistance was refused them by the captain of the fort." These were the very tribes that had welcomed Lewis and Clark and supported them through a long, bitter winter.

On this same, extensive trip, De Smet writes: "In all the public speeches of the chiefs and in all the private talks I had with them, they all showed a friendly disposition toward the whites and a strong determination to keep aloof from the hostile bands. We kept a strict list of all the complaints made by the Indians, which has been transmitted to the Department of the Interior. I am firmly convinced that if the just claims of the Indians are attended to, if their annuities are paid them at the proper time and place, if the agents and other employees of the Government treat them with honesty and justice, if they are supplied with the necessary tools for carpentry and agriculture, the Indian tribes of the Upper Missouri...would maintain peace." That, of course, is an almost insurmountable mountain of *ifs*. Later, even De Smet's good disposition and hearty hopefulness would end in sarcasm and anger.

ASH HOLLOW AGAIN

Only three years after the Fort Laramie Treaty, an incident occurred that would wreck the hopes of peaceful coexistence. It happened near Ash Hollow. De Smet tells the story in a letter to friends in Belgium. In this letter you hear the angry sarcasm brought on by the events he describes:

April 17, 1855

My very dear Gustave and Marie:

I have received your good letter of the 4th of October last in response to mine of September 12th. Thank you for it most sincerely. I cannot tell you how much good your letters, going into such details and so full of family news, do for me...

I told you in my last letter that I proposed to return to the desert in the course of this spring. That was sincerely my desire and I regret that serious difficulties have come up which compel me to put off my visits to the savages to more favorable times and circumstances. For you must know that the grand and glorious Republic is going to appear on the stage of the great Indian desert to give a representation of the lovely fable of the Wolf and the Lamb. The moral is, "The wicked and the strong always find plenty of pretexts to oppress the innocent and the weak; and when they lack good reasons they have recourse to lies and calumnies." An unpardonable offense, it appears, has been committed in the eyes of our civilized people by the Indians. They had repaired, to the number of 2000, to the appointed spot at the time fixed by the Government agent to receive their annuities and presents [promised in the Laramie Treaty]. They waited several days for the commissioner to arrive and in the meantime they ran out of provisions. Then a Mormon wagon-train, on its way to the Territory of Utah, came peaceably by the Indian camp. One of the party was dragging after him a lame cow hardly able to walk. A famished savage, out of pity for his wife and children, and perhaps, also, from compassion for the suffering animal, killed the cow and offered the Mormon double value for it in a horse or a mule.

Such an act with such an offer under such circumstances passes for very honest, very fair and very polite, in a wild country. Still the Mormon refused the proffered exchange and went and filed a complaint with the commandant of Fort Laramie, which is in the neighborhood. Like the wolf who leaped upon the lamb to devour it, crying: "I know very well that you hate me, and you shall pay," the illustrious commandant straightway sent out a young officer with twenty soldiers armed to the teeth and with a cannon loaded with grapeshot. He was absolutely determined to capture the so-called robber and make an example of him. The savages were astonished at the menacing turn that the affair of the cow, so frivolously begun, had taken; they begged the officer to take one, two, three horses in exchange, a hundred times the value of the cow, if necessary. They wished at any price to "bury" the affair, as they express it; that is to arrange it peaceably and quietly, but without giving up to him their brother, innocent according to their code. The officer was inflexible, refused all offers; he must absolutely have his prisoner; and when the latter did not appear, he fired his cannon into the midst of the savages. The head chief, whom I knew well, the noblest heart of his nation, fell mortally wounded and a number of his braves beside him. At this unexpected massacre the Indians sprang to arms; and letting fly hundreds of arrows from all sides they instantly annihilated the aggressors and provocateurs. Will you in Europe believe this tale of a cow? And yet such is the origin of a fresh war of extermination upon the Indians which is to be carried out in the course of the present year. An army of 3000 to 4000 men is being got ready in Missouri at this moment to penetrate the desert. A very large number of whites will lose their lives without a doubt, but in the end the savages will have to yield, for they are without fire-arms, without powder and lead and without provisions.

Of course De Smet was right. The government saw what the newspapers called The Grattan Massacre (after the foolish lieutenant who died with his soldiers during the attempted arrest) as a pretext to attack. Secretary of War Jefferson Davis (soon to be president of the Confederate States during the Civil War) believed that the Sioux should be taught a lesson, so he sent General William Harney and 700 soldiers to punish them. While pretending a negotiation with the Sioux chief Little Thunder, Harney circled his cavalry behind the village and charged the encampment of Brule and Oglala Sioux, just northwest of Ash Hollow, killing around 100 men and women and destroying the camp. (One of the young men in the camp that day was Crazy Horse, who would, twenty years later, help lead the attack that destroyed Custer and his men at the Battle of the Little Bighorn.)

The Harney Massacre was the beginning of 25 years of intermittent warfare on the northern plains: men, women, and children on all sides gunned down, beaten, sliced, scalped, burned, tortured, raped, decapitated. And it started with a cow.

BASQUE FESTIVAL

Alex and I find a motel called the Blue Gable in Buffalo, a town just east of the Big Horn Mountains. The next morning we unload our mountain bikes and take a spin around and out of town along a winding trail that follows the beautiful, dashing stream through groves of trees and flowered meadows. We surprise two does that bound away over tall grass into the tree line. Miles to the west the Big Horn Mountains rise distinct and detailed against a clear sky. The morning sun is bright, the sky a perfect blue. We pedal back into town just before a parade begins. It turns out we've happened upon the Buffalo Basque Festival. We park our bikes and join the crowds lining the street.

The parade begins with a black-and-white police pickup whooping its siren. Then comes the honor guard strutting with the flags, followed by a grey-haired drum major stomping down the street leading the Seventh Cavalry Drum and Bugle Corps (Custer's failed command) marching with two Indian maidens in buckskins (both of them blond and very white). The band is playing "When the Saints Go Marching In." Miss Wyoming sits prettily waving from a passing blue Corvette convertible. Then comes a line of antique cars. A man dressed in robes like an Arab leads a real camel that strides along, looking lazily left and right at the crowds as if unutterably bored. Shriners—middle-aged men squatting in red-white-and-blue go-carts putt-putt circles around each other, followed by the Buffalo High School Marching Band, which is playing the theme from the cowboy television show *Bonanza*. Two girls carry a sign that reads, "Start em young/ Raise em right/ Teach em to eat beef with all their might." Loud motorcycles pop wheelies. From shiny cars, girls throw water bottles and candy at the crowd. A little boy makes a run for the candy, but his mother grabs his arm and pulls him up short. Pet owners display their leashed dogs. They stop and laugh and talk to friends along the street as one dog keeps lunging and barking fiercely. Then come tall-tired pickups, a flatbed carrying the Kalif Oriental Band playing strange music, followed by local gymnasts in tights doing graceful leaps down the pavement. The Big Horn Basque Club appears, girls with white bandanas on their heads, black and red dresses flowing to their feet, dancing in pairs. A boy runs from a side yard and sprays the girls with an oversized water gun. They scatter and shriek, and return quietly to ranks. Then come the horses: horses pulling carts, ponies painted pastel blues, yellows, and greens, horses carrying cowboys and cowgirls, The Blue Sky Saddle Club. Four big, dappled whites clop by pulling an old freight wagon, followed by five Cub Scouts with a red wagon, shoveling up horse dung.

Late that afternoon we're walking past storefronts and bronze statues of horses and cowboys when we hear a country-western band playing somewhere behind the main street stores. We walk the sidewalk beside the clear, rushing stream to a big field, surrounded by chain link. The field is filling with people. They've set up a stage to one side of the field where a band called Chancey Williams and the Younger Brothers is playing. A pretty blonde in a miniskirt and jean jacket takes the microphone and sings a song about wild horses, as the drummer, the base, and guitar players keep the rhythms moving. A tall father and a short daughter two-step on the grass in front of the stage. A mother carries a little girl with blond pigtails that stick straight up, swaying the girl on her hip. A middle-school boy in a black T-shirt and black sunglasses is trying to dance with a girl who will not look at him.

Alex and I pay our six dollars apiece and walk in among the beer and hamburger stands. Billboards surround the field: Rifleman Propane, MineRite Technologies, Joy's Appliance and Video. It's cowboy country; almost everyone wears boots. Families are setting up folding chairs or spreading blankets on the grass. A Native American family on folding chairs nods to the beat of the band. Two girls are trying cartwheels; the heavier one spins gracefully, heels over hands. A big, bald man with a dark tan and a bull neck pays for a longneck beer and joins his laughing friends. A yellow-and-white ice cream truck squawks recorded calls of cows, roosters, ducks, the mew of a cat. There are a lot of young couples that look to have married right out of high school, many have babies and toddlers. Almost everyone in the growing crowd is white. There's a great absence of tattoos, and no one is texting.

I walk by two women talking: "Did he beat you?" "No, no, no. I don't know why I left him. I guess I run away once a year."

An old man with a white, handlebar moustache and a cowboy hat is saying, "I just don't know. Can't sleep with that pillow. Hurts my shoulder. Nights are long."

A middle-aged woman aims a squirt gun and shoots a cowboy. He backs off laughing, takes off his white hat and shakes the water from it.

We walk by a man talking about a burgundy, cherry-red pickup truck. "He'd shoot you five times if you put a scratch on it."

A thunderstorm is building over the snow-streaked mountains west of town, but the storm is still a long way off. The music plays on and the sinking sun silhouettes the blowing cottonwoods along the rushing stream.

These are hardworking people with deep tans; almost no one is overweight. Hundreds of local people sit in folding chairs eating hot dogs, drinking beer, occasionally getting up to dance.

Alex looks around and says, "I can't locate a girl my age!"

I point out that there are a quite a few (though most have an arm firmly hitched to a boy). He laughs and moves off to join some boys throwing a football.

In time the mountain shadows reach quietly over the town as they once embraced the villages of the Teton Sioux. A silver moon sliver is rising, and a cool wind picks up. I call Alex away from his football and we walk back to the motel. It's a line of one-room log cabins, and it has an outdoor barbecue. We buy steaks and a small bottle of bourbon to marinate them, then cook under the stars and eat baked potatoes and medium-rare steaks before the wind drives the rain into town.

THE WANDERER

De Smet traveled east and south and north and west, crossing the Atlantic, meeting kings and nobles, reporting to the pope in Rome, meeting the Irish orator and freedom fighter Daniel O'Connell in Ireland. De Smet seemed to be everywhere.

On one return trip from the Rockies, he met Brigham Young, who, with his Mormon refugees from Nauvoo, was contemplating where they should go. About 10,000 Mormons were camped near Council Bluffs, preparing their wagons and carts for the long trip west. "They had resolved," writes De Smet, "to put distance between themselves and their persecutors, without even knowing at that time the goal of their long wanderings...They asked me a thousand questions about the regions I had explored and the [basin of the Great Salt Lake] pleased them greatly from the account I gave them of it...Was that what determined them?" asks De Smet. "I would not dare to assert it. They are there."

He returned from Europe to New York just as the nation went wild with the news of the bombing of Fort Sumter, the beginning of the Civil War. He was in the nation's capitol again during the Union disaster at Bull Run, when the capitol seemed in serious danger of being overrun, and again in 1862 when he could hear the cannons of Antietam.

He made long trips to the nation's capital to lobby for the missions and the Indians they served. He spent an hour with Abraham Lincoln after the outbreak of the Civil War, trying to convince him that the Indian tribes of the West who had settled on reservations needed their promised supplies or they might lose faith in the federal government and side with the Confederates. Lincoln, a storyteller himself, listened to De Smet's tales of the West, and De Smet left with not only a $1000 down payment for the mission schools the Jesuits were supporting among the tribes on the Missouri River, but also a promise of more funds. He returned the next year to persuade Lincoln that priests should not be drafted as combatants in the war and won a compromise: they would be drafted, but not forced to carry arms. He ate with ambassadors from France, Russia, and Spain, remarking that they were all splendidly dressed while his worn frock coat was missing buttons. "I did the best I could among these great personages," he writes, "but I remain of the opinion that I shall always be more at ease sitting on the grass and surrounded by savages, each one making his jokes [while] eating with good appetite a bear rib, or roasting a piece of buffalo or fat dog."

On a steamboat on the Missouri River he met the naturalist Audubon and other notable scientists, painters, and travelers. An 1867 journey up the Missouri to send supplies to the mountain missions was the subject of one of the most detailed descriptions of steamboat travel extant. He records the jobs of the nearly 40-person crew from the captain to nineteen negroes "for all the work of the boat." On board were "Catholics, Protestants of diverse shadings, free thinkers or infidels and a few Jews. All this mixture is wafted in peace over the American waters."

He himself tried to be congenial, "all things to all men," answering hundreds of questions about Catholicism and about the West: "The long days are passed," he writes, "in social conversations, sometimes political, sometimes scientific or religious. Storytellers or jokers are never lacking in an assemblage of American travelers. Some read, others play cards or dice, or perhaps checkers...Evenings we amuse ourselves by proposing charades, somebody imitates some animal or other, as the antelope or buffalo, or suggests some word or question." In the evenings, came music and dancing, "concerts on the deck, with mirth and refreshments."

By day travelers watched for wildlife ashore. Once a herd of buffalo trapped in a steep valley feeding on the spring grasses were panicked by the approach of the noisy, smoking steamboat. The herd rushed up 60-degree slopes in long, zig-zag lines, but three bulls were caught halfway up "an almost vertical slope:" "At the approach of the boat they made prodigious efforts to clamber up and gain the top. All eyes were fixed upon them; our cheers were a powerful encouragement to high speed. One reached the goal, and received the applause of the spectators; his two companions strained their best, but still they slipped down; and beginning to slide with their enormous weight, they rolled head over heels, and by a long series of bumps and pirouettes, at a height of 400 or 500 feet they came tumbling into the river within a few yards of the boat...We supposed they were killed; but...to our great astonishment and admiration they rose to the surface and, snorting, blew water from their nostrils. We saw them both reach shore, shake the water from their shaggy heads and necks, and each triumphantly hoisting his standard (his tail), they disappeared at full gallop."

***

In 1868, after two years of battles and skirmishes, raids, killings, and victories by Red Cloud's and Crazy Horse's bands of Brule and Oglala Sioux, Sitting Bull's and Gall's Hunkpapa Sioux, and their Cheyenne and Arapaho allies, De Smet was again called upon to be an envoy to the hostile tribes. Officials thought that he alone stood a chance of receiving safe passage to the Sioux bands of Sitting Bull, Black Moon, and Crazy Horse.

De Smet was 67 years old. His once strong and agile body was much reduced by the years of travel, malaria, office work and other ailments, yet he readily agreed to take on the mission, once again refusing government pay.

At Fort Rice, a military base established four years before on the Missouri River in what is now North Dakota, De Smet met with the more peaceful bands of Sioux who were gathered there. His plan to ride into hostile territory astonished them. They advised him that after the broken promises, the battles and killings, even the black robe's scalp was insecure. "The Plains Indians," writes historians Bob Drury and Tom Clavin, "had honed their war ethic for centuries, and their martial logic... was accepted by all tribes without challenge—no quarter asked, none given; to every enemy, death, the slower and more excruciating the better. A defeated [enemy] not immediately killed in battle would be subjected to unimaginable torments for as long as he could stand the pain."

De Smet responded that six lamps were burning night and day before an image of the Holy Virgin Mary and that a thousand children were "imploring every day, before these burning lamps, the favor and protection of heaven upon all the band who accompany me. I intrust myself with all my fears to the hands of the Lord."

"All of them then," writes De Smet, "as by one impulse, raised their hands toward heaven crying out, 'Oh! That is fine! We will go with you! When shall we start?'"

"Tomorrow at sunrise!" said De Smet.

He took with him Galpin, an old Indian trader who had spent 30 years in the country as interpreter; Galpin's old wife, a Sioux by birth, and Catholic convert "who," says De Smet "has great influence among all the tribes of her nation. He was accompanied by Two Bears, head chief of a large band of the Yankton Sioux, and Running Antelope, head of a large band of Hunkpapas, along with chiefs of the Blackfeet Sioux, Miniconjous, Oglalas, Sissetons, and Santees.

They set out early, riding into wide, rolling prairie. A heavy rain muddied the way for the two wagons that hauled their supplies, and the winds blew hard, but this didn't seem to dampen the spirits of the traveling horsemen. "When we reached our camping place, it did not take us long to make ourselves at home. All seemed animated and enchanted and went joyously to work. The hunters came in with four fine antelope. While some busied themselves about the arrangement of their beds, composed of the small branches of willows and cottonwoods, others hastened to kindle fires, fill the kettles and coffee pots and arrange rows of roasts on sharpened sticks, to content the inner man."

After eating, the Indians danced, accompanied "with joyful songs at the top of their voices." They must have loved escaping the idle life of the reservations and been glad to run free again into their native wilderness, whatever the risks. Long into the night, as De Smet lay rolled up in his buffalo robe, the chanting of the Sioux rose and fell to the thumping of drums that must have felt like the ancient pulse of the land.

They traveled on, a happy band of horsemen, marking their long journey into hostile territory by the buttes that rose in the distance: Rainy Buttes, Three Buttes, Dog-Tooth Butte, White Butte, Blue Stone Butte. The party covered over 250 miles in six days.

Having found no trace of the hostiles, four chiefs led a few followers in different directions to scout the country. "Each of them," writes De Smet, "was bearer of a small charge of tobacco. I should mention that sending tobacco is the same thing as a formal invitation...If the tobacco is accepted, it is a sure sign that you will be admitted among them; if on the contrary, it is refused, you may understand that all communication is forbidden, and govern yourself accordingly."

Late the first afternoon, the scouting bands returned with members of the hostiles. De Smet's tobacco had apparently been accepted, though the hostiles warned that no white man but De Smet would be allowed into Sitting Bull's camp three days away on the Powder River. That night, in their own camp, De Smet and his friends feasted the newcomers "with joyful songs and fraternal rounds of the calumet. They were uproarious reunions, *a la savuage*, but harmony and cordiality prevailed."

Days later, the combined party rode up the hills above the Powder River and down toward the wide and sandy river that pours into the Yellowstone "and mingles its waters with those of a great cataract or rapid above its mouth, the dull sound of which is heard from afar, resembling the distant roll of thunder."

Below them 400 to 500 warriors rode up to meet the little column. De Smet quickly hoisted his standard, a flag bearing an image of the Virgin Mary surrounded by stars. De Smet says that, "They took it at first sight for the hated flag of the United States." The hundreds of horsemen below milled about and seemed to be consulting what to do, then four chiefs galloped toward them "and seemed to flit around the banner. They considered it, and perceiving its meaning and high importance, they came up and shook my hand and made signals to all their warriors to advance. They then formed into a single long line or phalanx; we did the same, and with the flag at our head we went to meet them."

Shouts and songs broke out everywhere. "Everything was wild and noisy, but at the same time everything was carried out in admirable order." They shook hands all around, exchanged presents of weapons and garments, then were escorted down among the 600 tepees that lay scattered in clusters among the tall cottonwoods.

The Indians were painted for war: "Each one had his visage daubed according to his own ideas, with black, yellow or blue, streaked and spotted in every imaginable shade. Feathers of the eagle and of other birds were tied to their hair or in the manes of their horses, scalps and silk ribbons hung from their lances and saddles." These were the men who had long fought the whites, yet De Smet says, "my heart was as tranquil and my mind as calm as if I had been in the midst of [you, my readers]."

There were four to five thousand Indians in camp, hundreds and hundreds hurrying near to see the visiting chiefs and this black-robe. The hostile chiefs surrounded De Smet to protect him from the code of vengeance by which any Indian who has lost a family member "is obliged to avenge himself on the first white he meets. Well, there were a good many of them," says De Smet, "in this position at the time of my arrival." Sitting Bull placed warriors around the tepee provided for De Smet to protect him night and day.

De Smet was worn out from journeying over 300 miles. He ate a little and lay down, falling immediately to sleep in the hostile camp.

"When I awoke, I found Sitting Bull beside me, together with Four Horns, head chief of the camp, Black Moon, his great orator, and No Neck. Sitting Bull presently addressed me, saying: 'Black robe, I hardly sustain myself beneath the weight of white men's blood that I have shed. The whites provoked the war; their injustices, their indignities to our families, the cruel, unheard of and wholly unprovoked massacre at Fort Lyon (where Chivington commanded) of 600 or 700 women, children and old men, shook all the veins which bind and support me. I rose, tomahawk in hand, and I have done all the hurt to the whites that I could. Today thou art amongst us, and in thy presence my arms stretch to the ground as if dead. I will listen to thy good words, and as bad as I have been to the whites, just so good am I ready to become toward them."

The next day, thousands of Indians gathered for a council. After the ceremony of the calumet, led by Four Horns, the orator Black Moon arose and presented the grievances that had led to war and cried out, "We are determined to resist or die! Thou, messenger of peace, thou hast given us a glimpse of a better future. Very well; so be it; let us hope." He then announced that some of their men would accompany De Smet to Fort Rice and hear "the words and the propositions of the Great Father's commissioners. If their words are acceptable, peace shall be made."

Sitting Bull arose and touched on the same matters, along with De Smet's companions Two Bears and Running Antelope. All said they were in favor of peace if the conditions were right. They asked for De Smet's flag as a symbol and remembrance of their council, and De Smet gave it to them willingly. He also gave Sitting Bull a crucifix (that can be seen hanging around his neck in one of the famous photographs of the chief).

De Smet returned to his lodge, followed by a rabble of children who reached out their little hands to shake his. "The mothers were not satisfied until I had laid my hands upon the heads of all the babies and little ones around me." He was exhausted and ill, but he mentions nothing of this in his letters. He entered the tepee, found a buffalo robe and slept.

The next day, a delegation of the hostiles joined De Smet and his chiefs and returned to Fort Rice to negotiate a treaty to end the war. One of the men sent from Sitting Bull's camp was a notable war chief named Gall. His story is a microcosm of these years:

"He told me the story of his troubles," writes De Smet, "and I touched with my fingers the scars he bears. He had been arrested on a charge of stealing horses [by a troop of U.S. cavalry whose scout was an old Aricaree enemy of Gall's]. It was the dead of winter, and the ground was covered with snow. On the road to the prison at the fort, the soldiers thought or feared that he intended to escape, and they ran him through the body twice with bayonets. He fell, bathed in blood, but being still conscious, he counterfeited death. They trampled him and kicked him, covering him with bruises. To finish their cowardly and cruel work upon the prisoner, they thrust a third bayonet through his neck, and at last threw him into a deep ravine. Here he lay unconscious for quite a while, entirely naked, on the drifted snow. When he came to himself, it was already far into the night. He got up and walked 20 miles. When he reached the timber, on the bank of the Missouri, he found a fire, at which he warmed his limbs, stiffened by the cold. The hope of life returned to him then, and he implored the Great Spirit to 'take pity on him and preserve him.' He then quenched his burning and feverish thirst and washed from his body the clotted blood that covered it. In the hope of meeting someone, he continued to drag himself on, and after traveling some miles farther he discovered an Indian lodge. It was that of old Peter [a Catholic convert De Smet had encountered at Sitting Bull's camp] who treated him like a veritable Samaritan. When it was daylight, his host conveyed him on a stretcher to the main camp, where he was received with all the honors of a great warrior. Upon hearing his tale of the soldiers' cruelty and seeing his wounds, the rage of the warriors knew no bounds, and a great number of unhappy whites fell victim to it. In less than a year, Gall himself set out on his war of vengeance, and returned to camp amid acclamations, with seven white scalps on the end of his lance."

At Fort Rice, Gall gave the first speech rejecting the agreement, but eventually he changed his mind and signed the peace treaty. He was given presents, and returned to his people apparently satisfied. Red Cloud, principal leader of the hostiles over the last two years, would sign the treaty that November, not returning to war even when Sitting Bull, Crazy Horse, and Gall later picked up arms again.

De Smet was ill. This was his last trip into Indian lands; he died five years later in St. Louis. His efforts at peace and the great council of 1868 where the hostile bands agreed to peace all came to bitter ends. The government had promised the Sioux a vast land that included much of South Dakota, including their sacred land, the Black Hills, but after gold was discovered in the Black Hills, the government radically diminished the size of the reservation. It was the Nez Perce story repeated. Provocations continued and war broke out again.

STANDING BEAR AND IRON HAIL

Our white car with its green canoe roped on top is singing out of the shortgrass prairies of Montana into the dry hills of Wyoming and then east toward Spearfish and Deadwood. Far off to the south and west, a strange sky leans over strange land. A darkness, a scarcely seen wall, brooding beyond the sunlight, tall, impersonal, private—looming up from this treeless prairie of high hills and thin grass as if the sky were dreaming its own landscape.

Beside me, Alex leans his head against the window, half asleep, his long legs folded beneath the dash. Earlier that afternoon, driving through Montana, we passed the Crow Indian Agency and for a few miles followed the Little Bighorn River along the dry hills where George Armstrong Custer and his 210 men, on a hot day in June,

1876, scrambled up through sagebrush and grass to escape their deaths. Surrounded, cut off, cut down, they were backing along the highest ridge they could find. They must have seen rather quickly that there was no way out, no way out at all.

Custer has become an icon of those surprised by death. Thirty minutes before his retreat, he was sitting his horse on a bluff over that river valley, surveying with his field glasses the turning of the little river the Indians called Greasy Grass. He could see hundreds and hundreds of tepees clustered in tribal groupings for maybe four miles among the cottonwoods and willows and bullberry bushes. He told his orderly, young Sergeant Windolph, that women and children were tending campfires and some boys were hurrying horses to the far hills to join a herd of 15,000 to 20,000 ponies. A Crow scout had told Custer it was the largest encampment he had ever seen.

Custer thought he had his quarry trapped. According to Windolph, Custer took off his wide-brimmed hat and waved to the 200 men waiting below him. "Hurrah, boys!" he called, "we've got them. We'll finish them up and then go home to our station."

The sun had passed its zenith. Not seeing the 800 warriors he had been told were in the camp, he told Windolph they might be sleeping in their tepees. Custer took off his buckskin jacket in the heat, tied it to his saddle, then rode down the grassy hill to rejoin his men. He led them at a trot down a wide, dry ravine that circled behind the hills then down a ravine toward the river. He turned to Windolph and ordered him to return the way they'd come and take a message to Captain Benteen's detachment, telling him to bring up ammunition. That order saved young Windolph's life.

In fact, not 800, but perhaps 2,000 warriors were already on the attack some three or four miles down the valley behind and below Custer, hitting Major Reno's smaller detachment hard after Reno's men had splashed across the river and attacked the southern end of the camp. By the time Custer's horses moved down through rocks and sage and rabbitbrush toward the river, mounted warriors had already thrown

Reno's cavalry back across the river and into the bluffs.

As Custer approached the flowing water, hundreds of Hunkpapa, Sihasapa, Miniconjou, Sans Arc, Oglala, Two Kettles, and Brule Lakota Sioux, with Wahpekute Dakota Sioux, Northern Cheyenne, and bands of Arapaho burst out of the riverside trees and brush, riding with such leaders as Gall, Hump, Black Moon, Rain-in-the-Face, Red Horse, Lame Deer, Crazy Horse, Ice Bear, Lame White Man, Little Shield, Runs the Enemy, Chased by Owls, Two Moons, Little Shield, Wooden Leg, American Horse, Antelope Women, Little Shield, Waterman, Sage, Left Hand, and a Cheyenne woman named Buffalo Calf Road Woman who, according to Cheyenne storytellers, would knock Custer off his horse.

***

Standing Bear and his brother awake in their tepee, two teenagers sleeping late on a summer morning. Standing Bear is just sixteen years old. His brother Iron Hail is eighteen (about Alex's age). They are Miniconjous. The women in Standing Bear's tepee have left to dig turnips, but their old, feeble grandmother and one of their uncles are still inside when the boys sit up. With the sun high and hot, the two boys leave the tepee and walk down to the river to swim. There are other boys there wading and laughing and splashing in the cool water, horses drinking, dogs yapping and snapping, women and girls filling clay water pots, a raven on a dead limb of a thorn tree watches, nervously flicking its wings.

It seems just another nameless day in camp. Such a large buffalo hunt camp will soon disperse, and the day will pass and be forgotten. The current is waist-high, cold and fast when the boys step in. After swimming, they are hungry. Still barefoot, Standing Bear puts on his buckskin shirt and with his brother, walks back to the tepee.

When they stoop into the shadows of the hot tepee, they smell meat cooking and see that their old grandmother is roasting pieces of buffalo in the ashes. They're chewing the roasted buffalo when their uncle looks over and says, "When you have eaten, you must go to the horses right away. Something might happen. I can feel it in the air." (The boys' older brother and another man are herding horses in two bunches on Muskrat Creek below the Santee camp.)

Standing Bear says he will go bring back their horses, but before they've finished eating, they hear sudden shouts outside. Someone is running. Then the familiar voice of the camp crier is shouting that soldiers are charging the camp. His uncle looks at him again and says, "I told you before that something might happen. You'd better go right away and help bring in the horses."

Both boys jump up and duck out of the tepee. Young Standing Bear sprints to the river and splashes and swims across to get to the horses. By then there are shouts that there are soldiers to the south. The boy scrambles up the bluff to take a look. Away south, beyond the camp of the Hunkpapas, Sitting Bull's camp, maybe four miles away, he sees tiny horsemen fanning out as they ride down a slope to the river. Dust is already rising from the southern camps of the Hunkpapa and Oglala as men scramble to find their horses. He turns and starts down the slope, but his feet are still bare and he has to pick his way slowly through a big bed of cactus. Then he catches sight of something that makes his heart skip. Behind him and to his left, up along the ridge of hills: more soldiers on horseback—much closer. He leaps from stones and dodges through cactus, deciding he has no time to look for the horses. He splashes again into the river. Everyone is shouting and running around, dogs barking. He finds his uncle and reports he's seen soldiers, then ducks into the tepee to find his heavy six-shooter and his bow and arrows. He is only sixteen and his heart is pounding. He slings the bow and quiver over his shoulder, finds the skin of the red-and-yellow oriole he has killed a few days before, and ties it into his hair. He makes a quick vow that he will make an offering if the bird's *wothaw* (its protection) will keep him from getting hurt. He steps out of the tepee. His brother Iron Hail has already fingered white paint spots representing hail onto his forehead for protection and is hurriedly braiding the tail of his buckskin pony he calls *Zi Chischila*. In the dust and confusion, their older brother rides up driving their horses and his uncle calls out, "Hurry! Let's go!" They hear rifle fire explode near the river. Iron Hail mounts *Zi Chischila* and his uncle hits the buckskin on its butt with a stick. The wild little pony bolts, knocking over an old woman. Standing Bear catches his own grey horse, loops a thong around its lower jaw and leaps on its back; he's still barefoot and naked except for his wet shirt.

They kick their horses along the river to the mouth of Muskrat Creek toward the approaching band of cavalry Standing Bear has seen. Already there is a continuous rattle of rifle fire above with warriors from the south still galloping up along the river and splashing across. The boys force their way across the river, then, drumming the ribs of their horses with their heels, they lean forward and gallop up the wide ravine through rabbit brush and rocks. They meet a Lakota man riding down the slope with blood running out of his mouth and all over his horse's shoulders. His name is Long Elk, and they hurry past him.

The boys rein in their ponies to let the more experienced fighters, the "fronters," pass by them and lead the charge, then they follow up the slope onto the ridgeline. They feel themselves moving fast into a dry, heaving storm of flashing guns and smoke and drumming hooves, dust and shouts and eagle-bone war whistles shrieking insanely, men barking out warnings.

Hundreds of warriors whip their horses through broken brush, blasted cactus and prairie grass. Bullets whip by, arrows leap from ravines. Smoke everywhere, the acrid taste of gunpowder in their throats, their wild-eyed ponies snorting and panting as they pound along, gun-fire banging beside them—a Crow scout later said the sound of rifle fire was like the snapping of threads in the tearing of a blanket.

They meet another Lakota Sioux walking on foot. He is bleeding and dizzy. He walks a little ways and then sits down, then gets up again before falling.

Farther along the ridge, Standing Bear can finally see the soldiers through the smoke. They are kneeling and firing from in front of their horses. Over a hundred of them have dismounted and are trying to form a rough perimeter with the reins of their horses tied to their wrists or elbows, their horses jerking and screaming and going down before squalls of incoming arrows and a hail of bullets. The soldiers are firing rapidly, fumbling for cartridges, reloading, backing together onto the highest hill they can find, their retreat cut off completely.

The boys urge their horses up through the hot, smoky air. Someone shouts, "They are gone!" and Standing Bear spots a number of the cavalry's grey horses breaking from the soldiers and galloping away. The warriors shout, "Hoka hey! Hurry! Hurry!"

They thunder toward the soldiers, and the day goes dark with dust and smoke. Riding his grey pony into chaos, young Standing Bear sees men flitting by this way and that way like shadows amid the pounding of hooves and crashing rifles—all so terribly loud that "it seemed quiet in there," he says, "and the voices seemed to be on the top of the cloud. It was like a bad dream. All at once I saw a soldier right beside me, and I leaned over and knocked him off his horse with the butt of the six-shooter. I think I already shot it empty, but I don't remember when. The soldier fell off and was under the hoofs. There were so many of us that I think we did not need guns. Just the hoofs would have been enough."

The firing eventually dies away, and they find themselves walking their horses among the dead and wounded along the crests of the hills, their hearts still pounding, sweat beading on their foreheads. When they turn their ponies back toward camp and ride past the bodies—Iron Hail on his buckskin pony, Standing Bear on his grey—the white painted spots on eighteen-year-old Iron Hail's forehead are streaked with grime and sweat; Standing Bear's oriole skin is twisted in his dark hair. Bodies are scattered through the brush and dry grass: Dog's Backbone, a fellow Miniconjou, two Cheyenne: Lame White Man and Noisy Walking, a Lakota named Long Road. Many more. Custer's own brothers Boston and Thomas are dead. His brother-in-law James Calhoun, dead. Custer's eighteen-year-old nephew, the flag carrier, dead and scalped.

"We were all crazy," says Standing Bear. "And I will tell you something to show how crazy we were. There was a dead Indian lying there on his face, and someone said, 'Scalp that Ree!'" thinking it was one of Custer's Aricara scouts. "A man got off and scalped him, and when they turned the dead man over, it was a Shyela [a Cheyenne], one of our friends. We were all crazy."

And so that day has not been forgotten. The stories have been repeated and collected, preserved as a witness to courage and victory, to horror and sudden death.

THESE VANISHING HILLS

As we drive, there is still sunlight behind us, but that mottled, almost-seen barrier far to the southwest rears up, looming higher into mist and storm. After a while it seems to move toward us, and soon the thin grasses on the hills begin whipping about in the wind and the shadowed hills seem to be blowing toward us, mixed into a thickening sky moving low and fast from that distant shadowland. *Must be mountains*, I tell myself. *They don't look like mountains.*

Alex is staring out the window.

Now the road is rising into higher hills that are gathering dark pines in clotted groups with the grass gone greener. In a quick-passing meadow there is a single deer, peacefully grazing. Now, dark forests are moving down out of the Black Hills and crowding left and right, and the massive mountain substance south is moving quickly. Then suddenly, a heavy wind beats us sideways, and the canoe atop our car screeches and bounces against the ropes. A low black running ceiling of cloud rushes over us, and then a slashing, lashing rain. Hard. Harsh. Blinding. Tearing at us. Shaking us. A terrific noise. I hit the brake, slowing us down.

And then, as if in a nightmare, an old man is pedaling a bicycle in front of us, miles from any town, bent over and pedaling. His grey rain gear flaps hard in the dark rain. Yet he doesn't stop, pedaling alone, his balding head like a thin crockery bowl turned against the battering rain, but not stopping, pedaling patiently, neck and shoulders braced grimly against it all, and our white car eases past his maybe seventy-year-old figure bent and flapping behind us now like a storm-driven pelican. Our windshield washers are jumping back and forth, and I'm thinking we should stop and pick him up, but he is clearly not asking for help. I think of old King Lear caught in a terrible storm, betrayed by his daughters and yelling, "Blow, winds, and crack your cheeks! Rage, blow!" And yet Lear chose to leave protection and "wage against the enmity 'o the air, to be comrade with the wolf and owl." Perhaps this old man has chosen this way and this storm, as Alex and I chose four weeks of cold mountains and rushing rivers in the Bitterroots. And now he is behind us, gone forever, and the windshield wipers leap to the flood—with a heigh, ho! the wind and the rain!—and now the clouds darker and chasing the rain gusts in rapid succession across the highway and other cars resolving into shapes out of rampaging rain and cloud, some cars pulled over on the shoulders, others easing along, and the rain battering us all, and Alex beside me peering into madness.

His mother had called hours earlier, worried we were in trouble. She had awoken from a dream in which she had seen an airplane go down in a lake. Alex took the call on his cell phone. I saw him lean back and smile, and rub the soft stubble on his cheek as he told her we'd keep an eye out for low-flying airplanes near lakes.

But I know that her dreams are not to be taken lightly. One night

Justin was driving his convertible through a thunderstorm at 70 miles-an-hour, not wearing his seatbelt. He hydroplaned, slammed the little car into a concrete wall, flipped it and shattered every window. His mother had been lying in bed in my mother's trailer house 200 miles from her son. She awoke sweating, gripped with a terrible worry, her mind fixed on Justin. Outside the trailer house, violent winds were thrashing the hickory trees and rain drummed down on the tarred tin roof. She knew Justin, specifically Justin, was in terrible trouble. She prayed for his life. He survived, though for weeks, after she returned home, she kept pulling pieces of glass from his body as they worked their way to the surface.

One morning, after running my nighttime paper route, I walked into our bedroom and found her sitting upright in bed, demanding to know what had happened. Someone had clicked off five or six shots at me from behind a house. She had awakened about the time the bullets were skipping across the asphalt around my car, certain I was in trouble.

Days before the Battle of the Little Bighorn, Sitting Bull told a dream. He saw U. S. cavalry soldiers falling from the sky, shorn of their ears, dropping like locusts into their camp. Sitting Bull told his nephew it was a sign that the Sioux would soon have a great victory, though many would die.

We all know, with or without dreams, that death rides with us. And we accept death because we have no alternative. Perhaps we even take pride in our ability to face the inevitable. But how can I believe that this boy beside me, this single boy, so full of adventure and camaraderie, of jokes and sympathy, can be exterminated. He loves me. He loves his mother. He loves his brothers and sisters, and we love him. Can love be exterminated? Will he leave us, not only for months, for years, but cease to exist, come to nothing? His courage and all his many friendships snuffed out with nothing but the fading, blowing smoke of a memory spiraling away till even that lingering scent is driven away in storm?

How can this be? Surely the personality so evident in that smile and speech resists extinction.

Fatuous fool, you say. Creating hope where none exists. Perhaps, but no explorer that I am aware of has found an indigenous tribe that does not believe in an afterlife. The tribesmen of Southern Sudan, where I grew up spoke of spirits that lived in a baobab tree, of little black dwarves that came up out of the ground and spoke to them. The Cheyenne believed that when the breath leaves, the spirit travels up the long fork of the Milky Way to *Seana*, the camp of the dead. Why do we so thirst for the ineffable? Hilaire Belloc says that thirst indicates the existence of water and that spiritual longing indicates the existence of spiritual fulfillment.

Some argue that these beliefs are coping mechanisms. Our minds, recalling the past and contemplating the future, would prefer that our lives not end, so we propose an afterlife, we suppose a resting place.

Yet even our scientists long for life beyond our temporal place. They stand beneath the reflective mirrors of their massive telescopes peering into that barren cosmos and long for planets like our own, yearn for communion with other life, intelligent life, somewhere out there. We should know by this time that the distances are prohibitive. Speculating of hypothetical wormholes or practicable space travel to nearest stars seems delusional; it would take a spaceship 700,000 years to reach our nearest star after the sun. Having rejected gods and devils, many writers and movie-makers, even scientists, have invented a romantic and frightening cosmos filled with aliens. If there is life in the "crushing black vacuum of the universe" beyond our tiny system of circling rocks, we will find it only in our imaginations. We are physically alone. The vast distances of space provide room for the afterlife fantasies of scientists, but we will never encounter a passing star rover, nor hear on the wind a hymn from Orion.

And what of these hills? A billion years from now, what reminders? What remainders? A fossilized bone in a gravel pit? Worn shards of glass blown bare on a creek bank? Dust of brick and concrete sweeping by in a nameless wind? Can it be that all human history and every memory will so crumble and calcify? No record left of all humanity and its long sojourn on this spinning, swirling, globe of amethyst and emerald, of blowing clouds and rushing rivers, of dry hills and humid jungles, of quiet ponds and booming oceans?

In time they tell us there will be nothing here but hot, dry rocks staring blind and dumb across lifeless deserts as our sun grows old and monstrously pregnant with vast fires, swelling till she gives raging birth to a growing red giant who consumes his most beautiful child, this sweet, sweet Earth.

I look at my son. This leaping, bounding, surging current of a boy will bounce down through pebbles, swirl and crash around boulders, push his way through sedges and reeds, laughing and leaping over log-jams and ledges. He will join others like himself, running and shouting beneath starlight and sunsets. But one day his life will age like mine, like Lear's, and sink like a desert seep into cracked clay and sand and dust. We know this. But if this is all, it is an atrocity.

To be, then never to be, is the problem.

* * *

Alex and I spend the night in Spearfish, then drive the canyon route through the Black Hills, turning and curving just above the sunlit stream that jumps and turns, catches the light, and ducks into shadows beneath cliffs of grey stone thatched with pine trees. The Precambrian granite cliffs and outcroppings are two to three billion years old. Volcanic activity caused by the shifting of three supercontinents and as many as nine micro-continents forced huge magma intrusions of granite and pegmatite, and over the eons titanic pressures squeezed and crushed later sediments into stone, then buckled and folded, twisting the rock, thrusting it all upwards over 7000 feet into this strange mottled island of rock and pine standing alone within a surrounding sea of treeless hills. For millions and millions of years, the place was just another aggregate of eroding stone and of blowing winds and harsh sunlight. Who then could have dreamed a place of such vitality and beauty as now thrives among these ancient rocks? Not just the larger life: the pines and junipers and cotttonwoods, mule deer and pronghorns, bighorn sheep and mountain goats, coyotes and cougars and bears—but also the grasses and cattails, pink anemones, clustered broomrape, black snakeroot, curled dock, with dung beetles and tiger beetles scrabbling over pebbles and ebony jewel-wing butterflies alighting on green knobby twigs and dirty-orange skippers and black-laced monarchs and cabbage-white butterflies sucking sweet nectars before flitting erratically away. And the green bottleflies and bluebottles swerving onto a cluster of fresh deer scat, a black-and-gold spider hanging from a torn, spiral web laced to standing thistles, a fat tick sucking the diaphanous ear of a rabbit, a black squirrel high up a ponderosa pine blinking, scratching its hip, a bullock's oriole (which young Standing Bear believed had once protected him) hanging upside down from its woven, feather-lined globe of grass, hair, and twine, and yes, even a flying squirrel leaping now, gliding now, from a high oak, slap into a lower trunk of pine; and chipmunks and mice skittering through dead leaves and dried grass, and a western meadowlark pouring out its lilting liquid call and two dark vultures hunched on a high rock observing, while a red-tailed hawk drifts along an eroded escarpment maybe two billion years old, and three brown horses that took 50 million years to evolve, cropping the meadow grasses, and suddenly a falcon flashes straight down through the limbs of an oak in direct pursuit of a screaming jay—a thousand forms of life all acting and reacting and interacting through and around and above and below this remarkable island of life called the Black Hills.

The Lakota Sioux, forced westward from their woodland homes by Algonquin tribes around the Great Lakes, warred with the Cheyenne who lived here, wresting it away by 1776, driving the Cheyenne west and south. Having acquired the place, The Lakota felt its magic. They prayed to the spirits of wind and rock and beast. They said that at the creation of the universe, a song was sung that only in these hills finds its completion. They made this outpost of life a central, sacred way of living.

A hundred years passed. An expedition under that same George Armstrong Custer discovered gold on French Creek, and the Americans tore the place away from the Lakota—who even today cannot bring themselves to give it up, rejecting millions and millions of dollars the government has offered for the land it has already taken.

* * *

Road work up ahead slows a long line of cars. I don't mind. I would love to spend a summer here, a winter, a lifetime, several lifetimes.

In the little gold-mining town of Deadwood, we stop and eat a gourmet breakfast at a cafe called the Deadwood Thymes: a Swiss, ham, and mushroom omelet and fine coffee for me; quiche and orange juice for Alex, which he follows up with a slice of creamy peanut butter pie that the waitress says has been written up in the *San Francisco Chronicle*. Alex gives me a bite. Smooth and very tasty.

THE BEAR

After taking in the granite monuments of presidents not yet forgotten at Mount Rushmore and the rocky stare of Crazy Horse
at the Crazy Horse Monument, we leave the Black Hills heading
south. Alex is driving now and listening as I again read aloud from *The
Fellowship of the Ring* of the wizard Saruman's betrayal of his old friend
Gandalf: "'So you have come, Gandalf,'... but in his eyes there seemed
to be a white light, as if a cold laughter was in his heart."

I look up and see a storm far off to our right, seeming to run with
us, pouring out of the Black Hills, while beyond the running clouds the
prairie spreads out, bright in the afternoon sunlight. We are heading
south and away into the rolling, treeless hills. I tell Alex we are leaving
Tolkien's Land of Mordor and its black gates behind us, but the clouds

brooding over those dark, magical hills these last two days will not let us escape. A grey, patchy string of clouds seems to be keeping pace with us, running like an outrider of the building storm flowing out of the Black Hills. Driving at 70 miles per hour, I know the storm cannot keep up with us and I say so, then return to Tolkien's story.

When I look up again, the storm has drawn closer and long, dark strands of ragged cloud seem to be reaching out toward the prairie grasses with a great darkness filling behind.

"I can't believe that storm is keeping up with us," I say. "Look at it, Alex. Looks like Mordor has sent a dragon."

Alex glances over for a moment, then returns his attention to the highway. "Keep reading, Dad."

I return to Gandalf's imprisonment by his old friend Saruman: "They took me and they set me alone on the pinnacle of Orthanc, in the place where Saruman was accustomed to watch the stars...Over all Saruman's works a dark smoke hung and wrapped itself about the sides of Orthanc. I stood alone on an island in the clouds; and I had no chance of escape, and my days were bitter."

After a few pages, I glance up. The storm is still running with us, miles to our right, but not falling behind. "Look, Alex. It looks like a bony hand reaching out." As we watch, the hand slowly fists and humps into the shape of a great bear snarling. I stop reading altogether and watch this bear that seems so intent on running us down. The wind is picking up and the canoe above us jumps and squeaks.

A half hour later, unexpectedly, the highway curves westward toward the storm and for the first time I think we might not outrun it. The canoe begins jumping and bucking above us in a strong wind and we pull over again to check the ropes. The wind is powerful. Two men on motorcycles fly by us, leaning sideways into the growing gale. We jump back into the car, and I say I'm glad not to be on a motorcycle in weather like this.

Within minutes the great black claws of the mutating bear are stretching toward us. A hundred yards ahead, we see a quick gust drive dust and torn grass across the two-lane highway.

"Look at that!" I say.

Then something heavy bangs off the cab of our car, and another, and another. I tell Alex to stop.

He says, "No, Dad! We've got to get away!"

I say, "The hail will smash our windshield. Pull over!"

He does. Huge balls of ice bang onto the roof, bounce off the windows, shatter the side mirror. Iceballs bound crazily over the blacktop all down the highway. At first there is only a scattering of golf-ball-sized clumps banging all around. (The weather service will report almost two-inch-diameter hail in this storm). A single tree near the fence line shudders for a few seconds, then shakes, then suddenly bends over before a weighty rush of wind and tearing hail. The noise is outrageous, like being attacked by crowds of roaring rioters armed with hammers and iron bars beating us down as they rush past. The wind is flying horizontally, whipping a white blizzard of rock-ice against us, bashing our windows, beating canoe and cab and hood and glass. Alex grabs a pillow from the back seat and covers his head. I follow his example, expecting the shattering of windows any second. The wind rises, a continuous shout of driven hail. We pull the pillows around our ears. We can see nothing at all outside. Our little white car sits there rocking anxiously as the great gusts shake us. (I will read later of whole trailer houses lifted and thrown one on top of another just a few miles south). The roar, if possible, grows louder. The grizzly is batting us around in his hard claws. For a long ten minutes we endure this tension, waiting for glass to shatter or the car to overturn or get shoved across the blacktop, and then, suddenly, the hail ceases.

We look up from our pillows. It's still raining hard, but the wind is dying. Then the storm turns and takes another look at us. The wind that had broadsided our right side now swings behind us and hits us again. Then a new sound arises, a low, heavy moaning.

Alex yells, "It's a tornado, Dad!"

I turn quickly to look out the back window. I can see nothing but wind-driven rain. We are blind. Blind and helpless. The moaning increases to a nasal howl. No refuge, no escape.

"Dad! What do we do?"

I look at my son and shake my head. "Nothing we *can* do."

We wrap the pillows around our heads and wait for disaster, that strange moan coming and going and coming and going like an old man's labored breathing, and I think of that old, precarious man pedaling by on his bicycle. I think of the two men leaning into the wind on their motorcycles as they flew by. I think of Lear, his battle lost, his beloved child dead. I think of the centuries when Indian encampments on these open plains were ripped apart by hail and wind or stampeded by storm-maddened buffalo, or run down by thundering horsemen slaughtering men and boys and women and girls with their whips and their spears and their guns and their scorn and their fears. I think of two Sioux boys and a teenage color bearer caught by the sudden roar of war.

I can accept the death of a jewelwing butterfly because there are many more. But as every parent knows, my son is unrepeatable. Unique. A singularity. In astronomy a *singularity* refers to the death of a burning star. Its heat and light gone, the mass of the star collapses and crushes into a point of zero volume and infinite density, an impossible place in which space and time become infinitely distorted, which is an image as incomprehensible as the final loss of my son, or the final ruin of the lovely Black Hills, or the extinction of all life on this planet.

After a time, the moaning gives way to a rumbling growl, then to a long, low sigh, as if the rampaging bear has grown weary of breaking our shell and has wandered away.

The outside world comes back to us. The lone tree beside the fence stands up like an old man with a wrenched back, its limp limbs and torn leaves dripping quietly in the last passing showers. Hail lies like white gravel in the ditches and across the pastures.

We open our doors and step out into clean, fresh air. We check the ropes and readjust the canoe, run our fingers over the dents that pit the windward sides of the car: $6000 worth of damage. But the hills are cool and wet and you can see a hundred miles.

I put my hand on Alex's shoulder and say, "Quite a storm."

He smiles and shakes his head. "I thought it *was* a tornado," he says.

"Maybe it was," I say. "Maybe it was."

We climb back into the car and within minutes stop in little Chadron, Nebraska: north-facing windows shattered, glass and pieces of roofing scattered, gutters ripped away, wet little mounds of hail beneath remaining downspouts, vinyl siding chewed up as if by a great machine, bits and pieces spit out into streets and yards.

We drive westward to take a look at the damage. Along the creek, trees have suffered little damage. In a nearby field, a 50-million-year-old horse lifts its head and looks at us.

Then Alex, who is still driving, points south: "Dad. Dad, look."

We pull over and step out.

Just beyond the hills the dark clouds are in full retreat. The hills stand green and golden in the evening sun, with a few black pines scattered across their slopes. Beyond the hills, against that thick, rolling cloudbank is what you'd expect to see—yet somehow always unexpected—rising out of this quiet prairie of high hills and thin grass, vivid against the storm, a rainbow. Tall, complete, intense. Upon the cloak of chaos, a quiet hem of light—so bright, so still. A living light. A windfall word.

By ritual and reenactment, we enter into words. Words that hold great power. A journey can be a kind of ritual reenactment. Stopping to honor times long gone in places still present, we enter the past and experience it more fully if we take with us the words of those who lived it. When we attend to words, they attend us, and we find ourselves within the story and the story rewriting our lives. Carrying words, we walk out of the infinite night, onto the horizons of history.

We step back into the car, make a U-turn, and drive back to Chadron. Then, hungry for life, we turn south to follow the storm.